JAPAN
The Ultimate Samurai Guide

An Insider Looks at the Japanese Martial Arts and Surviving in the Land of Bushido and Zen

ALEXANDER BENNETT

TUTTLE Publishing

Tokyo | Rutland, Vermont | Singapore

Contents

BUDO FOR THE SOUL
A GUIDE FOR THE MODERN GAIJIN SAMURAI (GAI-SAM)

I first came to Japan from New Zealand in 1987 as a 17-year-old high school exchange student. It was then that I decided to try my hand at Kendo. I had never seen it before, nor did I have any intention of taking up a martial art before arriving in Japan. But Kendo just looked "cool," like a scene out of *Star Wars*. I joined the school's club with little inkling of what Budo (Japanese martial arts) were, let alone the physical and mental ordeal I was about to be subjected to over the ensuing 12 months.

Despite the initial language and cultural barriers, I survived the arduous training sessions meted out by the club's *sensei*, and the more I learned the more I realized that there was so much more to it than meets the eye. Acutely aware of only having scratched the surface, and being a sucker for punishment, I felt a burning desire to stay in Japan and embark on a personal quest of martial discovery.

With a mixture of trepidation and excitement, I set forth on my "spiritual journey" and immersed myself completely in the world of Budo. I was pretty naïve in those days but I had a purity of mind and intent that kept me going through good times and bad.

Many questions whirled in my brain. Is Japanese culture, as most people seem to believe (including the Japanese themselves), truly impenetrable for foreigners? Can a foreigner learn the esoteric secrets of Samurai philosophy? Is it even relevant in Japan today, let alone outside of Japan? What's the difference between Budo and Bushido? Is Bushido really a tangible code of ethics that permeates the Japanese lifestyle? What's the difference between Budo and other sports? Are Japanese Budo masters superhuman? What should I look for in a teacher? What are realistic goals for a foreigner in Japan? Are the traditional training methods still valid? Where do I start and what should my priorities be?

The author, Alex Bennett, has been living and studying the martial arts in Japan for 30 years. Holding the rank of 7th Dan in Kendo and high grades in several other martial arts, he has dedicated his career to researching and practicing Japan's traditional Budo culture. He lives in Kyoto and teaches the theory and techniques of martial arts at Kansai University in Osaka.

What is genuine Budo and what is fake? Am I allowed to question my teachers? Are the harsh methods of training that characterize Budo really necessary? More than anything else, what the hell do I think I'm doing here?

I have chipped away at these questions over the past three decades of training and studying in Japan and, dare I say it, figured out most of the answers. I can confidently say that Budo is relevant to me, a *gaijin* (foreigner) living in Japan in the twenty-first century, and it has enhanced my life in many ways. It took time but I learned to distinguish fact from fiction and fantasy from reality. I have seen Budo from every angle— the good, the bad and the ugly—and my fascination with it keeps growing.

The purpose of this book is to provide the kind of information that I wish I had when I started out. It is designed to demystify Budo for young non-Japanese who are about to set out on a similar path, or contemplating it. Think of it as the fundamental knowledge a "*gaijin*-samurai" (*gai-sam* for short) needs to know.

I use this term with a degree of tongue in cheek. Although ubiquitous, *gaijin* is not a particularly nice word. Sometimes it is downright discriminatory but I have come to embrace it all the same. The G-word is a part of my identity in Japan, as is Budo. It's from this standpoint—an unashamed non-Japanese Budo nut—that I explain the ins and outs of surviving this challenging but rewarding world.

I wrote this book from the heart. It's not a technical manual but a guide which aims to dispel false ideas and unrealistic hopes that might otherwise hinder you, the reader, in finding your own path of discovery through Budo. Many young (and not-so-young) Budo aficionados come to Japan harboring Samurai fantasies nurtured through films and manga comics. Alas, they often end up abandon-

Spelling Conventions

Japanese words and expressions have been divided into their most logical components to assist reading and pronunciation. Japanese terms have been Romanized according to the Hepburn system and italicized, but macrons have not been used to approximate long vowel sounds. Japanese names are listed in the conventional Japanese order with the surname first. Japanese words found in most standard English dictionaries and names of the modern Budo disciplines are treated as Anglicized words or proper nouns. Organizations such as the Nippon Budokan and the Dai-Nippon Butokukai are commonly referred to as Budokan and Butokukai and are sometimes shortened as such. All era dates in this book are quoted according to conventions used in the "Kodansha Encyclopedia of Japan." Many of the historical figures mentioned in the text changed their names during their lives but I have used the most familiar versions. The birth and death dates for a number of historical figures are impossible to verify but I have also used the generally accepted dates.

ing their pursuit of Budo soon after they start, either because their expectations are unreasonable or because they fail to find the Budo experience they are seeking. Based on my years of first-hand trials and tribulations, this book provides readers with the basic knowledge required to succeed in any Budo discipline in Japan. It targets Budo enthusiasts but I also hope it will be of interest to non-practitioners who are curious about Japan and the meaning behind the Budo cultural phenomenon. You might even feel compelled to give it a go!

To the uninitiated, Budo may seem like the domain of athletic meatheads but that's not what it is supposed to be about. Like a fine wine, the Budoka gets better with age and you are never too old to start.

Top Woodblock print by Utagawa Kuniyoshi of Yoshida Sedaemon Kanesada, one of the 47 loyal Samurai.

Above left A Westerner dressed as a Samurai. Painted by Goseda Horyu, probably in the 1870s when Japan saw an influx of foreign visitors.

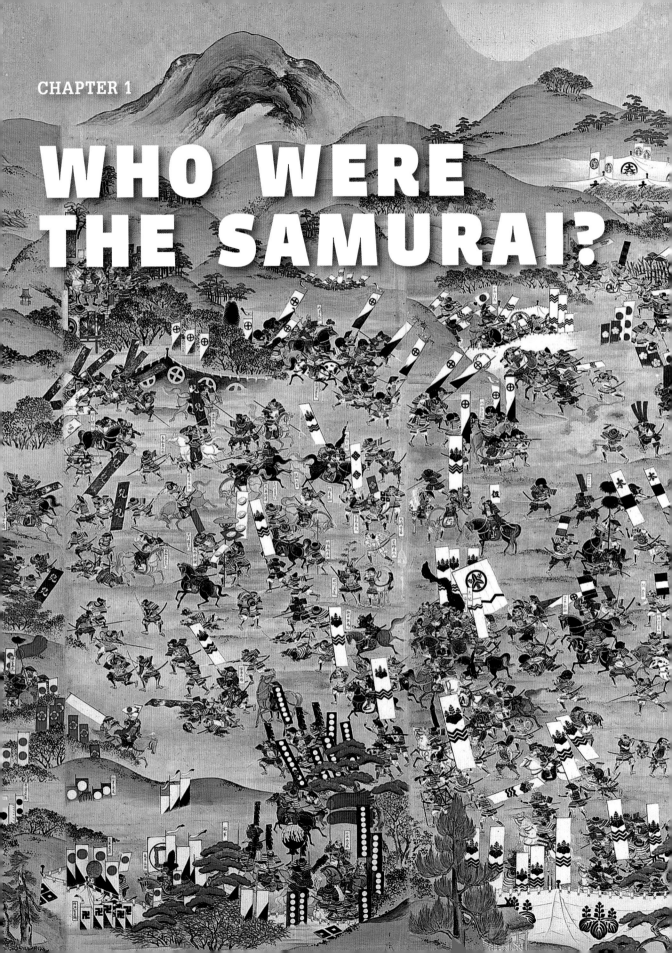

CHAPTER 1

WHO WERE
THE SAMURAI?

The word "Samurai" represents all that is considered noble by the Japanese people—bravery, humility, honor, loyalty and selflessness. National Japanese sports teams are sometimes referred to as Samurai. For example, Japan's soccer team is called the "Samurai Blue." In spite of their heroic image, it must be said that much of Japan's warrior past was not particularly honorable. Moreover, the prevailing notion that modern Japanese people are heirs of the "Samurai spirit" by virtue of their DNA is problematic, to say the least. What you believe and take on board is up to you, but if you live in Japan you should make an effort to learn the basics of Japanese history. Coming to terms with the complexities of this fascinating subject is not easy, so this chapter will provide the fundamental knowledge needed to put it all in context. There is no room to give bios on all the Samurai I find interesting. But at the very least the *gai-sam* should know a little bit about the five I have included in the following pages. It's also a good idea to learn about famous Samurai who feature in the lore of the place where you live in Japan. Modern Japanese are very proud of local Samurai legends and still harbor bitter one-eyed prejudices against their heroes' historical foes.

INTRODUCING THE REAL SAMURAI

The Samurai—also known as Bushi—were elite warriors who eventually became the ruling class in Japan from the end of the twelfth century. Although characterized by much killing and chaos along the way, warrior dominion remained intact until the Meiji Restoration of 1868. This was when Japan shed its feudal culture and embarked on a topsy-turvy journey to become a modern nation state competing with other colonial powers on the world stage. Long after the Samurai class was dismantled, the image of Samurai as indomitable paragons of strength and morality continued as a powerful symbolic force.

The Heian Period (794–1185):
Go East Young Man

Where did the Samurai come from? In a nutshell.... Professional men-at-arms emerged in the Heian era through the reluctance of Kyoto-based courtiers to get their hands dirty overseeing private estates in the provinces. After all, who wants to live in the boondocks when there are tantalizing linked-verse competitions, plum blossom parties and moon viewing events to attend with the rest of Kyoto's glittering elite? Instead, they called on lesser mortals in the pecking order to oversee provincial affairs. Young noblemen who stood little chance of career advancement because of family rank, or rank within their own family, were encouraged to go to the eastern frontier lands. There they would eke out a living managing the estates, developing new lands and keeping peasants in line, rivals at bay and local "strongmen" with long-established roots on their side.

The Heian period saw the privatization of various government functions, including military operations, and a tug-of-war between the leading noble houses for power and wealth. Men with proven martial ability became a sought-after commodity. They were hired to make up numbers in independent aristocratic armies, much like private security firms. Those with the wherewithal, including retired emperors, nobles, temple and provincial officials, maintained their own little militias. These consisted of a core group of salaried personnel. Mercenaries would be hired when required for specific campaigns.

Clansmen from two imperial offshoot families—the Taira (aka Heike or Heiji) and the Minamoto (aka Genji)—were at the forefront of the warrior rise to dominance. There were 17 major lines in the Minamoto clan stemming from the sons of Emperor Seiwa (850–78), and four Taira lines from Emperor Kammu (707–836). Factions of the Taira family set down roots in the Kanto region in the east and further to the north from as early as 900. The Minamoto followed suit a

Above Most of the warrior gentry trace their family lines back to illustrious aristocratic houses.

Left Warrior monks of the Ishiyama Temple armed with *naginata* (glaives) during the Kamakura period.

century or two later. Minamoto warriors began to dominate military matters in the capital from the late tenth century through a nepotistic relationship with the Fujiwaras, a clan of powerful nobles who monopolized important positions in court by marrying their daughters off to generations of emperors. As we shall see, it was the Minamoto, however, who were to prevail in the end.

The Late Heian Period: Trouble in Paradise

A string of violent episodes in the late Heian period brought warriors to greater political prominence. First, the Hogen Disturbance of 1156 erupted over an imperial accession dispute. Taira and Minamoto bigwigs tangled on both sides of the squabble. Minamoto Yoshitomo and Taira Kiyomori bet on the right racehorse by choosing to support the reigning emperor Go-Shirakawa over the retired emperor Sutoku. Sutoku and his allies were vanquished. Taira Kiyomori was especially well rewarded for his loyalty. A few years later, in 1160, Yoshitomo, a little green-eyed at Kiyomori's special treatment, became involved in a hamfisted *coup d'etat* attempt (the Heiji Disturbance) against Taira dominance at court.

The hapless Yoshitomo was killed and the Minamotos were relegated to court outsiders. The Taira (led by Kiyomori) were now free to rule the roost unopposed. Although victorious, Kiyomori made a fatal mistake—he showed clemency to Yoshitomo's young sons (Yoritomo and Yoshitsune) by sending them into exile rather than murdering them in cold blood.

Bushi or Samurai?

Both! Samurai and Bushi are largely interchangeable terms now but the latter once denoted men-at-arms in general rather than someone in the service of a lord. During the Kamakura period (1185–1333) and earlier, warriors were called *mononofu* or *tsuwamono*. *Mononofu* can be written with the same *kanji* as Bushi (武士 = military + gentry). Warriors were also called *saburai*, stemming from the verb *saburau*—to wait on or serve—because they were originally in the service of the nobility as retainers or bodyguards. *Saburai* became pronounced as *samurai* (侍) from around the sixteenth century. In the Tokugawa period (1603–1868), the "Way of the Warrior" was given various designations, such as Bushido, Shido or Budo. Shido was the most prevalent term, and *shi* on its own (士) has the alternative reading of Samurai. Commonly used among visiting foreigners during the Meiji period (1868–1912), Samurai is the usual term used in the West. Bushi is heard more frequently in Japan.

A pictorial scroll depicting the *Heiji Monogatari*, a war tale about the eclipse of Fujiwara power and the rise of the Taira clan over the Minamoto family in the 12th century.

Right Emperor Antoku (1178–85) reigned from 1180 until his demise at the battle against Minamoto forces at Dannoura. His grandmother, Taira Tokiko, plunged into the ocean to commit suicide with the infant emperor in her arms.

Below A broader section of one of the five "Heiji Monogatari" scrolls. The colorful pictures of the Heiji Disturbance of 1160 are dramatic and incredibly detailed works of art.

Strutting about like proud peacocks, the Taira dominated court politics. Kiyomori then sought to cement his dynasty by marrying off his daughter to the emperor in 1171. He installed Antoku, his two-year-old grandson, as emperor in 1180 instead of the incumbent emperor's brother, Prince Mochihito.

Ejected from the throne before he got to sit on it, Prince Mochihito was not impressed. He issued a call to arms and summoned the Minamotos to help him rid the world of the troublesome Taira clan once and for all. This was just what Yoritomo was waiting for. He wanted to avenge his murdered father and led a Minamoto uprising that came to a head with the bloody Genpei War (1180–85).

The Kamakura Period (1185–1333): Tent Government

Yoritomo amassed a large following in the eastern provinces far away from Kyoto and plotted his revenge albeit under the guise of "rescuing" the court from Taira clutches. He promised his band of Minamoto kin to dutifully negotiate any claim to lands if they swore him allegiance. This was a juicy prospect for disenfranchised Minamoto scions.

Softened by a luxurious life at court, the Taira were eventually crushed in the five-year Genpei War. The final clash was a naval battle in the seas around Dannoura in 1185. Realizing that the end was nigh, Taira Kiyomori's wife, Tokiko, grabbed her grandson Antoku along with the imperial regalia and

An Edo period print of the final battle in the Genpei War (1180–85). The Taira forces were routed by the Minamoto at Dannoura.

chose death over the humiliation of capture by jumping off her vessel into the briny swirl below.

Mission accomplished, Yoritomo then established Japan's first warrior government in Kamakura, not far from modern day Tokyo. It was essentially an independent state in the east run by warriors for warriors and was in no way a replacement of the imperial government in Kyoto. Yoritomo cleverly utilized the emperor to legitimize his military supremacy. He was granted the lofty title *seii tai shogun* or "barbarian-quelling generalissimo," along with carte blanche to pretty much do whatever he wanted.

Minamoto-no-Yoritomo (1147-99): The Jealous Genius

Yoritomo is most certainly a Samurai bigwig *gai-sam* need to know. As we have seen, he was the Minamoto warrior chieftain who set up the first warrior government in the small seaside village of Kamakura after the successful uprising against the Taira who were running amok in court politics in Kyoto. Yoritomo was careful to receive imperial support to avoid being branded a rebel traitor. He was "Mr Just," and after he had vanquished the tyrannical Taira, the emperor bestowed upon him the title of shogun and legitimized his operation on the other side of the country.

He was clearly a shrewd tactician who knew the importance of keeping the boys happy. To this end, he established landholdings and titles to reward his loyal vassals, and to keep them loyal. In return, they pledged fealty and military service in a "you scratch my back, and I'll scratch yours" lord-vassal relationship. In spite of his skill as an administrator and military commander, he was insanely suspicious of any perceived contender and summarily exterminated a number of his relatives. He only had two very young sons to fill his boots when he died aged 59 after falling off a horse. They were also extinguished rather viciously by rivals—well, close relatives actually. Such were the times.

Speaking of Bigwigs: The Chonmage Topknot

Well, not wigs, but strange hairstyles that were popular among Samurai—the *chonmage*. The pate of the head was shaved like a reverse Brazilian and the hair at the back and sides was grown long and tied into a topknot. It was originally designed to make the wearing of battle helmets (*kabuto*) a more comfortable and hygienic affair. Shaving the pate of the head made it less stuffy. The topknot also served as a layer of padding inside the *kabuto* to stop the scalp chafing on the metal. Besides, a full head of hair was sweaty and smelly, a source of embarrassment if one's noggin happened to be removed as a trophy in battle. Even posthumous appearance was a question of honor!

As Japan modernized during the Meiji period, the government tried to remove symbols of their feudal past. They issued the "Cropped Hair Edict" in 1871, which encouraged all men to adopt Western hairstyles. Many former Samurai rushed to new-fangled photo studios to get photographs of their topknots before lopping them off.

Nowadays, professional Sumo wrestlers have topknots but without shaved pates. Occasionally you will see one reminiscent of the old Samurai style, but this is because he is genuinely going bald! Removal of the topknot is an important custom for retiring sumo wrestlers, and dignitaries and patrons are invited to take it off one snip at a time with much pomp and ceremony.

Minamoto-no-Yoshitsune (1159–89): Japan's Tragic Hero

Yoshitsune was Yoritomo's younger sibling whose star still shines brilliantly as Japan's classic tragic hero. He was one of Yoritomo's most successful generals in the Genpei War but his popularity proved to be his downfall. When the infant Minamoto brothers were sent into exile by Taira Kiyomori, Yoshitsune was placed in a temple in Kuramayama, Kyoto. It is there, generations of storytellers tell us, that he learned the art of swordsmanship from the mythical Tengu. Little is known about his childhood. But his prowess as a warrior, although useful in war, left him open to slander in the aftermath. One of Yoshitsune's rivals hinted to Yoritomo that his brother was readying himself for the top job. The sibling friction was picked up on by yet another meddling emperor, Go-Shirakawa, who played the brothers against each other.

By late 1185 Yoshitsune knew that the paranoid Yoritomo was after his head and decided to retaliate. Uncle Yukiie sided with Yoshitsune but both were ultimately betrayed and Yoshitsune was reduced to hiding out in and around Kyoto. He managed to find shelter with Fujiwara Hidehira, his childhood custodian. When Hidehira died in 1187, his last will and testament declared that Yoshitsune was to inherit the "governorship of Mutsu."

Enter Hidehira's resentful son and a medieval telegram to Kamakura to nark him out. An attack was ordered. Holed up in a mansion, Yoshitsune's legendary chum, Denkibo Benkei, held off the attacking force single-handedly, giving Yoshitsune time to mercy-kill his wife and then commit suicide. Yoshitsune's head was preserved and transported back to Kamakura for confirmation. Those who saw it lamented at the heart-rending demise of this great hero of the Genpei War. In fact, when Yoritomo fell off his horse and died, they attributed it to the angry ghost of Yoshitsune. There was even a popular theory that he escaped with his life and made his way to the land of the Mongols. And that he was, in fact, Genghis Khan (Genji = Genghis)!

After Yoshitsune's death, a supporter of Yoritomo wrote in his diary: "In bravery, benevolence, and justice, Yoshitsune is bound to leave a great name to posterity. In this he can only be admired and praised. The only thing is that he decided to rebel against Yoritomo. This was a great traitorous crime." The poor guy was probably framed. Incidentally, the term *hogan biiki* (sympathy for the lieutenant [Yoshitsune]) is still used today and means "to support the underdog."

Oda Nobunaga (1534–82): The Ruthless Strategist

Oda the "Nobster" Nobunaga was the great chieftain who successfully brought the feudal lords (Daimyo) into line after a century of civil war. Although he met a grisly end at the hands of his own "trusted" vassal, by the time of his death he controlled a whopping one-third of Japan and had set a wave of unification in motion which his two henchmen, Toyotomi Hideyoshi and Tokugawa Ieyasu, would later get to ride.

His brilliance as a strategist, and his tyrannical ruthlessness, knew no bounds. After the death of his father in 1551, Nobunaga took control of Nagoya Castle and then started his campaign of violent expansion. He outwitted his opponents, made the right alliances, obliterated his enemies and was always on the lookout for new technology and systems to further his cause. His infamous legacy included the extermination of Buddhists who opposed him. The Buddhists were not a particularly peaceful bunch, either, and were a major thorn in Nobunaga's side. He went to great pains to snuff out the secular power of Tendai Buddhism by burning the Enryakuji Temple on Mount Hiei to the ground, and killed thousands of men, women and children in rebellious groups affiliated with the Jodo Shin sect.

Nobunaga was on the verge of defeating the last bastions of opposition. On his way to the front to support Hideyoshi against the Shimizu and Mori forces in Takamatsu, he stopped off in Kyoto and stayed where he always did, at the Honnoji Temple. Two days later, the temple was attacked by one of his generals, the "dastardly" Akechi Mitsuhide. As the temple burned, Nobunaga apparently disemboweled himself in a back room.

Modern sentiments would surely categorize him as a Class-A war criminal, and his sudden demise was undoubtedly the result of some seriously bad karma. Still, he was the alpha male of his times and is thus remembered as a hero of Japanese history. In classic medieval "whodunit" fashion, controversy still surrounds his death. People love to blame the perfidious Akechi Mitsuhide but was it really him, and if so, why? Knowledge of the following theories will impress any Japanese over a cup of *sake*.

Who greased the Nobster? Various theories have been proposed...

The Remonstrance Theory	Mitsuhide was frequently berated by Nobunaga and harbored a grudge against him because of it.
The Ambition Theory	Mitsuhide had lofty ambitions to take power for himself.
The Fixation with Tradition Theory	Mitsuhide was a great believer in tradition whereas his lord had no compunction in disposing of traditional institutions in his way.
The Hideyoshi and Mitsuhide Conspiracy Theory	Hideyoshi and Mitsuhide conspired to assassinate Nobunaga. Hideyoshi then betrayed Mitsuhide by rushing back from Takamatsu in record time to kill him at the battle of Yamazaki.
The Frightened Noble Theory	Court nobles felt threatened by Nobunaga and were behind the plot to have him killed.
The Tokugawa Treachery Theory	Ieyasu wanted revenge for the death of his wife and child whom he had been forced to kill to prove his allegiance to Nobunaga.
The Catholic Conspiracy Theory	The most unlikely theory—but Dan Brown might be interested—Catholic missionaries saw him as a major barrier in their mission to convert Japan.

BUDO CALLIGRAPHY:
Fu-rin-ka-zan "Wind, Forest, Fire, Mountain"

風
林
火
山

Something that perhaps evokes images of brave Californian fire-fighters. In the Japanese context, however, it was the motto of Takeda Shingen, one the greatest warlords of the Warring States period (1467–c. 1603) and Oda Nobunaga's nemesis. Originally from Sun Tzu's *Art of War*, which was mandatory reading for Samurai, it is explained in the *Koyo-gunkan* as epitomizing the military philosophy of the Takeda: "Be as rapid as the wind and as silent as a forest. Attack like a raging fire and be as immovable as a mountain."

His government was called the Bakufu (Shogunate or tent government in English) and it coexisted with the imperial government. In essence, Kyoto represented a kind of Ministry of Cultural Affairs and Nice Things while Kamakura was the Ministry of Security and Nasty Things. This heralded the beginning of the Kamakura period (1185–1333).

Before the emergence of the Shogunate, nobles at court would control small independent armies. With the rise of Yoritomo's tent government, however, the rules were changed and court influence began to evaporate.

Unfortunately for Yoritomo, he did not live long enough to really enjoy his meteoric rise. He died when he fell off a horse in 1199. His son Yoriie became the second shogun, but not for long. He was replaced by his younger brother Sanetomo after another coup instigated by his mother Hojo Masako and her father Hojo Tokimasa, who then assumed the role of regent (shogun manager). Yoriie was murdered (probably by Tokimasa) in 1204 and Sanetomo was killed by his nephew Kugyo, Yoriie's son, in 1219. It really was Game of Thrones on steroids. The rest of the period saw a succession of six titular shoguns controlled by Hojo regents.

Although Yoritomo's time at the top was short-lived, he was successful in creating a "government within a government" that had exclusive rights over military matters. Yoritomo also set clear protocols in place for reciprocal obligations binding warriors to their masters in service.

Yoritomo was instrumental in spawning an honor code for the Samurai community, and rewarded his supporters with official positions throughout the country. Aspirations for wealth and power, along with the shared experience of living in the harsh hinterland conditions, saw the evolution of a patriarchal warrior subculture very different to the effete court culture of their brethren in Kyoto.

Apart from a couple of miraculous victories against Mongol invaders in 1274 and 1281, the Kamakura Shogunate was not an overly effective government and it ended abruptly in 1333. The Kamakura demise was sparked by the machinations of an uppity emperor (Go-Daigo) who sought to restore full imperial power. He was joined by a couple of high-ranking Shogunate vassals in what became known as the Kemmu Restoration (1333–36).

First, Ashikaga Takauji was sent to Kyoto to teach the mutinous emperor a lesson but ended up joining Go-Daigo instead. Nitta Yoshisada was then dispatched to Kyoto to punish them both but he too decided that the time was right for a change.

Eventually, the Muromachi Shogunate (1336–1573) was established in the Muromachi area of southern Kyoto. This came to pass when Ashikaga Takauji turned against his two co-conspirators and took power for himself. Even the imperial family was thrown into disarray; from 1333 to 1392, rival Southern (Nara) and Northern (Kyoto) courts both claimed sovereignty.

The Muromachi (Ashikaga) Period (1336–1573): Getting Some Culture

As the Shogunate was now located in Kyoto, hordes of bucolic Samurai moved into the city. Derided as belligerent bumpkins, they were desperately in need of a crash course in manners to fit into the snobbish aristocratic world of Kyoto. Indeed, the Muromachi period (aka Ashikaga period) was a time in which the Samurai began to excel in arts in addition to the martial variety. Patronage of the tea ceremony, Noh theatre, poetry and the like added a veneer of refinement to the more violent disposition burning in their souls.

Samurai concern for propriety is evident in another Muromachi period trend—the promulgation of "House codes" (*kakun*). These were family documents that advised Samurai on practical matters such as appropriate apparel, etiquette in front of VIPs, everyday interaction and the treatment and use of arms and armor.

Peace was always hanging by a thread, but it was an accession dispute that thrust the country into chaos once more with the outbreak of the Onin War (1467–77). Actually, it was more a domestic squabble between the eighth shogun, Ashikaga Yoshimasa, and his wife Tomiko that plunged Japan into the depths of bloody bedlam.

Because she couldn't conceive a son, he asked his brother to take over the mantle of shogunship. With the pressure to produce an heir gone, Tomiko got pregnant! Of course she wanted her precious son to inherit his rightful place as supreme ruler. "But honey, I promised my brother...." Whammo! All manner of family infighting broke out. High-ranking vassals chose to support one side or the other to settle their own personal, unrelated grievances.

The Warring States Period (1467–c. 1603): The Strong Eat the Weak

By the end of the Onin War, nobody could actually remember why it had even started. Kyoto was burnt to the ground and the Shogunate was left barely intact. Being a coalition, the Shogunate had no standing army of its own, and exerted

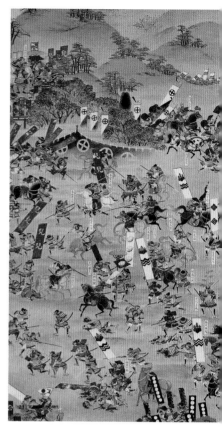

Far left Medieval foot soldier (*ashigaru*) armed with a musket.

Left A high-ranking Samurai of the Muromachi period on his horse ready for battle.

Right A scene from the Battle of Sekigahara in 1600. Victory paved the way for Tokugawa Ieyasu to establish the third Shogunate in Edo.

virtually no control over pugnacious vassals seeking to improve their lot in the world. Japan degenerated into an anarchic free-for-all known as the Sengoku (Warring States) period.

From around the beginning of the sixteenth century, self-made warlords (Daimyo, literally "big names") vied to become even bigger names. They entered and exited alliances at the drop of an arrow, always looking for a larger slice of the cherry pie. Pandemonium engulfed the country for over a century and a half. Fortune or failure was a mere back stab away and subordinates were not averse to overthrowing their masters when the opportunity presented itself.

Needless to say, the "art of war" burgeoned as warriors honed their skills and resources for maximum destructive effect. Different to the small-scale melees of the Kamakura period, where extroverted individuals took the "Look at me, aren't I just fabulous" approach to make a name for themselves, war became large-scale and highly regimented.

When they weren't growing rice, umpteen thousands of beleaguered peasants were drafted into armies as infantrymen. They didn't receive professional warrior training in the use of halberds, swords or bows, but with the introduction of easy-to-use pointy sticks (*yari*) and firearms in the mid-1500s, peasants provided a formidable addition to the ever-expanding warring armies as *ashigaru* (light foots). Raise crops in the spring and summer months and poke people's eyes out during the off season.

The Azuchi-Momoyama Period (c. 1573–1600): Killer Pâtissiers

In the end, a handful of super ruthless Daimyo steered the country towards some semblance of unity by brutally quashing any and all opposition. "Join us or be butchered" was their mantra. "And if I don't like you, I might butcher you anyway." The unification of Japan was achieved incrementally by three legendary Daimyo: Oda Nobunaga and his two right-hand men, peasant-to-regent Toyotomi Hideyoshi, and his astute associate, Tokugawa Ieyasu.

After Nobunaga was deceived by his vassal Akechi Mitsuhide and killed as he rested in the Honnoji Temple, Toyotomi Hideyoshi inherited the leadership of Japan. When he went slightly mad and died in 1595, Tokugawa Ieyasu broke his promise to support Hideyoshi's young son Hideyori. Toyotomi supporters (led by Ishida Mitsunari) and Ieyasu's forces met on the crowded,

muddy battlefield of Sekigahara in 1600. Ieyasu won the day as fencesitters and turncoats defected from the western army loyal to the Toyotomis to join Ieyasu's eastern force. The realm was now Ieyasu's. It is said that Nobunaga "made the cake," Hideyoshi "baked the cake" and Ieyasu "gorged himself on the cake," licking his plate with gusto.

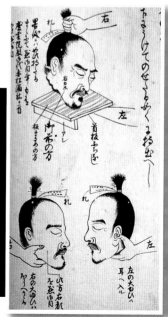

Left Battle helmets called *kabuto* provided protection but the decorations also made them an important means of identification.

Right The unenviable task of cleaning and grooming heads for presentation to the lord was usually assigned to women.

Tokugawa Ieyasu (1543–1616): The Canny Politician

Tokugawa "Easy Rider" Ieyasu, the third hero, outwitted and outlasted all of his competitors to usher Japan into a lasting era of peace. Ieyasu spent most of his childhood as a hostage, first of his father's enemy, the Oda family, and then of his father's ally, the Imagawa family! This somewhat unhealthy upbringing made him adept in the art of winning friends and influencing (or killing) people.

He entered into an alliance with Oda Nobunaga. Nobunaga made Ieyasu kill his wife and first-born son to prove his allegiance as he suspected that the poor woman may have been in cahoots with his mortal enemy, the Takeda clan.

Although central in the Nobunaga alliance, Ieyasu's relationship with Hideyoshi was not particularly amicable at first. They eventually decided that nobody stood to gain much through petty rivalry and bickering and even a façade of friendship was better than fighting. To this end, Ieyasu gave Hideyoshi one of his sons and Hideyoshi reciprocated by betrothing his 43-year-old sister to Ieyasu.

With Hideyoshi's ascendancy to top dog following the Nobster's demise, Ieyasu was required to forfeit some of his territories and relocate to the east. He chose a sleepy little fishing village called Edo—now the sleepless city of Tokyo—as his HQ. Just before Hideyoshi died, he made his generals, including Ieyasu, swear an oath to protect his son and heir. Of course, Ieyasu broke his promise within two years as splits formed between the vassals. This led to a massive showdown at Sekigahara in October 1600. Ieyasu's political maneuvering and tactical nous resulted in a decisive victory for his army.

In 1603, Ieyasu established the Tokugawa Shogunate in Edo. He was the lucky one who had his cake and could eat it too. Actually, it was rumored that he died of food poisoning after eating his favorite dish, sea-bream *tempura*, but it was probably stomach cancer that got him.

Left The Kiheitai was a crack volunteer militia unit organized by the Choshu domain in 1863. It was made up of 300–400 men of all social classes, including farmers. **Right** A group of Satsuma domain warriors making battle plans during the Boshin War.

The Tokugawa (Edo) Period (1603–1868): Peace Finally

Japan enjoyed an era of relative peace after Tokugawa Ieyasu established the Shogunate in Edo (modern-day Tokyo). Society was loosely divided into four classes—warrior, farmer, artisan and merchant—but the lines were often blurred.

Peace was somewhat problematic for the Samurai who, constituting only around 6 percent of the population, lorded over everyone in their position at the top of the social pyramid. Peace was a tad boring. After all, their status was based on war and killing people. Some Samurai were reduced to brush-wielding bureaucrats working for the Shogunate, while most others lived in their domains and received stipends for doing, well, very little. The devil finds work for idle hands and gambling, drinking, prostitution and fighting were common vices for the volatile Samurai. Enter Confucian intellectuals and military scholars who redefined the social duty of Samurai in peace and formulated codes of behavior collectively referred to now as Bushido (the "Way of the Warrior.") Needless to say, the Tokugawa period (aka Edo period) was a time of great cultural refinement.

The Bakumatsu Period: Samurai Social Seppuku

The twilight years (1820s–) of the Tokugawa period saw growing dissatisfaction with the Shogunate's feeble reaction to possible foreign incursion. This intensified with the arrival of the American Commodore Matthew Perry's flotilla of "Black Ships" to Japan's shores in 1853 and the "insolent" demands that Japan open its ports for trade. Japan's long-lived peace deteriorated as xenophobic fanaticism reared its head. Samurai

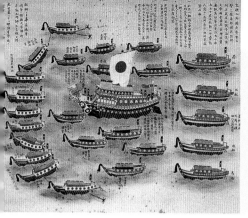

The National Flag and Anthem

The Hinomaru flag was officially adopted for merchant ships in 1870. It may come as some surprise that it only became the official flag of Japan in 1999. Until then, no legislation actually specified a national flag. At the same time, an old poem now known as "Kimigayo" was officially made the national anthem. "May the reign of the Emperor continue for all generations and for all eternity—the time it takes for small pebbles to grow into a great rock and become covered with moss." The *gai-sam* will be expected to sing along to the national anthem at the start of any Budo tournament.

from the Satsuma, Choshu and Tosa domains (now Kagoshima, Yamaguchi and Kochi prefectures) rallied national support as they headed an anti-Shogunate movement. They promoted an imperial-loyalist alternative, which championed the *gaijin*-unfriendly ideal of *sono-joi* (expel the barbarians and revere the emperor). A short but sharp revolution (the Boshin War) ensued. It was driven by low-ranking Samurai and culminated with the Meiji Restoration of 1868. The Meiji Emperor was installed as head of state

and Japan embarked on a frantic mission to modernize and catch up with the West. Foreign experts were recruited to advise, and even Tom Cruise lent a helping hand (see *The Last Samurai*).

The Meiji Period (1868–1912): Japanese Spirit, Western Technology

Class distinctions were dismantled soon after the Meiji Restoration and replaced with two categories of *shizoku* (former Samurai) and *heimin* (com-

moners). The *shizoku* gradually lost all of their privileges, including government stipends, and in 1876 were forbidden to carry swords in public. A conscript system was introduced in 1873, and although a few disgruntled diehards vented their frustration in a handful of armed insurgencies, the Samurai were finally tamed for good with the quelling of the Satsuma Rebellion in 1877, covered in *The Last Samurai* movie.

With the Meiji Emperor steering the ship of state, politics, religion and the military were combined into one potent

Toyotomi Hideyoshi (1537–98): The Cautious Consolidator

Toyotomi the "Hideous" Hideyoshi is considered the second "great hero." His rise was a remarkable story of peasantry to pageantry. Thanks to his brilliance in strategic matters and politics, he rose from obscurity to become Oda Nobunaga's right-hand man. He was not nearly as ruthless as his overlord but did demonstrate a strong tendency for paranoia.

He entered Nobunaga's entourage in 1558. Nobunaga took an immediate liking to him, reputedly nicknaming him "Saru" or monkey. A passage in the *Hagakure* text describes him in less than flattering terms: "Lord Hideyoshi was a small man with big eyes, and his face and limbs were red, as if they had been painted in vermillion." If anything, perhaps he looked more like a gelada baboon. Apparently, his wife used to call him the "Bald Rat"! Monkey or rat, Hideyoshi led one of Nobunaga's armies from the mid-1570s and proved his worth in battle time and time again. After Nobunaga was betrayed and killed in 1582, Hideyoshi took over (hmmm ... see

Nobster greasing theories) and systematically brought the last pockets of resistance under his control. A decade later he had Japan. He legitimized his power over civil and military matters by getting the emperor to bestow upon him the title of "imperial regent."

Following in Nobunaga's footsteps, Hideyoshi instigated a number of social changes to consolidate his rule. The "sword hunt" was an attempt to disarm the general population and define the roles of agriculture and military. He was decidedly suspicious of Christians and had a fair few missionaries and their converts crucified. In a fit of rage, he even ordered the great tea master Sen-no-Rikyu to commit ritual suicide. Nobody really knows why as they were supposedly good friends. It may have been that Rikyu overheard one too many secret discussions conducted

in his tea room (occupational hazard), and he offered his ten yen's worth when it wasn't welcome. A sad end for Rikyu, and a decision that Hideyoshi later regretted. Who would make him a cuppa now?

Having unified Japan, Hideyoshi needed a new supply of booty to keep throngs of rough and ready warriors happy and occupied. To this end, he launched invasions of Korea in 1592 and 1597, with the second one being abandoned following his death in 1598. Although records indicate that he was generally an affable fellow, he was clearly a megalomaniac. He even ordered his favorite nephew to commit suicide in 1595 (plus many of his family members) when Hideyoshi's concubine (Nobunaga's niece) successfully bore him a son and heir, Hideyori, to whom he made his vassals swear allegiance. He should have known this would never work.

Left The first plutonium bomb, dropped on Naga-saki, Japan, on August 9, 1945, was named "Fat Boy."

Far left Tokyo in the after-math of the magnitude 7.9 Great Kanto Earthquake of 1923. Over 100,000 people died.

entity. The emperor was seen as repre-senting Japan's mythical past by virtue of being a direct descendant of the Sun Goddess. He became the symbol of the "enlightened government" (*meiji*) which built a modern army and navy ready to expand Japan's colonial interests.

Japan reinvented itself as a "divine" nation in no way inferior to the West. It exploited Samurai culture to forge a new cultural identity for its citizens. The defeat of China in the first Sino-Japanese War of 1894–95, and success against the superpower Russia over the Korean peninsula in 1904–05, saw a surge of patriotism and the growing belief that Samurai DNA constituted the moral backbone and vitality of the Japanese people. Bushido was promoted and readily accepted as the quintessence of an immutable "Japanese spirit."

The defeat of Russia by the Japanese truly shocked the world. The victory was lauded as a David versus Goliath marvel and cemented Japan's position as the big boys on the Asian block. Japan had already gained control of Taiwan in 1895 after the first Sino-Japanese War. The victory over Russia cleared the way for Japan's annexation of Korea in 1910, an act of aggression that the Koreans have never forgiven.

Above Two fencers face off with bamboo swords. The style of Kendo armor used today has changed little in 300 years.

Left The phrase *kirisute-gomen* refers to the right of Samurai to cut down commoners for any perceived affronts to their honor. Apparently, this right was justified as "self-defense."

The Taisho Period (1912–26):
Trendsetters Take Over

After the Meiji Emperor died in 1912, his son Yoshihito became the next sovereign of the Greater Japanese Empire. He was a sickly lad and his strange behavior has been attributed to lead poisoning from the white make-up smeared on his wet nurse's breast.

His interest in foreign languages and his penchant for odd and unpredictable behavior fitted nicely with the era of his reign. The Taisho period is remembered as a brief sojourn into liberal democracy preceding Japan's slide down the slippery slope of militarism and totalitarianism in the early Showa period.

Japan enjoyed a time of economic prosperity thanks to markets opened up by World War I in Europe. Money meant fun. Hedonism was in and bourgeois cultural trends, described as *ero-guro-nansensu* (erotic, grotesque nonsense), captured the age. Young trendsetters became interested in bizarre contemporary art and went on extravagant shopping sprees at newly constructed department stores, and enjoyed Western popular music, movies and fashion. *Modan gaaru* or *moga* (modern girls) enraged the conservative establishment with their unbridled adop-tion of Western frivolities.

It wasn't all fun and games though. With increased wealth came more socio-economic disparity and calls for worker rights. This sparked the infamous rice riots of 1918, burgeoning interest in Western liberalism, socialism, communism and other 'isms. With the influx of less than desirable Western ideals came an inevitable backlash through the rise of ultra-nationalism and militarism. Goodbye roaring twenties. It must have been fun for a while.

A group of middle-school girls practicing Naginata during a Physical Education class in the early 1940s.

Kamikaze Fighters

Kamikaze means "divine wind." The term was coined after typhoons saved Japan from imminent Mongol invasion on two occasions in the thirteenth century. The word was revived to describe the "Tokubetsu Kogekitai" ("Special Attack Unit") during World War II. These were young men drafted to carry out suicide attacks in planes, speed boats and human-driven torpedoes laden with explosives against Allied naval vessels in the closing months of the Pacific campaign. According to records, about 3,860 *kamikaze* pilots died, with a successful target hit rate of around 20 percent. Many more were drafted into the units but escaped imminent death with Japan's surrender. The *kamikaze* pilots are remembered today as tragic—often reluctant more than fanatical—young men who represent the Bushido ideals of loyalty, gallantry and self-sacrifice. Although admired, it is a chapter in Japanese history that is rarely talked about now other than in terms of incredible sadness.

The Showa Period (1926–89):
War and Peace

The passing of the Taisho Emperor in 1926 saw the enthronement of Hirohito (1901–89). The Showa period, as his reign is known, really was a game of two halves. Ironically meaning "period of enlightened peace," the 1930s saw Japan constantly embroiled in conflict with other nations. This started with the invasion of Manchuria in 1931, followed by military and economic expansionism throughout Asia and then the Pacific.

In 1940, Japan became the third Axis wheel in the Tripartite Pact with Nazi Germany and Italy. In 1941, Japan set about "liberating" Indo-China from the French and Indonesia from the Dutch, and invaded British colonies, Hong Kong, Burma, North Borneo, the Philippines, Singapore and various Pacific islands. And, of course, there was the audacious bombing of Pearl Harbor in December 1941.

The bloody battle for Okinawa in 1945, with its shocking mass suicides by soldiers and civilians in the face of the enemy, not to mention the frenzied *kamikaze* pilots smashing their planes into enemy ships, was all the justification the US high command needed to finish the war with a bang. By unleashing the Kraken, the US also sent a chilling warning to future foe. The cities of Hiroshima and Nagasaki were obliterated with atomic bombs nicknamed "Little Boy" and "Fat Man."

In the aftermath, Emperor Hirohito spoke "directly" to the Japanese people for the very first time on August 14 via a crackly phonograph record on the radio. Without ordering them to surrender per se, he spoke in archaic court language that few understood: "According to the dictates of time and fate, we have resolved to pave the way for a grand peace for all the generations to come by *enduring the unendurable and suffering what is insufferable.*" That meant unconditional surrender to the Allies.

Postwar Japan: Rising From the Ashes of War

Following the US-led Occupation headed by McArthur's General Headquarters, Japan began the process of purging itself of militarism and refashioning the country as a modern democratic state. All martial arts were banned at this time. They were viewed suspiciously as aggressive accouterments of a very dark yesteryear. Budo penance continued until around 1952 with the

Demonstrators at the Meiji Jingu Shrine's classical Budo Embu held yearly on November 3 to mark Culture Day.

signing of the San Francisco Treaty.

Picking itself up from the ashes and anguish of defeat, Japan focused on developing its economy and industry. The Tokyo Olympic Games in 1964 and the Osaka Expo of 1970 were events designed to show the world how far Japan had come since the regrettable war years. Japan's famous Shinkansen Bullet Train linking Osaka and Tokyo was unveiled at the time of the Olympics and symbolized rapid economic growth and newfound prosperity. The yen was cheap and exports surged. Goods "Made in Japan" came to mean "excellent" rather than "excrement."

Japan was on a roll, but where did this resilience come from? After a few years in the cold, the trusty old Samurai spirit was back in vogue. The new Samurai were the legions of *salariman*—corporate *ashigaru* foot soldiers—who put company and country above any of their own "selfish" interests.

In spite of severe environmental pollution and a few high-profile industrial fiascoes like the appalling mercury poisoning in Minamata, Japan's economy went from strength to strength. Showa Japan came to an end in January 1989 with the passing of Hirohito. By the time of his death, Japan was riding a wave of success that was surely inconceivable in those fateful days in August 1945.

The Heisei Period (1989~): Bubbles and Other Troubles

Although it will change in April 2019, the current era in Japan is called Heisei. Hirohito's son Akihito ascended the imperial throne when Japan's economy was peaking. The so-called "Bubble Economy," which started to sparkle around 1985, was an era when the yen soared and Japan suddenly became "economic animal" wealthy. Such was the extent of ridiculously inflated land values, the Imperial Palace where the emperor resides in central Tokyo was rumored to have a value greater than the entire state of California. Banks were only too happy to lend customers as much money as they desired to buy things beyond their

Left and above Dignitaries dressed in Samurai garb for the annual New Year Kagami Biraki celebration held at the Nippon Budokan in Tokyo. Kagami Biraki ceremonies are held in many *dojo* to signify the first training of the year.

actual means. Japanese companies expanded by buying assets overseas. Although wary of Japan's economic belligerence, the world was besotted by the Japanese "miracle" of ashes to riches. It resulted in a worldwide craze for things Japanese. This was occurring about the time I first arrived in Japan.

But, as we all know, bubbles eventually burst. And boy, did this one go J-Pop! Land prices tanked. Average Joe Tanaka who bought into the affluence on the illusion of inexhaustible wealth and security was left with debts amounting to millions of dollars in some cases. There was no way to sell their white elephant assets to repay their mortgages. The mid-1990s saw a rapid downward spiral in the sumptuous lifestyle enjoyed in the 1980s. The poor old salaryman at the vanguard of Japan's economic growth was cast off like trash. Words such as *ristora* (restructuring) heralded in a new age of belt-tightening (= firing) and frugality. Japan has never quite recovered from this crash and looks on with trepidation as its population ages and shrinks.

Postwar tensions have arguably never been greater between Japan and its Asian neighbors than they are now. In May 2017, hawkish Prime Minister Abe Shinzo set a 2020 deadline for the revision of the post-war Japanese Constitution's ambiguous Article 9. The article in question says: "The Japanese people forever renounce war as a

sovereign right of the nation" and assures that "land, sea and air forces, as well as other war potential, will never be maintained." The change would legitimize the deployment of the Japanese Self-Defense Forces to exercise military action outside Japan if allies required assistance. The Japanese government already ended its total ban on the export of arms in 2014.

Critics point out that such monumental changes are not being made through a transparent democratic process. But that is not surprising when you look at the nature of postwar Japanese politics! Factionalism, corruption, scandals, nepotism and entrenched constituent apathy all contribute.

Economic and military issues aside, Japanese soft power is still gaining traction and winning Japan a new generation of admirers around the world. I am referring, of course, to the allure of Japanese popular culture—food, music, manga and anime, video games, cosplay, films, fashion, cuteness and, of course, its fabled Samurai culture and martial arts. The term "Cool Japan" is now a common expression denoting the country's status as a "cultural superpower." In June 2010, the Japanese Ministry of Economy, Trade and Industry established the Creative Industries Promotion Office to stimulate the private sector to develop "Cool Japan" for worldwide consumption. And consume it does.

WOMEN WARRIORS, NINJA AND RONIN

Always floating on the fringe of Bushido culture, the role of women, "wave men" and *ninja* in Samurai society is hazy. Were there women combatants in Japan? Was being a masterless Samurai really that bad? Did those black-hooded *ninja* really have superhuman powers? Did they even have black hoods?

Women Warriors: The Ones Without the Moustaches

As the wives, mothers and daughters of Samurai, women were positioned to exert significant influence in the lives of their menfolk, both directly and indirectly. There are also a handful of celebrated women warriors. Luminaries such as Tomoe Gozen feature in the old literary war saga *The Tale of the Heike*. Hangaku Gozen was known for her sublime archery and leadership skills. Then there were the countless inconspicuous women moved as pawns in marriages to forge alliances between warrior houses. Their function in the maintenance of the warrior code is, for the most part, overlooked.

There is interesting archaeological data from old battle sites showing that

A woodblock print of a woman practicing forms with a *naginata*.

women were active participants in the front lines. Without stating it explicitly, a passage in the *Hagakure* offers a clue: "Warriors in olden times used to grow mustaches because their ears and noses would be removed and taken by the enemy as proof of their

triumph in battle. The mustache was cut off together with the nose to confirm that the trophy head was that of a man and not a woman. If the head was found to be clean-shaven, it was just left to rot in the mud. A Samurai cultivated his drooping mustache to ensure that his head, once removed, was not unceremoniously discarded." Could this mean that women were also in the thick of things? A mountain of evidence certainly points this way but it has never really been acknowledged.

Far left Tomoe Gozen in the fray, clutching a trophy of her exploits.

Left A woman burns incense in her husband's battle helmet to ensure the fragrance is pleasant should his head be taken by an enemy warrior.

It is no great secret that women trained in the martial arts, albeit behind the scenes. There are many stories of Samurai wives defending their fortresses from besieging armies while their men-folk were engaged in a campaign else-where. There are also records of women who avenged murdered relatives and chilling eyewitness accounts of women committing suicide the traditional way to avoid the shame of capture. It was commonly accepted that one of the most important jobs for women of warrior houses was educating their sons in how to behave and act honorably and pre-pare them to make the ultimate sacrifice for their lord. The adage "Behind every great man there stands a great woman" could not have been truer of Samurai society. They were just as much "protec-tors of the Way" as any man. Although Bushido is masculine on the outside it is very much counterbalanced by femi-nine qualities internally. Maybe this is why Bushido is a topic of fascination for modern Japanese women, arguably even more so than for the average guy.

Who Were the Ninja?

Yes, *ninja* (aka *shinobi*) did exist but they were not as conspicuously inconspicuous as they are typically made out to be. The rise of the *ninja* begins in the two neighboring regions of Iga and Koga, located in modern-day Shiga prefecture. It is an interesting but surprisingly unknown story because of all the hype and "bullshido" that engulfs the modern *ninja* myth. In the late fourteenth century, Iga and Koga, off the beaten track and surrounded by treacherous mountains and rugged terrain, were plagued by unruly ruffians and bad eggs passing through. Of more concern to locals, however, were the big Daimyo armies threatening to carve up their part of the countryside. To protect their way of life, farmers and rustic Samurai (*jizamurai*) in the region formed leagues (*ikki*). They banded together to fight common enemies who threat-ened their havens. These Samurai were not associated with any warlord's army

and trained the farmers in the martial arts to lend a hand when needed. The system worked well and they became highly proficient at guerilla warfare.

One day, a certain Nobster came a calling. He sent his son Nobukatsu into the region to sort out this annoying farmer-warrior league. Against all odds, Nobukatsu was beaten! Nobunaga decided to crush the fly with a sledge hammer and dispatched 50,000 troops to end the "insurgency" once and for all. The Iga and Koga freedom fighters were soundly defeated by Nobunaga. The local Samurai who led the insurgencies were reviled by Nobunaga and other Daimyo. They were never going to be accepted into the real Samurai hierarchy. Too proud to become cogs in his new political order anyway, they continued to operate covertly as resistance fighters. This was the beginning of the *ninja*.

Eventually, 200 of the Iga militia members were employed by Tokugawa Ieyasu as guards. This relationship came about through Hattori Hanzo, progenitor of the Iga-ryu, who was greatly admired by Ieyasu. Koga *ninja* were also used as spies in the 1637 Shimabara Uprising and took orders to engage in various acts of espionage hoping that they be made real Samurai, just as Pinocchio wanted to be a real boy.

This was never to be. In 1745, the Shogun Yoshi-mune dismissed them all from his service. They con-tinued to peddle their skills as mountain guides, spies and assassins. Schools of *ninjutsu* sprang up around the country through the hype they created to market their magical, superhuman powers. Perception of their

Left A young Samurai in formal attire.
Below A rather strange photo of a woman posing with a *katana*. The popularity of Kendo among women is very much a postwar phenomenon.

mysterious skills—walking on water, magic spells, shape-shifting and the ability to vanish into thin air, etc.—became a mainstay of their highly ro-manticized image in fictional literature. They did have some neat tricks like using their scabbards as snorkels or feelers in the dark. Like Samurai, they were adept at using many different weapons, including swords, daggers and spears. Thanks mainly to movie portrayals, they are also renowned for their "lethal" *shuriken* skills. For start-

Left A couple of *ninja* performers getting ready to entertain a group of foreign tourists.

Below The typical image of a *ninja* dressed in black, *ninja*-blade in hand, and *shuriken* in his belt. Blue eyes? The martial art of *ninjutsu* is infinitely more popular outside Japan than in.

Who Were the Ronin?

Ronin (or *roshi*) literally means "wave man." They were masterless Samurai who roamed the country looking for a job, or trouble. The reasons for becoming masterless were many. The Samurai's lord may have died, he could have been disassociated because of bad behavior or he may have just absconded. Sometimes it was simply a matter of being red-carded for a bad attitude with the possibility of reinstatement when the lord lightened up a bit.

The Edo period saw hordes of *ronin* slinking around the countryside and in the cities. It is estimated that there were as many as 500,000 *ronin* looking for work after the Battle of Sekigahara in 1600!

The cream of the crop in terms of martial arts sometimes fell on their feet and they were employed to instruct swordsmanship at a domain school or private *dojo*, or hired as bodyguards. Others took to a life of crime and thuggery and moonlighted as hired muscle for gambling joints, brothels and other activities of ill repute.

As such, *ronin* were often feared as impulsive cut throats who had veered from the "Way of the Samurai." Interestingly, though, depending on the domain, *ronin*-ship was not necessarily the end of the road. For example, one Samurai from Saga commented, "When I was a *ronin*, I found it was not at all that bad. It was different than what I expected, and to be honest I wouldn't mind being a *ronin* again."

ers, "throwing-stars" were not lethal, just a painful hindrance; and small projectiles were not unique to *ninja*.

Samurai also studied the arts of espionage and spying, and some traditional martial art schools like the Tenshinshoden Katori Shinto-ryu include *ninjutsu*-esque teachings.

Ironically, foreigners tend to take *ninja* more seriously than Japanese, who are not even aware that a martial art called *ninjutsu* exists anymore, let alone that it has a big global following. Nowadays, the Bujinkan school founded by Masaaki Hatsumi is the most recognizable internationally. Apparently, he has 400,000 students around the world, including members of law enforcement agencies. A local TV station recently reported that his *dojo* in Chiba has

"overtaken Asakusa and the Ginza as a popular destination for foreign visitors." (Hang on.... As of 2015, that would mean around four million plus foreigners making their way to Noda City, which has a population of 155,644. Hmmm....)

In any case, it was the Iga and Koga *ninja* who started the rent-a-spy industry and there are still "*ninja* houses" set up for curious tourists which are worth going to if only because they are so incredibly tacky.

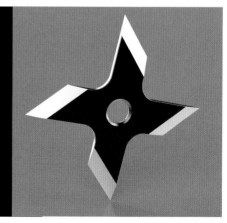

Left A real *shuriken*. They were not designed to kill but to hinder the enemy's advance. Who wants a multi-pronged razor blade whizzing at your face? Most throwing projectiles were not star shaped but more like oversized needles.

Right You are not allowed to carry a simple pocket-knife around in Japan now but you can still purchase these in souvenir shops!

FORMIDABLE SAMURAI WEAPONRY, ARMOR AND FORTIFICATIONS

"There is no country in the world where the sword has received so much honor and renown as in Japan. Regarded as of divine origin, dear to the general as a symbol of authority, cherished by the Samurai as a part of himself, considered by the common people as their protection against violence, how can we wonder to find it called the living soul of the Samurai?"
—Thomas McClatchie, talk given at the Asiatic Society of Japan (1873)

Above Early swords were called *tachi*. They were suspended at the left waist with the blade edge facing down.

Left Susanoo slays the eight-headed serpent and saves the maiden.

As professional men-at-arms, Samurai were familiar with a range of weapons. The bow and arrow was the mainstay of the Samurai arsenal for much of their history but other weapons came in and out of vogue depending on the era. The following overview merely scratches the surface but is a basic primer for *gai-sam*.

Swords of Mythical Power

An indication of the divine worth of swords can be seen in some of the myths and legends recorded in ancient chronicles such as *Kojiki* (712) and *Nihon Shoki* (720). For example, a well-known myth concerns the Kusanagi sword. Susanoo, the younger brother of the Sun Goddess Amaterasu Omikami, was kicked out of Heaven because of his bad attitude (he was the God of Storms). Wandering around Izumo in the Middle Reed County (earth), he came across an old couple crying as the eight-headed serpent, Yamata-no-Orochi, was about to take their last daughter away. Susanoo

The sword was actually an auxiliary weapon in the medieval Samurai's arsenal but no warrior would leave home without one.

devised a cunning plan and prepared eight big vats of *sake*. The serpent got drunk off its eight heads and Susanoo used his sword to slash the beast to pieces. Hearing the clunk of metal on metal, he dug into one of its tails and discovered a hidden sword—Ame-no-Murakumo-no-Tsurugi, so-named after the cloud that always followed the serpent around. The serpent now dead, Susanoo married the maiden and presented the sword to her older sister in Heaven as an apology for his ungodly behavior.

The sword was later passed back down to earth and used by the legendary Japanese warrior Prince Yamato Takeru (traditionally counted as the twelfth emperor of Japan), who conquered the eastern lands. When a treacherous warlord tricked him and set the grasslands he was in on fire, Takeru used the sword to mow the grass around him, thereby escaping a fiery end. From that time forth, the sword became known as Kusanagi, or the "Grass-cutter." It was included in the imperial regalia along with jewels and a mirror and still symbolizes imperial authority in Japan to this day. Incidentally, the original Kusanagi sword was lost beneath the waves at the Battle of Dannoura (Genpei War). A very old replica is enshrined in the Atsuta Jingu Shrine in Nagoya although nobody is allowed to see it.

Right Saito Katsuoki cutting flying arrows with his sword. Depicted in Utagawa Kuniyoshi's "Heroic Stories of the Taiheiki."

Far right Sword parts and their names.

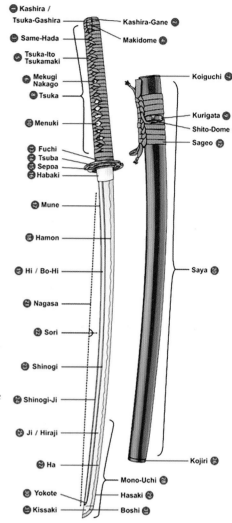

Kashira / Tsuka-Gashira
Kashira-Gane
Same-Hada
Makidome
Tsuka-Ito Tsukamaki
Koiguchi
Mekugi Nakago
Tsuka
Kurigata
Shito-Dome
Menuki
Sageo
Fuchi
Tsuba
Seppa
Habaki
Mune
Hamon
Saya
Hi / Bo-Hi
Nagasa
Sori
Shinogi
Shinogi-Ji
Kojiri
Ji / Hiraji
Mono-Uchi
Ha
Yokote
Hasaki
Kissaki
Boshi

At the Cutting Edge

Most people consider the *katana* as the representative weapon of Japan, but it was never the predominant weapon in battle. Bows and arrows really filled that role at first, and then pikes and firearms later on. In any case, following the introduction of straight double-edged swords in the ancient period (first to eighth centuries) from China, Japanese smiths began to develop a distinctive style of forging and blade design. Around the tenth century, specimens with curved blades and single cutting edges began to appear and were slung as a sidearm at the waist with the blade facing down. These were called *tachi* and were used from horseback by high-ranking warriors when arrows were no longer an option.

Around the fourteenth century, Samurai started wearing slightly shorter swords inserted firmly through their belts with the blades facing up. These were *katana*. They enabled more stability for fighting on foot and also made it possible to unsheathe the sword and strike in one quick motion. This was especially useful in daily life when not in armor. The appellation *nihonto* (Japanese sword) became widespread from the Tokugawa period to distinguish Japanese blades in general from Western or other swords.

Of the thousands of swordsmiths throughout Japanese history, Masamune (c. 1264–1343) was a legend. His blades were valued as the finest in the land. One of his disciples, Muramasa, dared to challenge his master. They both made blades and placed them in a river to test

them with the cutting edges facing the oncoming flow of water. Muramasa's sword sliced through everything that came down the stream—leaves, fish, plastic bottles. It was as if all objects were sucked into the blade. Masamune's, on the other hand, failed to attract anything; everything just seemed to flow around the blade's edge. Muramasa thought he'd won the encounter. A monk watching nearby appraised both swords. He said that Muramasa's sliced indiscriminately and was evil, whereas Masamune's was a compassionate blade that did not kill innocents and was obviously made by a truly enlightened master.

Forging a Samurai Blade:
Hold 'em and Fold 'em

The *katana* is made from *tamagahane* steel created by smelting iron sand. Low carbon metal forms the core and is encased with higher carbon metal. This mixture of metal is heated,

The process of forging a sword is long and labor intensive. After purification rituals are performed, the smith spends many hours hammering the lump of metal into shape, with sparks and sweat flying everywhere. It's little wonder few young people want to take up the craft these days.

Left Cutting through a straw roll like a hot knife through butter. It looks easy but the trajectory of the blade must be perfectly angled for a clean cut.

Above Swords were tested and graded on corpses and criminals.

hammered, folded, quenched, heated, hammered, folded and quenched for as many as 8 to 16 times. Each time the lump of steel is heated and folded, it is coated with a secret concoction of clay, water and straw-ash to prevent oxidation. Folding it up to 16 times will result in around 65,000 layers, which can be seen as the beautiful grain in a finely polished sword.

The metal is gradually crafted into the shape of a sword and continually refined. Before the final hot and cold treatment, a thin layer of clay is applied to the cutting edge and a thicker covering to the rest of the blade. Then it is heated again. The area with the thin covering will cool much quicker when doused in cold water, making it harder. This process creates the distinctive line on the blade edge called the *hamon*, which is revealed in the next stage of polishing. The style and shape of the *hamon* depends on how the thin layer of clay is applied and steadiness of hand!

The polishing is done by a *togishi* and it takes ages. Around seven polishing stones are used, starting with the coarsest, moving through to fine finishing stones. The finest are difficult to find in the natural environment these days and artificial polishing stones are becoming the norm. The polish is the icing on the cake and requires patience and skill. A bad polish will ruin the blade. No grinders are allowed.

Incidentally, a real sword must be registered at the local Board of Educa-tion, not the police. This is because a traditionally forged blade is classified as a "work of art" rather than a weapon. A license will be issued that must accompany the sword at all times. According to Japanese law, a sword-smith in Japan is allowed to make up to 24 blades a year as long as they are forged using traditional methods.

Cutting Power: The Granddaddy of Ginzu

Some say that the *katana* is the sharpest sword in the world. I've never worked out how such claims can be validated—all swords are sharp—but the hard exterior and flexible interior of the *katana* does give it astounding cutting power. I once missed the "carp's mouth" when sheathing my own sword—i.e. the hole where the sword tip is inserted into the scabbard—and accidentally sliced the area between my left thumb and forefinger. I didn't notice until the front of my white *gi* and *hakama* suddenly turned red! I shuddered to think what it could do with full force.

If you really want to test how sharp a sword is, you can try your hand at *tameshi-giri*, literally "test cutting," where rolls of *tatami* are soaked in water, placed vertically or horizontally and ceremoniously chopped from all angles. Cutting is a lot harder than it looks if your technique is askew. The angle of the blade must be perpendicular to the surface on impact, otherwise it won't cut through and may even bend. Vertical cuts are relatively easy to perform with a bit of practice, but backhand and diagonal cuts are a lot harder. Horizontal cuts are the hardest. Iaido probably won't do it for you if you're interested in actually using a sword to cut things. Joining a *battodo dojo* is your best bet but can be a bit expensive. By the way, although the cutting power of blades was tested on dead bodies or live criminals, and in the right hands could even cut through a metal *kabuto* (battle helmet), one thing a *katana* can't cut through is a big slab of chocolate. Go figure.

Symbolic Power of the Sword

With the dawn of the Iron Age in Japan, swords were originally used as implements in religious ceremonies. The shiny, hard quality of the metal imported from China represented

The first few years of training in Iaido, usually up to the grade of 4th Dan, will be conducted with a stainless steel replica sword with a blunted edge. These are called *iaito*.

advanced technology. Influenced by Taoist ideology, swords were believed to contain magical powers with the ability to ward off evil.

From around the fifteenth century, the Samurai developed a custom of rewarding warriors with swords for meritorious deeds. Medieval Samurai fought for prizes and hoped to receive parcels of land for their valiant service. As the land available for allocation became scarcer, they could also be rewarded with money or valuable items such as antique tea utensils (like getting socks for Christmas) or a sword. A specimen deemed extraordinary by virtue of having been forged by a legendary smith like Masamune, or maybe because it once belonged to some famous warrior, were called *meito*. Although an inanimate object, *meito* would even be given a name like "goblin slicer" or "drying pole" and were representative of the owner's political authority or gallantry.

Speaking of names, edicts stipulated that only Samurai were to carry two swords and have a surname. Privileged commoners were sometimes awarded these rights on occasion. And, although against the law, more than a few peasants actually possessed swords for self-protection against volatile vagrants and *ronin*. Officially, however, a long and short sword set of two became the membership badge for "Club Samurai."

Yabusame is a popular tourist attraction at some period events and festivals. The rider, I am told, must synchronize his mind with the horse's for the arrow to fly true.

The Yumi and the Ya

Samurai were originally called "adherents of the Way of the Bow and Arrow," such was the importance placed on archery by the earliest Samurai. Like swords, bows also had an important function in religious ceremonies and were considered to be more than just weapons. Battles would commence with the release of a *kaburaya*, an arrow that whistled as it flew through the air, only to plop back to earth like a spent firework. Awkward moment, and then all hell would break loose.

Feats in archery were lauded as proof of a superior warrior. When Yoshitsune dropped his bow into the water at the Battle of Yashima (1185), he risked life and limb to get it back. The bow was small and he did not want the enemy Taira warriors to get hold of it and think that the Minamoto commander was a weakling! A bit of a bow complex there. One of my favorite stories concerning arrows can be found in the

Tale of Hogen. "Kagemasa, who is now revered as a god, was only a youth of sixteen. When shot in the right eye with an arrow, Kagemasa, without even removing the arrow, shot an 'answering arrow' and killed an enemy. Thus did he bequeath his name to posterity." If only King Harold had been as robust.

There were two types of archery—mounted and on foot. The former was an indispensable skill for highly ranked warriors who would hone their abilities through *yabusame*, *inuoumono* and *kasagake*—three equestrian archery contests. *Yabusame* is still popular as a tourist attraction in Kyoto and Kamakura and involves a mounted archer who releases arrows at three stationary targets or boards while riding a straight course at full gallop. *Inuoumono* was a pitiless training method in which a large circular area was roped off with a smaller circle inside. Warriors galloped around the outer ring and fired their arrows at moving targets—hapless mutts placed in the inner circle. In the case of *kasagake*, mounted archers galloped down a causeway releasing hollow whistling *kaburaya* arrows at targets such as fans or suspended hats. The tradition of Samurai archery is maintained in the popular modern Budo of Kyudo. One of the important classical traditions of archery (*kyujutsu*) that led to the modern art was the Heki-ryu, created by Heki Danjo Matatsugu around 1480.

KEY BUDO CONCEPTS: *Kigurai* 気位 "Gravitas"

Some call it "loftiness of mind" while others call it "pride." It is essentially an aura of strength or a commanding presence that comes from having unfaltering confidence in one's capability. A person with true *kigurai* does not feel obligated in the slightest to boast of his or her talents. It just is. It is not something that can be emulated or pretended, for it is a natural by-product of years and years of diehard training—hell and back, and then back to hell again to spit on the devil. A person who radiates *kigurai* has a certain majesty and serenity about them. They have gravitas—an air of grace and nobility that makes people go "Oh, really nice dude, but I wouldn't want to mess with him!" It is not to be confused with arrogance or seething aggression, as it appears in those who try to fake it. Think of the difference between Mr Miyagi and hard-nosed Cobra Kai *sensei* John Kreese in the classic movie *The Karate Kid*.

Naginata and Pikes: More Than Pointy Sticks

The *naginata* was a relatively common weapon among early medieval Samurai. It was basically a sword on a stick and was particularly useful for slashing at horses or at foe from a safe distance. The butt end of the *naginata* could be used for coshing fallen enemies in the face. Being a bladed weapon, the *naginata* required skill to use. As was the case with swords, it wouldn't cut very well and could easily break if the angle of the blade was slightly off on impact. Then you would be left with a stick without a blade, which was how *bojutsu*—the art of the long staff—came about. The *naginata* became obsolete around the end of the fourteenth century with the introduction of pikes (*yari*). It remained the favored weapon of warrior-monks (*sohei*) and would later become a weapon studied primarily by women of warrior families. As such, the modern Budo art of Naginata is mainly practiced by women.

The revolutionary pike was in many ways the simplest weapon on medieval battlefields. Its use proliferated from the middle of the fourteenth century, and records indicate that in the period from 1467 to 1600, *yari* accounted for somewhere around 80 percent of inflicted casualties in pitched battle. Armies in this period had become huge semi-

professional units consisting of peasant conscripts who were trained to follow orders and stay in formation. A massive wall of bristling pointy sticks moving forward in unison was significantly more devastating than individual Samurai charging forth haphazardly in pursuit of personal glory. In other words, teamwork rather than individual play became the name of the game. When large lines of pikemen poked in unison it was like a giant angry porcupine trudging forth to impale all in its path.

Pikes could be from 4.5 to 6.5 meters (14.8 to 21.3 ft) in length, with straight metal tips that were not only pointy but had bladed edges as well. Various schools of *sojutsu* (pikemanship) arose. Of the most famous are the Hozoin-ryu and Owari-kan-ryu. The former uses *jumonji-yari*, which has a crescent-shaped hook to entangle attacker's weapons. The Owari Kan-ryu utilizes the *kudayari* (tube pike), characterized by its strong, rapid techniques for attack and defense by thrusting the shaft forward and back through a hand-held tube.

There is no modern incarnation of *sojustu* as a modern Budo. The closest is Jukendo (the "Way of the Bayonet"), which apparently borrowed some techniques from the art of the pike when it was developed in the nineteenth century.

Flashes, Bangs and Iron Balls

Conventional wisdom suggests that firearms were first introduced to Japan by Portuguese traders in the little southern island of Tanegashima (1543). Maybe this was not the only route, but by the end of the sixteenth century firearms were an integral part of any Daimyo's army. Nobunaga is known as one of the first to successfully integrate guns into his armory and used them to devastating effect. Not always that accurate, and time-consuming to load, they still made a lot of noise and must have frightened the living daylights out of horses.

For much of the Tokugawa period, guns were perceived more as farming tools than weapons. In spite of laws forbidding peasant possession of weapons, they used guns to scare off or kill dangerous animals like bears and wild boar. Although eschewed on the battlefield as

An entourage of Samurai posing with an array of different weapons. This is typical of photos staged in the Meiji period for foreign consumption.

Some classical martial art demonstrations will finish with a bang if a *hojutsu* school of gunnery, such as Morishige-ryu or Inatomi-ryu, is in attendance.

a weapon "not worthy of a Samurai" (it was mainly used by drafted peasants), the Tokugawa-period Samurai elite took pleasure in going on hunting excursions with guns as a display of status and prowess. Like other martial arts, *hojutsu* schools continued teaching the art of gunnery, complete with rituals, *kata*, arcane teachings and secret transmission scrolls.

From around the 1840s, guns were brandished by vulnerable peasants in self-defense against disenfranchised Samurai, outcasts and other unsavory elements who threatened the peace in this politically volatile age.

O-yoroi worn in the late Heian and Kamakura periods was designed for mounted warriors. Samurai of later periods wore armor that was still colorful but less bulky.

Samurai Armor

Early forms of armor, as seen on ancient clay figurines, consisted of iron plates fastened together with leather cords. The grandiose style of *o-yoroi*, synonymous with warriors of the Heian period, were later made of six main components—the *do* (torso protector), *kabuto* (battle helmet), *menpo* (freaky face mask), *kote* (protective gauntlets), *sune-ate* (shin protectors) and *hai-date* (thigh protectors). The suits were effective in mitigating the impact of arrows and slashes from cold steel. They also had moveable panels which provided the mounted archer with protection as he lined up his targets. The panels were fastened together in such a way that they were flexible enough to enable the warrior to release arrows from horseback, but there was a trade-off. It was cumbersome and difficult to move when forced to fight on foot.

One advantage of the *o-yoroi* over Western suits of armor was that they used very little iron. Instead, bamboo or leather panels were laced together with cord and covered with lacquer. This made the *o-yoroi* comparatively light and resistant to those embarrassing rusty patches at the back. The total weight was around 27 kg (60 lb).

The color of the armor, its design, lacing patterns, adornments on the helmet and pictures embossed on the torso were identifiers of the warrior's clan and rank. This was

particularly useful in the chaos of battle to ensure you didn't take a sword to one of your allies, or vice versa. Just as important to warriors was being recognized in battle when performing some heroic feat. This encouraged the design of some outrageously ostentatious suits. *Yoroi* served the absolute opposite function of modern camouflage gear.

From the late thirteenth through to the mid-fourteenth century, a gradual transition was made to a cheaper, lighter wrap-around style of armor called *hara-maki*. This suggested a shift away from mounted archers as the dominant factor in battle, since the simpler armor offered stability and the option of using longer weapons, such as *yari*, without impediment.

Sets of armor would often be passed on through the generations as family heirlooms. Many still survive today, and you can easily pick up a set in an antique shop for around $3,000. That's about the cost of a decent set of Kendo armor (*bogu*), which resembles traditional *yoroi* in terms of basic design.

合気

BUDO CALLIGRAPHY: *Ai-ki*
"Harmonizing the Chi"

Harmonizing one's *chi* or "inner-energy" with the opponent as they execute an attack or defensive maneuver. These are the first two ideograms in Aikido. *Ai-ki* was described as meaning "love" by the founder and is a common concept in all Budo.

KEY BUDO CONCEPTS: *Nanba* and *Suriashi* 摺足・歩行法
"The Importance of Footwork"

It doesn't matter what Budo you learn, the first thing you will be taught is footwork (*ashisabaki* or *taisabaki*). You can't build a house without a solid foundation and footwork is the foundation for all Budo movement. Although there are

various kinds of footwork, all Budo have *suriashi* in common. *Suriashi* is sliding across the ground as if there is a sheet of paper between the sole of the feet and floor. When I was at high school, I was constantly irritated by the way my Japanese classmates scuffed their feet noisily across the ground. Through Kendo I discovered that "feet scuffing" (sliding) was a peculiarly Japanese mode of moving, not only in bare feet but also when wearing traditional platform clogs and straw sandals.

Suriashi allows the warrior to maneuver evenly and react instantaneously to any situation. This is the same kind of footwork seen in Noh theater. If you placed a cup of coffee on the walker's head, not a drop would be spilled. The movement is very hip-centric, with no superfluous bobbing up and down. The lower body is perfectly balanced and the upper body is free to flourish a fan or a sword.

In recent years, the word *nanba* has come out of obscurity and is being applied to all manner of athletic pursuits as Japan's very own traditional style of movement. *Nanba* is a kind of *suriashi*. It is commonly defined as moving the right and left sides of the body through a vertical axis rather than right foot–left

arm, left foot–right arm. In other words, there is no twisting in the middle of the torso and hence no extra strain on the body. Apparently, the Japanese lost this style of movement with the introduction of Western marching and calisthenics in the nineteenth century. *Nanba* possibly originated in the agricultural lifestyle through planting the paddy fields, shuffling along with the right foot and right hand forward. It offers stability and the ability to sidestep an oncoming attacker with minimal effort. It is a common style of movement in most Budo.

No Tools? Yawara

Readers have probably heard of the term *jujitsu* before. Brazilian Jujitsu has a massive worldwide following in MMA circles and "sports Jujitsu" is quite popular in Europe (although mostly unheard of in Japan). Properly written as *jujutsu*, the "flexible art" is a generic term for unarmed grappling or immobilization of a weapon wielding adversary. Another common designation is *yawara* (also read as *ju*), and was a vital skill for Samurai. Early schools arose in the middle ages and incorporated the use of smaller weapons, such as daggers, and grappling in full armor. The *yawara* arts became less weapon oriented with the onset of the peaceful Tokugawa period.

The fundamental ideal is *ju-no-ri* or the "principle of yielding," that is, to combine one's strength with the opponent's and use it against them. In other words, flexibility overcomes firmness. The modern Budo disciplines of Judo and Aikido trace their lineage back to classical styles of *jujutsu*, of which there were many. One of Japan's most successful modern Judo athletes, Tani Ryoko, is affectionately referred to as "Yawara-chan" (Little Miss Yawara).

Bugei Juhappan: The 18 Critical Martial Skills

Bugei juhappan literally means the "18 martial arts" that were studied by Samurai during the Tokugawa period. The concept was basically copied from

earlier Chinese teachings but in Japan it came to mean all of the martial arts, not just 18. What the "18" martial arts were really depends. Each feudal domain or *ryuha* had its own twist on things. Generally speaking, the following 18 martial arts are usually cited: *kyujutsu* (archery), *bajutsu* (horsemanship), *suijutsu* (swimming), *naginata-jutsu* (glaive), *sojutsu* (pikemanship), *kenjutsu* (swordsmanship), *kogusoku* (grappling with armor on), *bojutsu* (long staff), *jojutsu* (short staff), *kusarigama-jutsu* (sickle and chain), *fundo-kusari* (weighted chain), *shuriken-jutsu* (hand-held projectile weapons), *fukumibari-jutsu* (spitting needles), *jutte-jutsu* (truncheon), *iaijutsu* or *battojutsu* (sword drawing),

Do Real Samurai Still Exist Today?

No! Well, no, but sort of.... At least as an ideal the emotive power of the word "Samurai" still evokes mostly positive images representing a model of strength, stoic resolve, selfless loyalty and compassion. Any Japanese who performs magnificently on the international stage is affectionately called a Samurai, never a townsman or a farmer. The Japanese national soccer team is referred to as the "Samurai Blue," and the poor old salaryman slaving away at the office is also a "Samurai." There are the odd—and I mean odd as in weird—right-wing ultra-nationalistic xenophobes who believe that they are incarnations of Samurai and the Bushido spirit. I have also met quite a few people in the martial arts world who somehow think that they are modern-day Samurai. In fairness, they do sort of dress like Samurai and carry swords around.

Interestingly, though, most of the Japanese people I know do not boast about their ancestors if they happened to be real Samurai. It might come up in conversation as an aside but it is never a point that is dwelled upon. The Samurai class was dismantled in 1869 and replaced with the new status of *shizoku*, albeit without their previous privileges. Even though Samurai only made up a small portion of the population during the Edo period, it's still claimed that, as a nation, the Japanese have inherited the warrior spirit. On a genealogical level, few people really care but from an idealistic and even nationalistic standpoint the Samurai spirit is very much the pride of Japan. Given my insatiable Budo habit, some people even call me the "Blue-eyed Samurai." I guess it's meant as a compliment but I prefer the "Lost Samurai" myself.

jujutsu (grappling), *mojiri-jutsu* (barbed staff or bear-hand), *sasumata-jutsu* (fork spear), *shinobi* (intelligence gathering and espionage), *hojutsu* (gunmanship). That makes 19. There were others as well, such as *chikujo-jutsu* (fortification), and one *ryuha* even had *yadome-jutsu* to deflect flying arrows! (Judged implausible by *MythBusters*.)

Kamon: Clan Logos™

The Japanese *kamon* ("house crest") was stitched on clothes, flags, tents and equipment to signify which clan one belonged to. Medieval battles were chaotic affairs, so easy identification was imperative to avoid friendly fire. And, of course, there was the matter of getting due credit for services rendered in the fray. Troupes of performers and merchant houses also adopted crests. Compared to Western coat of arms, Japanese *kamon* are generally mono-chrome, circular and feature stylized renditions of all manner of objects, such as plants, birds and ideograms. Even within the same clan, there might be stylistic variations of the same *kamon*. All Japanese families have a *kamon*, which is emblazoned on *kimono* or *haori* jackets for formal occasions. Kendo practitioners often put their *kamon* on the upper left chest area of their torso protector (*do*), as did Samurai on their *yoroi*. Some of the more famous *kamon* in Japan include the three diamonds used by the Mitsubishi group and the chrysanthe-mum blossom of the imperial family. Incidentally, the iconic Louis Vuitton monogram canvas uses *kamon* designs.

Although there are exceptions, most *kamon* are circular in shape and do not include a written motto.

Left Historical re-enactment is becoming popular as a form of entertainment in Japan these days. From behind, this guy looks more like a Viking than a Samurai.

Right With the onset of the Tokugawa period, the Shogunate only permitted one castle per domain. This was enough because it took more than the average mortgage to build!

Castles: Buttressing Butts

Many of Japan's major cities today have their origins as medieval castle towns. Nagoya is a prime example. As warlords sought to increase holdings, they needed to consolidate their military and their agricultural and commercial assets in defendable locations. A castle would typically be built at a strategic site, perhaps on a hill near an important river or port. It would be surrounded by farmlands with the area immediately below the castle serving as a busy hub for commerce and trade.

Early medieval fortresses were built of wood leaving them prone to fire in times of conflict! Towards the end of the sixteenth century massive castles constructed from stone adorned the landscape and were intended to intimidate invading armies as much as to protect the inhabitants. A fascinating characteristic of later castles were the designs which incorporated multiple gates and narrow pathways to confuse invaders and herd them into inescapable open spaces for slaughter from the walls above.

Although there were around 5,000 castles spread throughout Japan at one time or another, many were destroyed in the chaos of the Warring States period, during the Meiji period when Samurai domains were dismantled, and more recently in World War II air raids. There are 100 so-called "Famous Castles" left today in various states of (dis)repair. The one in Sakura City exists in name only, and only 12 are in their original state—Bitchu Matsuyama Castle, Hikone Castle, Himeji Castle, Hirosaki Castle, Inuyama Castle, Kochi Castle, Marugame Castle, Maruoka Castle, Matsue Castle, Matsumoto Castle, Matsuyama Castle in Iyo and Uwajima Castle. All are well worth a visit.

TEN LITTLE KNOWN SAMURAI FACTS

1. There were women combatants. Excavations of old battle sites have found female DNA among the bones.
2. Early armor was designed to allow firing arrows from the left, making it challenging when the target was to the right! This is also why the sword is traditionally worn on the left side. The US military produced the world's first modern flak jacket based on Samurai armor.
3. There have been a handful of Western Samurai. Notable among them were the Englishman William Adams, his Dutch associate Jan Joosten van Lodensteijn, French navy officer Eugene Collache and a Dutch/German arms dealer by the name of Henry Schnell.
4. Samurai were a minority group in the Tokugawa period at around 6 percent of the population.
5. Samurai were highly fashion conscious and as such were very much social trendsetters.
6. The Samurai of the early modern period were well educated and versed in the classics, poetry, garden design, painting and the tea ceremony.
7. Although portrayed in contemporary pop culture as burly specimens of masculine perfection, the average height of a sixteenth-century Samurai ranged from 160 to 165 cm (5 ft 3 in to 5 ft 5 in).
8. Samurai wrote death poems before committing *seppuku*.
9. Samurai were often bisexual. Toyotomi Hideyoshi was derided by his peers because he had no interest in boys.
10. Samurai used to burn incense in their helmets before departing for battle so that their heads smelled nice if removed by the enemy. Most thoughtful.

CHAPTER 2

CORE CONCEPTS OF BUSHIDO

"Bushido" is a word bandied about to signify all that is good about Japan. Following the 3/11 tragedy in 2011, for example, social commentators in Japan and around the world attributed the calm demeanor, selflessness and remarkable forbearance shown by the victims as being indicative of the "spirit of Bushido." Shelves in bookshops are adorned with a plethora of publications seeking to right the social, economic or cultural woes of Japan through rekindling the canon of Bushido. Ask the average Japanese "What is Bushido?" The reply will inevitably be "Why, that's the Japanese spirit," followed by a few mutterings about "Nitobe Inazo," and "Kinda like chivalry." Basically, there are three broad takes on Bushido. First, popular fanciful fiction that portrays adherents of Bushido as superhuman paragons of awesomeness. Second, scholastic surveys, often with a left-wing bent, that delve into the historical reality of the lives of professional men-of-arms but consider notions of Bushido as chimerical hocus-pocus not worthy of serious academic enquiry. Third, pseudo-scholastic surveys, usually with a heavy right-wing bent, that idealize a one-size-fits-all Samurai ideal as being the essence of "Japaneseness." Whatever the case, the following guide should help the *gai-sam* engage in an informed conversation about the topic from all angles as it will inevitably crop up frequently in Budo circles.

常川團十郎
行年 三十二紫
猿白院清成日田信士
嘉永七寅年
浪花天王寺村
八月六日自殺
一心寺ニ葬
辞世

Left A depiction of Ichikawa Danjuro VIII, the superstar Kabuki actor, taking his own life. Although he performed *seppuku* in theaters throughout his career, this method of suicide was reserved for Samurai. In actual fact, he slit his wrists in 1854, possibly because of debt incurred through his lavish celebrity lifestyle.

Below *Seppuku* staged at a studio during the Meiji period. Westerners had a morbid fascination with this custom.

THE SAMURAI CODE GLORIFYING HONOR, VIOLENCE AND DEATH

By the time Samurai warriors had set up a "tent government" during the Kamakura period (1185–1333), they had already developed a unique culture predicated on a ferocious appetite for fame, glory and honor. Although it was not codified at this early stage, warrior culture was referred to by an array of terms, such as *bando musha no narai* (customs of the Eastern warriors), *yumiya no michi* (the "Way of the Bow and Arrow") and *kyuba no michi* (the "Way of the Bow and Horse"). The term Bushido was not coined, in fact, until the late sixteenth century (first seen in the *Koyo-gunkan*), and only really became the prevalent word referring to Samurai ethics in the twentieth century.

The driving force behind Samurai culture has always been the pursuit of honor. Honor formed the basis of a unique cultural style for the Samurai's collective identity. Without implying that nobles and peasants lacked a sense of honor, there are comparatively few examples of any who strove to maintain it at the cost of their own lives. This made Samurai honor distinctive. The Samurai created unique rules for interacting with honorific expressions. These rules directed the relationships between Samurai of all ranks. It was the adhesive for Samurai politics and social life. They also harbored an unquenchable urge to enhance the name of their family and were fiercely competitive in ensuring that their reputation would last for posterity. In this sense, the quest for honor and avoiding shame became inextricably linked to combat prowess and unremitting valor.

Seppuku: The Gory "Gut Cut"

One of the first recorded instances of *seppuku*, commonly called *hara-kiri* and erroneously pronounced "harry-carry" in the West, was performed by Minamoto-no-Yorimasa during the Battle of Uji in 1180. Over time, the act of ritual suicide became highly refined and performed for various reasons.

1. Warriors committed suicide rather than suffer death at the hands of their enemies.
2. A naughty Samurai would be allowed to take his own life rather than suffer the humiliation of execution. This "privilege" was not afforded to other classes.
3. Some Samurai committed *seppuku* to protest their lord's behavior and make a point.
4. Some Samurai were ordered to commit *seppuku* to atone for their lord's transgressions!
5. Many Samurai in the seventeenth century committed *seppuku* upon the death of their lord as a show of loyalty. This was eventually outlawed because too many Samurai were doing it under duress.
6. Women in Samurai families were taught how to commit suicide in an act known as *jigai*. They would tie their knees together to avoid ending up in an immodest position after they stabbed themselves in the jugular with a *tanto* dagger.

Left A grisly illustration of a criminal about to be executed by decapitation. The picture provides details for setting up the execution site.

Below A curious scene of a Samurai disemboweling himself next to his bedding. In most cases, *seppuku* was performed in front of witnesses with a second standing by for the mercy blow.

An assistant (*kaishakunin*) became a part of the ritual from around the seventeenth century. The condemned man would don white robes, kneel down placing his sword in front of him and compose his mind by writing a death poem. The sword would then be plunged into the gut and drawn horizontally to slice through the intestines and flesh. Once the Samurai had finished the gut cut, he would extend his neck for his assistant to put him out of his misery through decapitation. The *kaishakunin* was not an executioner as such, but rather a trusted colleague. The role was supposedly a great honor but also a pain in the neck. If you can chop your mate's head off in one smooth swipe, then it was all good, but a less skilled or slightly nervous swordsman might need a couple of blows, which was seen as a terrible

embarrassment for all concerned. It was also considered a mark of skill if the head was not lopped entirely off as it tended to fly through the air toward spectators. Preferably, a little tag of skin would remain connecting the head to the neck.

Witnesses of the *seppuku* would report on the proceedings and grade the manner with which it was carried out. A particularly brave Samurai would perform a horizontal cut followed by a vertical cut from the solar plexus down

without the service of a *kaishakunin*. This was a certain A grade in the report card. The dying act of the Samurai was literally the culmination of his life and bespoke his merits as a man. Screaming or writhing in pain would be an abominable stain on his personal and family honor, not to mention the *tatami* mats.

The Emperor Meiji's funeral was held on September 13, 1912, and the national hero General Nogi Maresuke committed *seppuku* to repay his debt of honor and follow his lord in death. His wife joined him by cutting her own throat in a double suicide that shocked but simultaneously moved the nation. When Emperor Hirohito died in 1989, many old Japanese men committed *seppuku*. The great Japanese author Mishima Yukio committed *seppuku* in 1970 at the Japan Self Defense Force Ichigaya base in Tokyo as a protest against Japan's postwar "loss of spirit." The famous Japanese Judo champion Isao Inokuma, winner of the gold medal in the heavyweight division at the 1964 Olympics in Tokyo, committed *seppuku* after a monumental business failing in 2001. These examples represent *seppuku* as a show of loyalty, protest or atonement, respectively. So, it still happens in Japan, but what if you're asked to be the *kaishakunin*? A friend of mine actually received such a request. Thank goodness he turned it down. According to Japanese law, the role of *kaishakunin* is not treated as "assisted suicide" but as "contract murder."

KEY BUDO CONCEPTS:
Bunbu-ryodo 文武両道 "The Two Ways of Scholarship and Martial Arts"

Balance is crucial in Budo and is epitomized in the ideal of *bunbu-ryodo*. *Bu* refers to combat and denotes military valor. *Bun* implies scholarly pursuits and the arts—"The Brush and Sword in Accord." The warrior was expected to be skilled at arms and also in the arts. The term *bunbu-ryodo* is often mentioned in Japan today. It points to youths who show prowess in sports while throwing themselves into their studies. The kind of excellence expected in a modern Budo practitioner is essentially the same—strength in body and mind, a rounded, compassionate and affable personality and a high level of perception and powers of discernment. Muscle-bound ignoramuses fall far from the ideal. The warrior's education demands a balance. Spiritual, technical and intellectual cultivation are not considered to be exclusive but, rather, integrated components of a single whole.

Only high-ranking samurai rode horses. At 1.2–1.5 m (4–5 ft) tall, the Japanese horse was much smaller than Western breeds. They were not particularly fast either, but they got Samurai to their appointments with death on time.

The Good Old Days?

Despite the romantic depictions of Samurai in prominent medieval war tales, greed for land, power and self-advancement was always prevalent in the larger picture. This climaxed in one of the most turbulent times in Japanese history—the Warring States period of the fifteenth and sixteenth centuries—where multitudes of rival Daimyo warlords vied to conquer and rule Japan. It was a period when unquestioned loyalty to one's overlord was often conveniently forsaken for personal gain. Alliances and promises were broken as quickly as they were made. It was a volatile period where the rise or demise of a great Daimyo, his *ie* (house) and its members was only a treacherous back stab away.

The uncertainty led to a proliferation of "house rules" (*kakun*), laws (*hatto*) and prescripts outlining model Samurai behavior—a clear indication that model behavior was far from the norm. This resulted in efforts to codify the "Way of the Warrior." The warrior ideal became pragmatic, but was simultaneously cloaked in principles beseeching virtues such as loyalty to somehow safeguard the survival of the clan. Still, the Warring States period was revered by future generations as "the good old days" when Samurai were totally staunch dudes who would sacrifice all for the sake of honor.

War Tales: Gory Glory

Such images of the Samurai and the nebulous canon of Bushido were influenced by a genre of literature called "war tales" (*gunki monogatari*). War tales relayed the adventures of Samurai laughing in the face of death, their honor and sentiments of loyalty, and even dastardly acts of cowardice and betrayal. They embellish historic battles with gory sensationalism and heartstring plucking that would even make Hollywood storytellers wince. The genre was extremely popular among warriors who enjoyed hearing about the feats of their ancestors. Two of the most famous ones are *The Tale of the Heike* and the *Taiheiki*, both of which are available in English and are well worth a read. Many of the stories are depicted on beautifully painted golden screens. They inspired Noh plays and a culture of musical renditions by blind lute-playing itinerant troubadours.

House Precepts (Kakun)

"House precepts" were written by the patriarch of a clan to convey detailed advice for avoiding honor-destroying faux pas. They outlined many facets of daily life such as where to sit at a

---

KEY BUDO CONCEPTS:

Katsunin-ken Setsunin-to 活人剣・殺人刀 **"Life-giving Sword, Death Dealing Blade"**

On a practical level, as taught in the Yagyu Shinkage-ryu school of swordsmanship, *katsunin-ken* (also called *katsujin-ken*) involves coaxing the opponent into striking first, then countering when he is in full flight, or have him come to a standstill after a failed attempt. It means that you have to put your life on the line and manipulate the enemy's mind, controlling him like a puppet.

The "life-giving sword," or *ken*, uses the *kanji* 剣, which denotes a double-edged sword, that is, with cutting edges directed toward both the opponent and the wielder, the philosophical inference being that, although the swordsman tries to cut his enemy with the outward-facing blade, he is simultaneously seeking self-improvement through the ongoing act of self-castigation represented metaphorically by the inward-facing cutting edge. Therein lies the paradox of skills to kill connecting with the ideal of self-cultivation and peacefulness. Learn how to kill, develop the strength to choose not to, then become a better person who is an advocate for not killing. Thus, peace was seen as the ultimate goal of martial training.

The *to* in *setsunin-to* or "death-dealing blade" uses the same *kanji* as *katana* (刀). In other words, a single-edged blade, pointing in one direction only—the poor sucker in front of you. From a practical perspective, the "death-dealing blade" employed the strategy of overpowering or striking down an opponent before he could react. From a philosophical standpoint, dealing death with a sword was sometimes necessary in order to smite an evil man and purge the land of baddies. When a weapon is used for this purpose, it contributes to the greater good and thereby becomes a "life-giving" sword.

banquet, how to exchange *sake* cups, cleaning, travel etiquette and so on. For example, Imagawa Ryoshun beseeched his sons, "It is natural that a Samurai should learn the ways of war and apply himself to the acquisition of basic fighting skills needed for their occupation. But, neglecting the genteel arts will make it is impossible to be a worthy ruler...." In the *Chikubasho* (1383), Shiba Yoshimasa admonishes his descendants to pay attention to matters of propriety, self-cultivation and to detail. "Have a mind to improve one step at a time, and take care in speech so as not to be thought a fool by others." Further, "Be aware that men of insincere disposition will be unable to maintain control. All things should be done with singleness of mind. Warriors must be of calm disposition and have the ability to understand the measure of other people's minds. This is the secret to success in military matters." There are hundreds of examples of *kakun* dating back to

In the tenth month of 1185, Minamoto Yoritomo ordered a night attack on his younger brother Yoshitsune's mansion in the Horikawa district of Kyoto. A woodblock print by Utagawa Kuniyoshi.

Left Imagawa Ryoshun (1326–1420) was a prominent poet, military leader, Shogunate official and finally Buddhist monk.

Right Obata Kagenori compiled the *Koyo-gunkan*, the well-known chronicle of the Takeda clan.

the Muromachi period. They exemplify the first real codification of warrior ideals in line with the principle of *bunbu-ryodo*—proficiency in both the literary and military arts. The warrior's sensibilities, refined through appreciation and knowledge of the finer things in life, served as counterbalance to the cruel realties of the violent world he inhabited.

Koyo-gunkan: Silly Lords

Compiled in 1616, the *Koyo-gunkan* consists of 20 volumes with a total of 59 books. It was possibly the first book to ever use the word Bushido to describe the way a Samurai should live his

life. The text is centered on the life and times of Takeda Shingen (1521–73) and his son Takeda Katsuyori (1546–82), two famous Daimyo of the Warring States period. It covers the rise and fall of the Takeda clan, Takeda-style military tactics, constitution of the Takeda army, customs and weapons, laws and precepts. It is a rich source of information for the day-to-day living and culture of warriors in medieval Japan. The author is a point of much controversy and was thought to be Takeda Shingen's main counsellor (and male lover), Kosaka Danjo Masanobu. Tokugawa military strategist Obata Kagenori compiled the text, although

he is now considered by many scholars to be its main author. It was certainly a popular read among the Samurai of the Tokugawa period with its compelling commentary on human nature. Much of it seems perfectly relevant to our lives today, especially the section on the "four types of lords who ruin their

Above Yamaga Soko, one of the most influential scholars in redefining the Samurai's role in peacetime.

Right Facial armor that covered all or part of the face enabled the heavy helmet to be fastened securely to the head.

Below The 47 Ronin on their way back from assassinating Lord Kira in 1703.

domains and ultimately destroy their family lines."

The "foolish lord" is not only stupid but also conceited and selfish and infatuated with excursions, sightseeing, moon watching, flower viewing, poetry, linked verse and Noh. Wicked retainers become successful and everybody else imitates them to get ahead.

The lord who is "too smart" is generally vulgar and rude, arrogant and prone to depression. He harbors nefarious desires and will squeeze everything he can out of his vassals without considering their hardship. Convinced of his own cleverness, he will proclaim to have understood all after listening to only a little. He will be jealous of his bravest men, and afraid that his imperfections will be discovered, he will expel them or have most of them killed.

The "cowardly, weak lord" epitomizes all that runs counter to the "manly way"

of the Samurai. He moans a lot, is jealous of others, likes wealthy people and prefers subordinates who curry favor. He is unobservant, imprudent, uncompassionate, inconsiderate, not a good judge of character and only seeks to enhance his own reputation. His retainers soon lose their will to perform.

Strength would seem to be a virtue for a Samurai warlord, but not too much. The lord who is "too strong" is bold, astute, eloquent and persuasive. He is wiser than other men and despises any form of weakness. He rarely loses his temper and is never irrational. Being such an irreproachable fellow, if one of his counsellors feels obliged to offer advice, he will hesitate through fear of putting his lord in a bad mood. So, out of ten issues, he will only mention five, and even then three will not be explained adequately. The lord will become more obsessed with his own ideas, which will eventually result in failure. Many a good warrior will perish, and only "monkey Samurai" will be left.

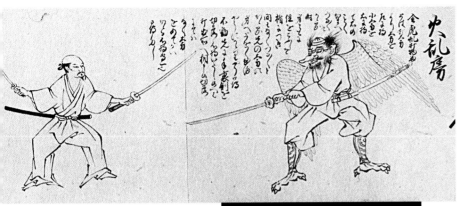

The Problem With Peace

When the Warring States period ended and Japan was ushered into a new era of peace under the Tokugawa, the Samurai found themselves in an unfamiliar situation. How could professional warriors justify their existence at the apex of society when there were no more wars to fight? A number of prominent scholars came to the rescue and independently formulated a new code of ethics for Samurai, which is now referred to collectively as Bushido. Arguments were circulated by Confucian scholars and military specialists (*gungakusha*) to justify the existence of military rule. For example, a virtuous ruler has the ability to use military force to protect the peace, and a "benevolent military government" was vital for the well-being of the realm. In other words, "the way of war is the way of peace." Such arguments were quickly accepted and helped solidify the resolve of the Shogunate.

Rank-and-file Samurai transformed into non-combatant civil servants, searching for meaning to their existence. Eventually, discipline and dedication to duty became the new measure for personal honor.

Scholarly Paragons

Prominent scholars such as Yamaga Soko (1622–85) and Daidoji Yuzan (1639–1730) provided the Samurai with much needed moral support and guidelines for behavior. For example, Yamaga Soko observed rhetorically, "The Samurai eats food without growing it, uses utensils without making it and profits without selling. What is the justification for this?" His solution was that the

A transmission scroll from a school of swordsmanship explaining techniques. The swordsman on the left faces a Tengu, a mythical goblin-like creature that excelled in martial arts.

Samurai's function in society was to serve his lord and to act as an exemplary moral example worthy of emulation by the masses. In other words, to live one's life in strict observance of correct moral behavior and etiquette, always maintaining a high level of military preparedness through practicing and perfecting the military arts. Proficiency in aesthetic and scholarly pursuits was also deemed as venerable as fighting bravely in battle. It was a far safer and less exciting substitute for war, but it served a need.

To this end, scholars and Samurai published step-by-step instruction booklets containing simple and practical advice on how a Samurai should act in any given situation. Getting out of bed early in the morning, moderation in food and drink, courtesy, education, grooming and respectability were redefined as the new warrior ideals. Even though death in the literal sense was not as likely as it once was, the concept was idealized to the effect that one was expected to fulfil one's duties with absolute selflessness.

There were several celebrated episodes during the Tokugawa period which demonstrated just how loyal to the point of death a true Samurai could be. The most famous example is the revenge of the 47 Ronin (Ako Affair). In 1701, a Daimyo (Lord Asano)

in attendance at the Shogun's castle in Edo drew his sword and assaulted an official because his honor had been slighted. The Daimyo was ordered to commit *seppuku* for this serious breach of protocol. His loyal retainers, who were greatly influenced by Yamaga Soko's ideals of duty, plotted and carried out a vendetta culminating in the successful assassination of the "antagonist" (Lord Kira) in the name of their master. This, in turn, led to the order of their own ritual suicide. The appropriateness of their actions attracted praise and criticism from all quarters. Some said it was an unforgivable criminal act, others said they should have done it quicker rather than plot for two years. Most people, however, admired them for their stubborn loyalty. They are still revered by modern Japanese for this reason and their legend is perpetuated in plays, films and books.

Art, War and Politics

In 1632, Yagyu Munenori, son of the great swordsman Yagyu Muneyoshi, finished his magnum opus, the *Heiho-kadensho* (Hereditary Book on the Art of War). The content was a fusion of Muneyoshi's and Kamiizumi Ise-no-Kami's (Muneyoshi's teacher and founder of the Shinkage-ryu) technical teachings on swordsmanship. This was spiced up with concepts borrowed from Noh and Zen. The influence of the celebrated Zen priest Takuan Soho (1573–1645), a personal friend of Munenori, is also evident throughout the text.

無
念
無
夢

BUDO CALLIGRAPHY:
Munen-muso
"No Design,
No Dream"

The spiritual state of selflessness, free from all worldly thoughts and desires.

It is divided into three sections: *Shinrikyo* (Shoe-offering Bridge), which outlines techniques; *Setsunin-to* (Death-dealing Blade) and *Katsunin-ken* (Life-giving Sword), which expounds on deep psychological concepts and philosophical ideals. Munenori points out that weapons are inherently "not nice" as killing runs counter to the "Way of Heaven." But there are times when force is justified to keep the peace: "Killing one man's evil so that ten thousand may live peaceably." This means that the warrior needs to be ready at all times. "Because of one man's evil, thousands suffer. So you kill that one man in order to let the thousands live. Here, truly, the blade that deals death becomes the sword that gives life."

Heiho-kadensho was one of the first books to promote the virtues of swordsmanship as a way of life and governance. The book was highly influential among Munenori's students. This is pertinent because he taught a couple of shoguns and a number of Daimyo lords! It provided them not only with an ideological basis for their study of *kenjutsu*, but some useful philosophical guidelines for ruling. He taught his students that the principles of warfare could be used to scrutinize the internal workings of the realm and to govern the people effectively.

Musashi's Book of Five Rings

Miyamoto Musashi wrote his classic *Gorin-no-sho* (Book of Five Rings) in 1645. It is often contrasted with Munenori's *Heiho-kadensho*. It consists of five chapters: *chi* (earth), *sui* (water), *ka* (fire), *fu* (wind) and *ku* (void). In *chi*, Musashi touches on his early career and the workings of his style of swordsmanship. In *sui*, he explains various aspects of individual combat, such as mental and physical posture, gaze, how to manipulate the sword, footwork and fighting stances. In *ka*, he expounds on how to choose the best site for dueling, how to control the enemy by taking the initiative and how to imple-

Miyamoto Musashi is arguably the most celebrated Japanese swordsman in history.

ment various stratagems. In *fu*, he criticizes other schools of swordsmanship and outlines their weaknesses. *Ku* is a short but nebulous chapter which explains how Musashi created his two-sword style, Niten Ichi-ryu, based on battle experience. He equates the supreme level of combat with all other arts and calls this realm "the void." "Through mastering the principles of sword work, the ability to triumph at will over one man means that you can defeat any man in the world. The mindset for defeating one is the same for beating one thousand or ten thousand. The strategy exercised by the general is to modify small-scale matters and apply them on a large scale, much like erecting a giant Buddha statue from a small thirty-centimeter model. It is not easy to write about such things in detail, but the principle underlying strategy is 'To know ten thousand things from knowing one thing.'"

Compared to Munenori's book, Musashi's is relatively short and simple and he doesn't dwell on complex Zen or Confucian concepts. There are similarities, however, such as the emphasis he places on mindset in combat and how mastery of the principles of strategy is a lifelong pursuit applicable to all facets of life. He also believes that the "Way of the Warrior" is not superior to

心身一如

BUDO CALLIGRAPHY:
Shin-shin-ichi-nyo
"Mind and Body As One"

The state in which the mind and body are juxtaposed rather than separate entities.

other Ways; the "Way of the Farmer" or the "Way of the Artisan" are essentially the same. The only difference is the that Way of the Warrior sought victory at all costs.

For this reason, the *Gorin-no-sho* is still a widely read and much appreciated book among modern Budo practitioners. Check out my translation.

☛ TUTTLE and BOOK OF FIVE RINGS

The Hagakure "Death Frenzy"

Properly titled *Hagakure-kikigaki* (literally "Dictations given hidden by leaves"), the *Hagakure* is undeniably the most infamous treatise on Bushido and the most misunderstood. Some even refer to it unfairly as the "evil book." Completed in 1716, it consists of 11 chapters containing approximately 1,300 aphorisms and contemplations concerning the people, history and culture of the Saga domain in Kyushu.

Some of the vignettes are short and to the point, but others are quite long and convoluted. They are difficult to make sense of without a contextual understanding of the dilemmas faced by Samurai in a time of peace.

In a nutshell, the *Hagakure* is a memoir of Yamamoto Jocho (aka Tsunetomo, 1659–1719) and his service to the Nabeshima clan. It chronicles feats of individual Samurai in the domain and the trials and tribulations of trying to succeed in the Samurai's community of honor. It serves as a fascinating window into the maelstrom of retainership and the strong emotional bonds that bound vassal and lord. It's quite violent in places, slightly erotic in others, but seeks to clarify the purest form of "hidden love" defined by absolute and selfless devotion to one's overlord.

Jocho was so enamored with his lord that his greatest desire was to martyr himself and follow him to the afterlife. To his chagrin, the practice of ritual disembowelment known as *junshi* had already been outlawed, so he retired from the mundane world and took the tonsure instead. It was at his hermitage shaded by trees that his junior clansman, Tashiro Tsuramoto, interviewed Jocho in his twilight years and wrote down his words for posterity.

Some of the stories are told with thoughtful reflection, while others are passionate rants about the ideal mindset of a warrior. Rather than a well-ordered philosophical discourse on Bushido, the book randomly plunges the reader into the darkest chasms of insanity. Then it restores in the reader a profound sense of equanimity and acceptance of the ephemeral nature of our existence. There is even the odd smattering of humor if one looks for it. The *Hagakure*'s underlying theme of absolute loyalty to the extent of being "prepared to die" in the course of duty is symbolized by the legendary phrase, "The Way of the Warrior is found in dying" (*Bushido to iu wa shinu koto to mitsuketari*). The anonymous hero of the book is the *kusemono*, a warrior who remains inconspicuous when things are calm but can be relied on in times of calamity when he will execute his duties with unmatched enthusiasm, without any concern for self-preservation.

Predictably, such notions of total self-sacrifice fitted well with the designs of Japan's militaristic machine before and during World War II. Most readers will immediately conjure up images of *kamikaze* pilots and their one-way missions to certain death. Indeed, pilots were not unknown to have pocket-sized editions of the *Hagakure* in their jackets as they zoomed to their doom. The *Hagakure* provided a powerful and emotive creed for wartime ultranationalists, in no small part due to its one-dimensional affirmation of loyalty to the point of "frenzied death" (*shini-gurui*). Was this, however, a fair interpretation of Jocho's actual intent? After painstakingly translating *Hagakure* over four years, I came to the realization that Jocho's morbid infatuation with death was actually an affirmation of life. By living as if you might die at any moment, each second on this earth becomes precious and is not to be wasted. If you want to know more about the *Hagakure*, please look for my translation.

☛ **TUTTLE and HAGAKURE**

Die on Your Futon

Often compared with the *Hagakure* is another book called *Budo Shoshinshu*. The *Hagakure* was written for warriors of one clan, whereas the *Budo Shoshinshu* was directed at all Samurai. There are several English translations of *Budo Shoshinshu*, such as *The Code of the Samurai* (Tuttle), but it literally means "A Collection for Novices in the Way of the Warrior." Budo in this context actually means Bushido, not the modern martial arts. It was written by Daidoji Yuzan (1639–1730) in his later years and was a handy how-to guide for Samurai who had to get along with each other in the city of Edo. Yuzan was a student of Yamaga Soko and carried on his work with a strong Confucian flavor. He could see the extreme tensions experienced by out-of-sorts warriors who were not quite sure what was expected of them. They were educated to be proud, noble and honorable and keep battle-ready through practicing the martial arts, but also had to keep a lid on it all. Meanwhile, merchants and townsmen were living prosperous lives without the shackles of duty imposed on them.

With the Shogunate-imposed requirement for all Daimyo to maintain a residence in Edo under a system of hostageship, the city was a melting pot of Samurai from rival clans. It wouldn't take much for tensions to explode, say, a drunken slip of the tongue at a blossom viewing party in Ueno, and if swords were drawn, somebody was sure to die. Anybody involved in a skirmish was punished by death, even if it was a matter of self-defense.

Yuzan's ideal for the Samurai was premised on the duty of loyalty. He differed from the more volatile doctrine in the *Hagakure* which advocated that Samurai always be prepared to take the most treacherous path. Yuzan taught that the Samurai should always be cognizant of death. If you accept the ever-present danger of dying, he argued, then you will do your

---

KEY BUDO CONCEPTS: *Koken-chiai* 交剣知愛
"Crossing Swords and Knowing Love"

Yep, it does sound a bit tree huggy. Perhaps too hippyish for a diehard martial artist, but this concept is the philosophical underpinning of all Japanese Budo. It's basically about learning respect and empathy. Even in competitive matches, etiquette is stressed as an expression of mutual respect, an ideal that sometimes gets overlooked in the excitement of intense competition. There is an understanding that all martial artists, irrespective of ability, shed the same blood, sweat and tears in the course of their arduous training regimes. Physical and mental barriers are smashed as the adherent develops skill, resilience and confidence in his or her ability. This experience encourages practitioners to develop a modest attitude to life and broaden their horizons through taking time to reflect upon and appreciate the cooperation of others in the quest for improvement. This ideal is known as *koken-chiai* (learning love and respect through crossing swords). It doesn't have to be just swords. It could be fists or feet. Train hard, learn and earn respect.

utmost to avoid it. Why? Because it is incumbent on a warrior to repay his obligations to his lord by living as long as possible to serve him. "No matter whether he be of high or low rank, if a man forgets about death, he will constantly eat and drink too much, will become involved in lasciviousness and all manner of unhealthy activities. This will be disastrous for his physical

condition and invite an unexpectedly early death. Even if he does live, he is destined to become a useless invalid."

Thus, the best way for a Samurai to die was not in a pointless street fight defending his honor but in a futon after a long lifetime of service.

Evolution of the ideogram *bu* (martial). The implication is to "stop" the use of weapons.

Nitobe Inazo's Bushido: Japanese DNA?

Although the Samurai class was dismantled after the Meiji Restoration, it did not mean the end of Bushido as a gripping emotive force. Samurai customs were temporarily suspended in the early Meiji surge toward modernization only to be revived from the mid-1880s as the cultural pendulum began to swing in a more nationalistic direction. It was a time when "Western technology" was complemented by "Japanese spirit" (*wakon-yosai*). One of the most influential purveyors of Bushido in the modern era was the Quaker convert Nitobe Inazo (1862–1933).

Nitobe was born into a Samurai family in Morioka, in the northeast of the country. His father apparently taught *jujutsu,* but Nitobe didn't have much experience in the martial arts. He was, however, a highly intelligent lad and was educated by foreign teachers almost entirely in English.

As a testament to his intellect and remarkable ability to navigate cultures, he became secretary of the League of Nations and was affectionately referred to as "the star of Geneva."

It is for his book, however, that he is most fondly remembered today. Following a conversation with a Belgian law professor in which Nitobe was at a loss to explain how Japanese children were taught morality in schools, he published *Bushido: The Soul of Japan* in English in 1900. In it, he depicted a wholesome interpretation of Samurai ethics to explain to the Western world that the Japanese, although not Christians, were certainly not barbarians devoid of moral fiber. One of his motives was to show

A general outline of distinctive warrior ideals divided by epoch.

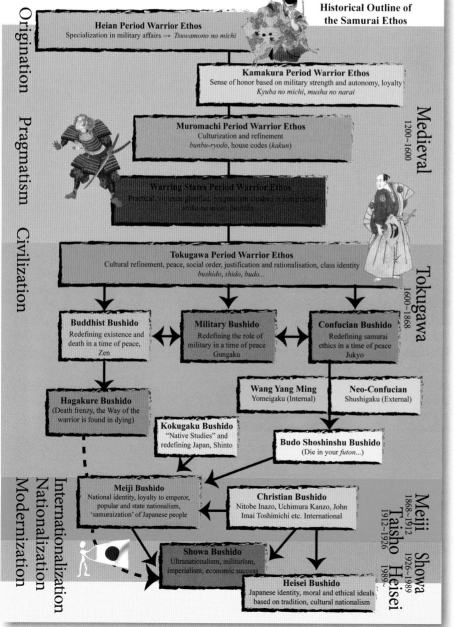

Historical Outline of the Samurai Ethos

Heian Period Warrior Ethos
Specialization in military affairs → *Tsuwamono no michi*

Kamakura Period Warrior Ethos
Sense of honor based on military strength and autonomy, loyalty
Kyuba no michi, musha no narai

Muromachi Period Warrior Ethos
Culturization and refinement
bunbu-ryodo, house codes (*kakun*)

Warring States Period Warrior Ethos
Practical, violence glorified, pragmatism cloaked in romanticism
ohuko no michi, bushido

Tokugawa Period Warrior Ethos
Cultural refinement, peace, social order, justification and rationalisation, class identity
bushido, shido, budo...

Buddhist Bushido
Redefining existence and death in a time of peace, Zen

Military Bushido
Redefining the role of military in a time of peace
Gungaku

Confucian Bushido
Redefining samurai ethics in a time of peace
Jukyo

Wang Yang Ming
Yomeigaku (Internal)

Neo-Confucian
Shushigaku (External)

Hagakure Bushido
(Death frenzy, the Way of the warrior is found in dying)

Kokugaku Bushido
"Native Studies" and redefining Japan, Shinto

Budo Shoshinshu Bushido
(Die in your *futon...*)

Meiji Bushido
National identity, loyalty to emperor, popular and state nationalism, 'samuraization' of Japanese people

Christian Bushido
Nitobe Inazo, Uchimura Kanzo, John Imai Toshimichi etc. International

Showa Bushido
Ultranationalism, militarism, imperialism, economic success

Heisei Bushido
Japanese identity, moral and ethical ideals based on tradition, cultural nationalism

Origination — Pragmatism — Civilization — Internationalization Nationalization Modernization

Medieval 1200~1600

Tokugawa 1600~1868

Meiji 1868–1912
Taisho 1912–1926
Showa 1926–1989
Heisei 1989–

Left A *jumonji-yari* or crescent spear. These were popular among medieval Samurai as they served the dual purpose of weapon and walking stick for long journeys on foot.

Below Nitobe Inazo, author of *Bushido: The Soul of Japan*, arguably one of the most influential books in the genre.

High school girls engaged in Naginata practice during the war years.

that Bushido was actually very similar to Christianity and that it could serve as a platform for Christian evangelism.

Highlighting virtues like honesty, justice, polite courtesy, courage, compassion, sincerity, honor, duty, loyalty and self-control, he argued that Bushido spread from the Samurai to other classes through popular culture (Kabuki, literature, etc.). He claimed it provided the moral backbone for Japan, evident in the physical endurance, fortitude and bravery of her people. He was by no means an expert in Japanese history or philosophy, and the book contains glaring inaccuracies, but it became an instant international bestseller after Japan's success in the Russo-Japanese War of 1904–05. US President Theodore Roosevelt is reported to have purchased dozens of copies to give to his friends.

Everybody wanted to know what made the Japanese tick and Nitobe provided some timely and easy answers. He essentially created his own interpretation of Bushido in line with Christian ideals. He hardly quotes from any recognized Japanese sources on Bushido, but his book should not be discounted

as inconsequential. He quite brilliantly crafted a universal ethos that people of all creeds could relate to. So popular did his book become internationally that it was translated into Japanese some years later (1908). In spite of some learned detractors, it has become the foundation for understanding Bushido in Japan today. Ironic as this is, especially considering that the book quotes extensively from Western rather than Japanese literature, religion and philosophy, it still remains a bestseller. Its prose is quite flowery but all *gai-sam* are advised to read it. The book will help you understand where the average Joe Tanaka's take on Bushido is coming from.

Postwar Bushido and Beyond

A more martial interpretation of Bushido came into vogue during the militarist 1930s. Copies of the *Hagakure* and Nitobe's *Bushido* were read to instill Samurai pride and fighting spirit. The empire's soldiers were expected to cede their lives for the emperor and state, just as the Samurai had done as loyal retainers in eras gone by.

In the aftermath of World War II, Bushido fell out of favor. Foreign and Japanese critics alike blamed it as

representing all that was loathsome in Japanese wartime behavior. The fanatical *kamikaze* pilots, the die-rather-than-surrender mentality and the abhorrent treatment of POWs were also attributed to the ultranationalistic tenets of Bushido. Japanese renounced Bushido as a poisonous ingredient in the erroneous militaristic ideology that dragged Japan into war. Such an ideology was deemed unsuitable for a new postwar democratic society.

Things began to change in the 1960s and 1970s when Japan's economic miracle took shape. "From whence does the vitality of the Japanese people spring to resurrect the phoenix from the ashes?" "Why, that must be the latent spirit of Bushido, of course." Loyalty to the company over family, working long hours to the extent that sometimes people die from overwork (*karoshi*) was, and still is, attributed to the spirit of Bushido.

The popularity of Samurai films and books suggests that no matter how old-fashioned or illogical the Bushido tradition seems on an intellectual level, it still wields considerable appeal on an emotional level. When in Japan, be prepared to listen to pious and impassioned sermons about the wonders of Bushido and why it makes Japan so "unique."

CHAPTER 3
KILLING AS AN ART FORM

In addition to mapping the creation of the earliest Japanese martial art traditions (Kobudo) to place the modern forms (Budo) in context, this chapter looks at the lives of representative masters of the classical and modern arts. It plots the evolutionary processes by which martial arts changed from techniques for killing into aesthetic pursuits seeking self-perfection, then into sports, and finally into standardized forms of physical education. Budo contains many concepts that originate directly in Samurai culture. As such, references to notions of "death" are common in Budo. Linked to this, the inherent danger of combat is clearly evident in Budo as the techniques can be lethal, and a special mindset is required in training which demands the practitioner maintains discipline and respect at all times. Being highly philosophical and spiritual in nature, these concepts are ideally applied to life outside the dojo as well. This is why there is a strong emphasis on etiquette, more perhaps than most other sports. To understand the significance of Budo in modern society, it is helpful to know about its violent history and how the techniques of death evolved into ways for living a fruitful life. Contemplating the past helps shed light on the present.

THE DEVELOPMENT OF JAPANESE MARTIAL ART SCHOOLS AND THE AESTHETIC OF DEATH

Traditional martial art schools are called *ryuha*. "Ryu" is the suffix attached to the name of each tradition and it means "to flow," that is, knowledge that cascades from one generation to the next, adapting to the times as it goes. Although the Ogasawara-ryu school of archery emerged early in the Kamakura period, comprehensive martial traditions with secret teachings and techniques really only materialized around the fourteenth century. There were three well-known traditions, in particular, that provided a model for hundreds of subsequent offshoot schools: Tenshinsho-den Katori Shinto-ryu, Nen-ryu and Kage-ryu. The teachings of these schools were often intentionally vague to ensure that the founder's "trade secrets" were not divulged to outsiders. They taught that success in combat could be achieved through fostering a coalescence of body, technique and mind, and indifference to the outcome. Understandably, such wisdom was zealously guarded by students of each *ryuha*, lest their techniques be rendered ineffective.

Two warriors of the Genpei War (1180–85) face off with swords. There were no known *ryuha* for swordsman-ship at this time. Trans-mission of martial skills was very much a family affair.

The battle-hardened founders of the prototypical martial art schools drew inspiration not only from their experiences in war but also from ideals of perfection gleaned from artistic pursuits such as Noh. Each school created its own distinctive form and philosophy by combining aesthetic, religious and technical teachings.

Establishing a Secret Ryuha

Ryuha didn't just appear randomly. It was certainly not a case of waking up one morning with a warm fuzzy feeling and suddenly deciding, "Oh my, what a beautiful day. I think I'll invent Alex-ryu™." History shows that there were several common requirements for the

successful creation and continuation of a *ryuha*. First, the founder needed a fearsome reputation predicated on extensive combat experience in the field of battle and in duels. His technical brilliance was peerless and he was dashingly charismatic—he walked the talk. Second, although his trademark techniques were honed and proven to be effective, they also had to be teachable. The founder would craft a methodological schematic for imparting his knowledge to disciples. Predetermined patterns of combat (*kata*), oral teachings (*kuden*) and transmission scrolls (*densho*) were

devised for this purpose. Another method for conveying knowledge was *ishin-denshin*, or "mind-to-mind transmission." Not quite a Vulcan mind-meld, secrets were inherited intuitively. Technical instruction was purposefully equivocal so that *ryuha* methods could not be readily imitated by rival martial artists.

The final ingredient for a successful operation was the founder's mandatory "spiritual revelation" through which the motivation to start the school was born. Stories abound of old schools that were inspired by some mysterious

BUDO CALLIGRAPHY: *Gokui* "Secret Teachings"

The essence, highest level or innermost knowledge of a martial art. The *gokui* represents the secret teachings of a school.

epiphany. Transcendental skills and principles were passed to the founder by a deity or some creepy apparition in a dream after an extended period of ascetic training at a shrine or temple. The founder then codified the arcane knowledge (*hiden*) and taught it to select disciples. The hidden *hiden* teachings were highly hush-hush. They afforded the master mystique and an aura of invincibility, and the disciple's reputation benefitted through association. Students would be accepted into the master's tutelage after making a blood oath not to leak the school's secrets. Such a breach of trust would be punished by divine retribution, like a thunderbolt strike to the head.

The Importance of Kata

Trembling in the face of death was never a good look for a Samurai. Learning to subdue psychological weakness was a fundamental concern in *ryuha*. The apical teachings were esoteric, spiritual and practical at the same time. They promised the holy grail of combat: a superlative combination of body and mind which made the warrior unassailable in battle. This corporeal and psychological synergy was taught and mastered through the vehicle of *kata*—preset sequences of movements usually performed in pairs. Through *kata*, the Samurai learned to control his weapon, to develop physical and mental fortitude and to hone

A transmission scroll for a school of swordsmanship. Scrolls contained codified technical and philosophical information and served as a teaching licence for the holder.

his understanding of timing, distance, respiration, rhythm and attacking opportunities.

The *kata* were physical manifestations of the school's sacred ideology and were jealously guarded by adherents of the tradition. They were a blueprint for the warrior's technical and spiritual development. The *kata* were often overtly ritualistic with bizarre titles (dragon's tail, angry goblin, dragonfly slicer, shock and awe…), outlandish vocalizations, complex ceremonial protocols and

KEY BUDO CONCEPTS: *Maai* 間合 "Distance and Timing"

Ma means time, space or distance. *Ma* + *ai* = meeting the *ma*. In other words, timing, distancing, spatial adjusting. Gauging the right distance to attack with maximum potency whilst maintaining perfect balance is key to success. All Budo have different *maai* depending on whether weapons are used or not, and the length of the weapon. Every individual's physique, height and reach are different, so there is always variation in terms of millimeters. The ideal is to not be too close (dangerous for both) or too far away (cannot attack). The optimal *maai* must feel close (= comfortably reachable) for you, and far (= uncomfortably unreachable) for your opponent. If you make the distance feel awkward for the opponent, s/he will immediately be on the back foot and you will be in control.

Taking your special *maai* is as much a psychological battle as it is a physical one. Confidently closing in to your optimal striking distance with intent will make the opponent lose his presence of mind and act rashly. If you can invoke such a reaction, you have won before even launching the attack. This is not to say that you run in randomly. Far from it. Accurately judging, adjusting and controlling *maai* is one of the most difficult aspects of any Budo and is an ability refined over many years of practice. You must know when to move in, when to move out and the exact distance and timing needed to land the strike with pinpoint accuracy. If you are too close, the strike will be weak. If you are too far away, it will not reach and will be weak. You must discern the distance well enough to avoid the opponent's attack by a whisker. *Maai* is always in flux, but whoever owns their *maai* owns the bout.

flashy movements which might camouflage the core principle. To the untrained eye, some *kata* simply looked like comical stick dances with no practical application at all. Indeed, not all *kata* were meant to be useful. Some were designed to impart divine wisdom of the school, like a kind of physical riddle.

In almost all *kata*, one of the protagonists is theoretically killed at the conclusion. The "death role" is usually enacted by the senior or teacher who, contemplating the reality of his mortality in a virtual sense, coaches his junior charges to identify and capitalize on genuine striking chances. By practicing the *kata* over and over, the Samurai programs his body and mind to maneuver unconsciously in relation to various technical situations and learns to rise above concerns of his own mortality. With absolute serenity of mind, spirit, weapon and body function as one unified entity. Eventually, the techniques became an expression of the warrior's own being. *Kata* training remains a central component of all modern Budo.

Top Secret Scrolls

Ryuha pedagogy made use of codified scrolls with pictures and cryptic texts to supplement the *kata* and verbal teachings. Only senior students would be able to join the dots and come to grips with the obscure meaning behind the instructions.

There were two kinds of scrolls. The first were catalogues of techniques and ancillary information awarded by the *ryuha* head to students as they mastered various levels of the syllabus: *shoden, chuden, gokui, kaiden, kirigami, mokuroku, menkyo, inka,* etc. Most of the time they made little sense to the uninitiated, but that was the point. The nomenclature and the duration of apprenticeship required depended entirely on the *ryuha*.

Even more secret in nature were the transcribed scrolls of the founder's oral teachings, or *kudensho*. These are enigmatic outlines of the school's most arcane knowledge, passed down to an exceptional student in each genera-

tion chosen to inherit the school. They were the sacred texts of the *ryuha* and were crucial for keeping future students on the true path. Just like the game of Chinese whispers, knowledge conveyed through techniques and verbal instruction was prone to corruption. *Kudensho* kept the subtle but all-important nuances intact down the generations.

KEY BUDO CONCEPTS: *Seiza* 正座 "Sitting Correctly"

Most houses these days have tables and chairs but old generations of Japanese spent most of their lives on the floor. This is why old ladies can sit for hundreds of hours at a time in *seiza*, that most painful of sitting styles in which you kneel with your butt on your heels. It literally means "correct sitting" and is used in all manner of formal occasions in Japan, including funerals, tea ceremonies and meeting the parents for the first time. When I was a high school student in Japan, an hour of *seiza* was standard punishment for those who misbehaved. Unfortunately, Budoka have to endure an awful lot of *seiza* and the subsequent agonizing pins and needles in their feet.

When sitting down in *seiza*, always go down from the left knee first followed by the right and rest your hands on your thighs. Standing is from the right foot first. Since Samurai carried their sword inserted at the left hip, the left knee would be lowered first to be able to draw if need be without slicing ham off their left thigh. Place the balls of both feet on the floor first when kneeling down or standing up. This will give you more stability and enable you to react if the situation goes pear shaped, that is, if you are suddenly attacked or if you suffer a loss of balance because of no feeling in your legs. Keep your back perfectly straight and be ready to stand up at any time. Don't grimace or fidget no matter how uncomfortable it might become. And it will.

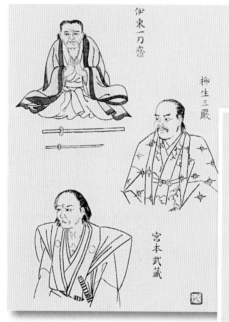

Left Three sword masters: Ito Ittosai (top), Yagyu Muneyoshi and Miyamoto Musashi.
Below Iizasa Choisai Ienao.

Three Granddaddy Traditions

Although the Ogasawara-ryu style of archery and ceremony is said to predate them, there are three pre-eminent traditions of swordsmanship, in particular, that provided the core teachings for hundreds of subsequent offshoot

Damn! What was that *kata* again?!

schools—the Tenshinsho-den Katori Shinto-ryu (lit. Direct and Correct Teachings from the Deity of the Katori Shrine), Nen-ryu (School of Perception) and the Kage-ryu (Shadow School). The origins of these early schools are hazy and their foundation stories often contradictory. Each is shrouded in mythical claims of divine inspiration, and the founders themselves were later deified by adherents of the schools.

In the case of the Tenshinsho-den Katori Shinto-ryu, legend has it that the founder, Iizasa Choisai (1387–1488), was a child prodigy acclaimed throughout the land for his prowess with the sword and spear. At the age of 60, he reckoned there must be more to life than killing and entered the precincts of the Katori Shrine to undergo a thousand-day training regime to purify his soul. While asleep one night, the shrine's deity, Futsunushi-no-Kami, appeared in a dream as a small boy standing atop a plum tree. He conveyed the secrets of military strategy to him saying, "Thou shalt be the master of all swordsmanship under the sun." He awoke and thought "Oh my, what a beautiful day. I hereby pronounce the establishment of Tenshinsho-den Katori Shinto-ryu!"

The Kashima Jingu and Katori Jingu Shrines

The closely adjacent regions of Kashima (Ibaraki prefecture) and Katori (Chiba prefecture) have seen hallowed grounds in the development of the military arts since Adam was a Samurai. Kashima-no-Tachi (the Sword [style] of Kashima) is the storied antecedent tradition conceived by a divinator at the Kashima Shrine, Kuninazu-no-Mahito. The standard theory is that he was awoken to the secret of *hitotsu-no-tachi* (also read *ichi* = Single Sword) or *shinmyo-ken* (Divine Sword), which became the foundation technique/philosophy for his clan-based tradition sometime in the seventh century. Nobody knows what this sword strategy actually entailed. Kashima-no-Tachi was also later referred to as the Kashima Shichi-ryu (Seven Schools of Kashima), redolent of the seven families associated with the Kashima Shrine, the inheritors of Kuninazu-no-Mahito's esoteric knowledge. The deity Takemikazuchi-no-Mikoto who is worshipped at the Kashima Shrine descended from the celestial plain to the Japanese islands together with his neighbor Futsunushi-no-Kami, the resident deity of the Katori shrine. According to Shinto mythology, the deities arrived ahead of Ninigi-no-Mikoto to orchestrate the transfer of the Japanese islands to the Sun Goddess Amaterasu Omikami and her descendants, that is, the subsequent emperors of Japan. Both deities are traditionally associated with military prowess and warriors came to worship at the shrines for protection and divine inspiration. This tradition continues today, with modern Budoka making a pilgrimage to either or both of these shrines to buy special Budo amulets.

A Samurai in the 1850s lugging his fencing armor and bamboo practice sword. Full-contact fencing evolved in the early eighteenth century. Until then, *kata* was the main means for studying swordsmanship.

Being famous far and wide for his martial prowess, many a young warrior sought Choisai out to try and extract some of his Budo juice. More than a few were determined to quash the mighty swordsman and stake their claim as the best in the land.

When confronted by such brash challengers, Choisai would quietly retreat to a *kumazasa* bamboo grove and sit down on top of the thin stalks. The bamboo would neither wilt nor buckle and it seemed as though he was levitating. "If you can sit here with me, I'll accept your challenge." Suspicious, amazed and frightened, the contender would slink away losing his will to fight altogether.

Choisai could not see the point of defeating foe who were obviously inferior in skill. To do so would only invite enmity. He said, "Hostility feeds hostility, and the vicious circle will continue perpetually. It is not until hostility is purged that peace can prevail. This is the natural way of things." This is the central paradox of the martial arts and remains the highest philosophical ideal for them all.

Aisu Ikosai (1452–1538) founded the Kage-ryu school. Sources about his background are scant and unreliable but he probably lived in Ise and engaged in piracy. Profiteering on

the high seas may have taken him to Korea, China and the Ryukyu Islands, but his overseas adventure came to an end around 1487 when his ship ran aground off the coast of Kyushu. He swam ashore near the Udo Daigongen Shrine where he spent 37 days in prayer. And lo, a "shadow-like apparition" came to him one night and passed on the esoteric secrets of combat.

He was instructed by the deity to go forth and duel with a local strongman named Sumiyoshi. Ikosai succeeded in defeating him and his reputation spread throughout the land. One of his star disciples, Kamiizumi Ise-no-Kami (1508–77), continued the "shadow" franchise when he formed the Shinkage-ryu (New Shadow School). This became one of the most illustrious schools of the Tokugawa period through the legendary swordsmen Yagyu Muneyoshi and his son Munenori.

Nen Ami Jion (c. 1350–c. 1408) founded the Nen-ryu school. As usual, it's difficult to separate fact from fiction with regard to his career, but he was formerly known as Soma Shiro Yoshitomo. He became a monk at a young age following the assassination of his father and was given the Buddhist name Nen Ami Jion. He moved

to the Kuramadera Temple in Kyoto when he was ten and began his apprenticeship in the martial arts there. Yes, Buddhist priests were expert combatants too, and the martial arts of Kuramadera were said to rival the Kashima traditions, sparking "the eight schools" of west Japan.

Jion demonstrated considerable aptitude and made his way to the Jufukuji Temple in Kamakura to study further under a priest named Eiyu. He received divine coaching from the Buddhist deity Marishiten via a Tengu (a mythical being with a long nose) whilst engaged in austere training at the Anryakuji Temple in Kyushu. He woke up the next morning, and you can guess the rest. Other versions of the story suggest he avenged his father's murder before taking Buddhist vows. Among his illustrious students was Chujo Nagahide of the Chujo-ryu, another school which was to have a massive influence on the development of swordsmanship.

The Art of Killing

The earliest modes of combat were family affairs, passed on from father to son. It was not until the fourteenth and fifteenth centuries that more sophisticated composite martial art schools emerged.

Bitter civil strife in the Warring States period elevated "combat artistry" to another level. A warrior needed to be skilled in the use of several weapons to ply his trade, but it was the sword that became the focus of many martial *ryuha*.

Fighting in the mayhem of a bloody battlefield and dueling with naked blades under more controlled circumstances had a degree of crossover in mindset and skill, but a differentiation was made between combat artistry and soldiery. Both skill sets were necessary to prevail and build a formidable reputation.

From the Tokugawa period (1603–1868), martial *ryuha* began to special-

BUDO CALLIGRAPHY:
Heiho "The Art of Combat"

兵法

This term also means swordsmanship or strategy. An alternative reading is *hyoho*.

ize in a particular weapon, whereas earlier schools were comprehensive and provided training in an array of weaponry, engineering and even magical spells and divination to provide a cutting edge in the art of war. The following sections analyze this evolution in more detail.

Noh, Zeami and Perfection

The Warring States epoch of incessant turmoil and instability was also the time warriors developed a profound appreciation for the finer things in life. Strength was tempered by refinement in spirit and thus warriors of the day sought solace in the arts.

One of the paragons of medieval artistry was Zeami Motokiyo (c. 1363–c. 1443), a Noh actor and playwright patronized by the highest echelons of warrior society. In the 30–50 odd plays that he wrote, he included themes of Zen Buddhism and impermanence, which appealed to their sensibilities.

Zeami also wrote ground-breaking treatises on the philosophy and intricacies of performing Noh and the flawlessness that was sought. The word *geido*—the "Way of Art"—first appeared in his book *Kyoraika* (1433), which has clear Zen influences and describes the actor's inner voice and mind. He considered Noh and the arts to be "Ways" through which the adept seeks perfection. The word *do* (way) was used as a suffix in various occupations during the Heian period and earlier but indicated the attainment of skills without any connotations of spirituality. The term *geido*, on the other hand, implies the procurement of spiritual awareness through perfecting the techniques of an art.

It was the genteel arts that inspired the aesthetic development of combat. Accomplished artists commanded respect in medieval society, so why not turn combat into an art form also? Martial arts (*bugei*) were practical, theatrical and easily adaptable to the holistic philosophies of perfection embraced in the performing arts like Noh.

Thus, truly exceptional warriors formulated their own brands of fighting arts and became bona fide celebrities by applying philosophical and religious insights to what was an otherwise vicious craft.

Samurai Dueling Tours

By the mid to late sixteenth century, Daimyo sought out notable martial artists to train their men. Individual warriors also searched for skilled teachers to guide them to new levels of martial prowess and employability. Itinerant Samurai roved the countryside on ascetic martial pilgrimages for months or years at a time, engaging not only in duels but also in austere physical and spiritual training in shrines and temples.

Japan was a dangerous place in medieval times. Masterless warriors hoped to peddle their services to the highest bidder as mercenaries or instructors for part-time peasant armies. First though, they had to prove their worth. They did this by travelling the provinces like carpetbaggers toting their weapon of choice, usually a sword or spear, and challenged anybody who would fight them.

Knocking a local legend off his perch was a sure-fire way of making an impression. Reputations were built on upsets and lives were lost as par for the course. If the challenger wasn't killed, he might ask for clemency and humbly request that his vanquisher accept him as a student.

The custom of *musha-shugyo*, as this practice was known, was outlawed in the Tokugawa period. It just wouldn't do to have warriors cruising the countryside looking for a scrap. Peace was a

precious commodity. The custom arose again, however, with the invention of safe-training equipment from the eighteenth century onward. Warriors could engage in fencing matches with Samurai from other schools and clans without anybody actually getting killed. Bruised pride was the most serious injury.

Fencing tours proved to be a fantastic way to see the world and collect important intelligence for the domain. A Samurai would receive a kind of passport and a letter of introduction from his lord: "To whom it may concern, Scrappernosuke, an expert in Alex-ryu, is hereby given permission to suspend his duties and polish his skills in the art of fencing. Please provide him with lodgings and a place to train and a beer afterwards. Best regards, Scrappernosuke's lord."

Along the way, he stayed at inns set up to serve those engaged in their swordsmanship sabbaticals. In some cases, accommodation costs were even covered by the host. Once checked in, he would be taken to the training ground and engage in any number of matches with the local fencers. At the end of the day, he might be taken to a nearby hot spring for a soak and an evening of convivial imbibing.

Not all requests were accepted with such hospitality, but when they were it was a great way to test one's ability against fresh opponents, learn a few new tricks and catch up on regional gossip.

This tradition was also related to the less friendly practice of *dojo-yaburi*, literally to "smash" a *dojo* ring by defeating all of its students. To add salt to the wound, the victorious challenger would defiantly commandeer the *dojo* signboard as a trophy of his conquest.

SOME BADASS SAMURAI SWORDSMEN

The second- and third-generation disciples from the three main source schools mentioned earlier took swordsmanship to new heights. After absorbing the celestial knowledge of their founders, these enlightened swordsmen crafted ever more sophisticated philosophical frameworks to supplement an evolving body of techniques. The cream of the crop were called *kengo*. They were skilled in many combat forms, such as pikes and grappling, but it was finesse with the sword that came to represent true warrior prowess. The sword fetish became even more pronounced with the onset of the peaceful Tokugawa period.

Tsukahara Bokuden

Tsukahara Bokuden (1490–1571) was a man whose reputation preceded him. He was born into a family of Kashima Jingu Shrine custodians. His adoptive father taught him Tenshinsho-den Katori Shinto-ryu. Some say he also studied under Kamiizumi Ise-no-Kami, but as Bokuden was approximately 20 years older it is more likely the opposite is true. As with so many swordsmen of his day, Bokuden sought guidance from the Katori deities. He also subjected himself to one thousand days of ascetic training and legend has it that he was enlightened in the secret of *Hitotsu-no-Tachi* (Sword of One). He named his school Shinto-ryu using different ideograms to the Katori Shinto-ryu.

Bokuden was one of the most important swordsmen of his era and contributed to elevating the status of swordsmanship as an art. Such was his notoriety, he was even employed as instructor to three successive generations of Muromachi shoguns—Ashikaga Yoshiharu, Ashikaga Yoshiteru and Ashikaga Yoshiaki—as well as the famous warlord Takeda Shingen.

He spent much of his time on the road seeking challengers and amassed a huge number of disciples who followed him through the provinces like rock star groupies. Many of his followers became famous martial artists in their own right. During his career, Bokuden is said to have participated in 19 life-or-death duels and 37 battles without receiving a scratch.

A famous Bokuden story concerns one of his top students who he planned to initiate into the secret of Hitotsu-no-Tachi. One day, this particular student happened to walk around the back of a horse that was blocking the way. The horse suddenly kicked its hind legs back. Through a magnificent show of agility, he was able to deftly dodge the horse's hooves. A witness to the spectacle was so impressed he immediately informed Bokuden of the feat. Bokuden, however, was not impressed. "This is not what I would expect from someone I was about to teach Hitotsu-no-Tachi to!" "Well, Bokkers, what would you have done?" Bokuden took him to a horse and showed him. He walked in

Tsukahara Bokuden. There is a famous story that Miyamoto Musashi attacked Bokuden as he was eating and he parried Musashi's sword with a pot lid. The truth is, Bokuden died long before Musashi was born.

front of the horse. "Horses kick! Avoiding a horse as it kicks back might be an impressive display of sprightliness, but forgetting that they kick in the first place is downright moronic."

Another well-known story demonstrates a similar point. He placed a pillow on top of a door so that it would fall down when opened. He called his three sons into the room one by one. The first son was able to draw his sword in time to cut the falling pillow. The second son was able to dodge the falling pillow without drawing his sword. The third son sensed that there was a pillow on the door and removed it before entering. Guess who became Bokuden's successor.

Kamiizumi Ise-no-Kami

Kamiizumi Ise-no-Kami (1508–73) founded the Shinkage-ryu. He based his school on the Kage-ryu and is thought to have studied directly under Ikosai, or possibly his son Genkosai. It was thanks to Ise-no-kami that the Kage-ryu school proliferated throughout the country. From his line arose many other illustrious martial traditions, such as the Yagyu-ryu, Jikishin Kage-ryu and so on.

Ise-no-Kami was born in Kazusa (modern-day Gunma prefecture) and showed flair in the martial arts from an early age. He made pilgrimages to the warrior shrines of Kashima and Katori and studied under Matsumoto Bizen-no-Kami. It is recorded that when he was 20 years of age he met and trained with Tsukahara Bokuden.

His fighting ability was respected by friend and foe alike and he was dubbed the "Spear of Kazusa." Many tried to recruit him but he turned down all offers from "Warlords Incorporated" and the benefits that came with gainful employment.

Instead, he embarked on a spiritual journey. "Old Ise's taken a few too many blows to the noggin," his friends would say but he saw things differently. He was in pursuit of artistic perfection.

Comparatively speaking, Ise-no-Kami's scorecard was less impressive than his contemporaries. This is not to say he couldn't walk the talk. Near the Myo-koji Temple in Owari (modern Aichi prefecture), he came across a group of excited villagers gathered around a farmhouse. A vagrant had broken into the house and was holding a child hostage. He was threatening to kill the child if anybody came near. "I will get the child back!" Ise-no-Kami proclaimed.

He asked a passing monk to lend him his robes and had his student shave his head. He then approached the house carrying some rice balls.

"Back! Get back I say! I have a sword and I'm not afraid to use it!" Ise-no-Kami ignored the vagrant's threats and continued to approach. "Dear fellow, I am but a humble monk and I fear the child may be hungry. In the name of Buddha's compassion, please allow me to offer you and the child a rice ball to alleviate the pains of hunger."

After throwing the child a rice ball, Ise-no-Kami turned to the vagrant and tossed him one too. Nice catch, silly move. Ise-no-Kami grabbed his arm and pinned him to the floor. The siege was over and not a drop of blood was shed. The monk was intrigued with Ise-no-Kami's unique method of conflict resolution. "You looked and acted as a monk. You were fearless and resolute putting yourself in danger for the sake of another. You surely must be an enlightened individual." Ise-no-Kami replied,

A rock called Itto-seki near the Yagyu family burial ground. Though it was most probably split through natural causes, legend has it that Muneyoshi cleaved through it with his sword.

Kamiizumi Ise-no-Kami assumes a stance with a *fukuro-shinai* practice sword. This was a leather sleeve with slats of bamboo inside. He invented it as a safe way for training in sword work.

"Even if the task at hand makes you look like a complete idiot, even if your body is engulfed in flames or even if it squashed by a great rock, it is only an indestructible mind that can provide the courage to do good."

Challengers dueled with him not so much to try and defeat him but more with the hope of receiving such gems of wisdom. He preferred to spar with swordsmen rather than cut them down. In fact, he is the man credited with inventing the bamboo practice sword.

Yagyu Muneyoshi

Yagyu Sekishusai Muneyoshi (aka Munetoshi) (1527–1606) was the founder of the Yagyu Shinkage-ryu. Yagyu-no-Sho village is in a beautiful mountainous district in the northeastern part of Nara. Muneyoshi was a superb fighter with swords and pikes. In 1563, In'ei, the chief priest of the Hozoin Temple in Nara, sent word that Kamiizumi Ise-no-Kami, the peerless warrior who created Shinkage-ryu, was planning a visit. In'ei was a fearsome pike fighter in his own right and a close friend of Muneyoshi. Both waited in anticipation for Ise-no-Kami's arrival. Muneyoshi was 37 years of age at the time and he relished the opportunity to test his mettle.

He first had to duel with the master's student, Hikita Bungoro. Muneyoshi was peeved at the indignity of having to fight the scruffy, scrawny Bungoro, yet was defeated convincingly three times

in a row. Having been put through his paces, Ise-no-Kami gave Muneyoshi a crack at the big prize. Predictably, however, Muneyoshi was defeated a further three times and had his wooden sword taken right off him. "Little boys mustn't play with big sticks!" Ise-no-Kami admonished him.

Humbled, Muneyoshi immediately requested to become an apostle. He stayed in the district for a while to teach, but hearing of the death of his son, Ise-no-Kami left Bungoro in his place. Muneyoshi's determination to improve eventually enabled him to surpass Bungoro by the time the master returned three years later. Ise-no-Kami presented him with a certificate of mastery and parted with the words, "I want you to become a man of sincerity." "What do you mean?" asked Muneyoshi. "I mean, *muto* my boy, *muto*…. No sword…. "

Muneyoshi pondered this riddle and finally worked out the answer. His epiphany formed the basis for what became known as *Muto-no-Kurai* in the Yagyu Shinkage-ryu. *Muto* can be explained at various levels—from a psychological mind game where an enemy forgets to slash at you because he is focused on not letting you take his sword, to the more mundane level where you entice an opponent to lunge across the perilous line of optimum striking distance and confiscate his sword when (if) it misses. So famous throughout the land did Muneyoshi's *muto* teaching become, even Tokugawa Ieyasu, the eventual unifier of Japan, requested to see it for himself. Ieyasu played the aggressor and to his astonishment was disarmed before he could even utter "It's mine. All mine!" Ieyasu, general supreme, immediately enrolled in Muneyoshi's school in 1594.

Miyamoto Musashi

Probably the most celebrated warrior in Japanese history was Miyamoto Musashi (1582–1645). He is remembered, among other things, for his combat style using two swords simultaneously. He called his school Niten Ichi-ryu (Two Heavens as One). There is so much mystery surrounding his life that very few details can be verified. Musashi declares in his famous book *Gorin-no-Sho* (Book of Five Rings) that he was born in Harima (present-day Hyogo prefecture). His adoptive father, Miyamoto Munisai, was a retainer of the Shinmen family in Mimasaka (present-day Okayama prefecture) and was accomplished in various weapons, including the sword and the truncheon.

Musashi had his first taste of mortal combat when he defeated Arima Kihei of the Shinto-ryu at the tender age of 13. By 30 he had fought over 60 duels, perhaps the most famous of which was his wrangle with Sasaki Kojiro on Ganryu Island in 1610. As the story goes, Musashi purposefully turned up late. Kojiro was irritated by this and it proved to be his downfall. Kojiro's mind was not in the right space and Musashi

Mystery man, Miyamoto Musashi. Undoubtedly Japan's most famous swordsman, much about his life is open to conjecture.

took advantage of his instability to bludgeon him fatally in the head with a wooden sword fashioned out of an oar. Like most things concerning Musashi, although he did duel Kojiro, this popular account is largely fictional

Even though he won all of his duels, Musashi confessed that it was more due to luck than a true understanding of the "Way of Combat." He knew there had to be something more to life. Apart from his skill as a swordsman, he was known for his expertise in painting, carving and other creative accomplishments.

Musashi left us a valuable treatise on combat and the meaning of life with *Gorin-no-sho*. It is one of the most famous of all martial art books although, like many aspects of his life, there are uncertainties surrounding its authorship. Some scholars claim that

it was written by a student after his death. This is most certainly not the case. He wrote it while meditating in the Reigando cave in Kumamoto and passed it to his student Terao Magonojo one week before passing away. The original scrolls written by Musashi no longer exist. Fortunately, his students made copies before the original perished in a castle fire.

His many teachings, such as "The Stance of No-Stance," "Seizing the Start [of the opponent's move]" and "Becoming the Enemy [to know what they are thinking]" are all based on combat experience and still translate fluidly into modern Budo. The strength of Musashi's swordsmanship is expressed in the teaching of *Iwao no Mi* (Body of a Rock). "When you have mastered the Way of Strategy you can suddenly make your body like a rock, and ten thousand things cannot touch you. This is the Body of a Rock." He was asked by his patron, Lord Hosokawa Tadanori, what the "body of a rock" meant. Musashi immediately summoned his student and ordered that he commit *seppuku*. It was very sudden but his student didn't flinch. He bowed deeply in deference and went to the next room to prepare for his imminent ritual suicide. Musashi turned to Lord Hosokawa and said, "That is the body of a rock." He then stopped his student from killing himself. "My fault, I was only joking."

Of course, a sword can easily pierce through flesh even if the body was a "rock." The point is that through

---

KEY BUDO CONCEPTS: *Mittsu-no-sen* 三つの先 "The Three Initiatives"

There are three timings (*sen*) in Budo in which techniques are unleashed. Understanding and utilizing these timings (*mittsu-no-sen*) is critical to success and lies at the heart of strategy. The first is called *sensen-no-sen*. Just as the opponent's technique is about to take form, you nip it in the bud and defeat it before it can take shape, moving earlier in anticipation of your attacker's intentions. The second is called *senzen-no-sen*. As the opponent sees an opening and attempts to attack, turn it against him with a parry or deflection. *Senzen-no-sen* is also called just *sen*. The third is *go-no-sen*, striking the opponent's attack down or dodging and then counterattacking immediately as his momentum is compromised.

connectedness with the universe, the mind becomes completely unperturbed and stone cold. Who can possibly defeat such an enemy? There is nothing to defeat. Pragmatically and philosophically speaking, his treatise is a valuable source of information for modern martial artists.

Ito Ittosai Kagehisa

Nobody knows for sure when or where Ito Ittosai Kagehisa (1560?–1653?) was born but it was sometime in the later Warring States period. His typically disheveled appearance, frightening gaze and peculiar behavior tended to startle people. But it was this young man of mysterious and probably humble beginnings who was to create one of the most influential martial art styles in Japanese history. The teachings of his school now permeate the thought of modern Budo. What made him special compared to other great *kengo* is that while they were all born into prominent families he was very much a dark horse.

He started his martial career in Kyoto where he learned from the famous Kanemaki Jisai (1536–1615) of the Toda-ryu school. After only a few years of apprenticeship, he rather superciliously proclaimed to his master, "Eureka! I now know the deep secrets of the mar-

tial arts!" Jisai was agitated by Kagehisa's conceit. "Bollocks, my son. How can you possibly have an understanding so soon? The cheek of it!" Kagehisa became even more emboldened. "It is not a matter of who one learns from, or how many years one has been studying. You either have it or you don't. How about I open a gourd of whoop-ass to prove my point?"

Indeed, this was not the kind of attitude a disciple should take to his mentor. Jisai had a reputation to uphold and was not about to let him off the hook for his brazen insolence. Taking a wooden sword, he prepared to teach

the young upstart a lesson in manners. Jisai's attack was countered successfully by Kagehisa, who drew first blood. "One more!" exclaimed Jisai. The same thing happened again and again.

Jisai was impressed by the prodigy who stood before him. "Ye gods and little fishes. I am truly humbled by your skill. Pray tell, how did you do it?" He explained, "Even in his sleep, a man with an itchy foot will not scratch his head. If there is an itch in his foot, he will scratch the foot. If it is his head that is itchy, it is his head that he will scratch. Wherever the itch, the hand is sure to go without hesitation. It is not the same for the martial arts? If there is an opening, the weapon should glide to the spot effortlessly, without a smidgen of indecision. It has to be subconscious, with no thought to it. That is what I have discovered."

Among the scrolls of Kagehisa's Itto-ryu, which means the One-strike School in reference to the idea that all things in the universe come back to "one," is the teaching of *mushin-muso* (no-mind, no-contemplation). This came from a revelation he had during his travels. While engaging in a period of austere circuit training and prayer at the Tsurugaoka Hachimangu Shrine in Kamakura, he was accosted by an unknown assailant with murderous intent. Without batting an eyelid, Kagehisa swiftly drew his sword and cut the man down in his tracks. He relayed this story to one of his students in his later years. "Although it is regrettable that I had to kill the man, it really was a superb example of what I call *muso-no-ken*, the sword of no-contemplation. In other words, it was a cut that was executed spontaneously without thinking, as if the sword was moving of its own volition." This ideal was to become the philosophical underpinning of the Itto-ryu, one of the most important schools of swordsmanship in Japan.

"GENTLEMEN" SAMURAI

With the onset of peace in the Tokugawa period, Japan's elite had time to indulge in all manner of artistic pursuits, fusing technique with religious ideals of heightened spiritual awareness. Government policies of national isolation and restrictions placed on Samurai to curb violence put Japan's military practitioners into a state of suspended animation. Samurai were obligated to be militarily prepared but the martial arts became more concerned with spirituality and beauty in form. Japan's military professionals trained to perfect archaic techniques but fell behind the technological advances seen in the rest of the world.

During the Tokugawa period, Kyoto's Sanjusangendo was the site of immensely popular archery contests known as *toshiya*.

Peace does peculiar things to martial arts. Samurai were still expected to be in peak condition but they rarely had a chance to test themselves in the cauldron of conflict. It was like training for the big game, then sitting on the bench because there is no game! A tad frustrating no doubt, but life goes on. And so the Samurai lifestyle was redefined, as were the martial arts and the reasons for practicing.

What changed? "Spiritualization" was seen in many schools from the late seventeenth century, with many *ryuha* incorporating ideals of *ki*, Zen and Confucian concepts, and an "idealistic" acceptance of death. After all, the likelihood of dying in battle was virtually non-existent, but the least a Samurai could do was imagine war and be ready to prove his valor if called upon. Martial training became increasingly seen as a vehicle for spiritual enlightenment, and this trend was linked to the "pacification" of the martial arts, that is, an inclination towards non-lethal techniques and an avoidance of confrontation altogether. The main objective in the martial arts became ascetic training—*shugyo*—rather than actual slicing and dicing. The art of winning without spilling blood became the mark of a superior warrior. There were many examples of new *kata* created by schools in the Tokugawa

period that omitted the coup de grace—the killing blow—signifying a trend toward pacifism.

Peace also led to the commercialization of martial arts. Samurai were still expected to be battle ready and needed to show certificates to prove they were doing their bit. With high market demand for instruction, the number of schools proliferated exponentially and each school tended to specialize in a specific weapon rather than the entire arsenal.

According to some guesstimates by Japanese scholars, by the late eighteenth century there were 51 schools

of *kyujutsu* (archery), 66 schools of *bajutsu* (horsemanship), 147 schools of *sojutsu* (spears), 192 schools of *hojutsu* (guns), 179 schools of *jujutsu* (grappling) and 743 schools of *kenjutsu*. Just like the martial arts of today, however, the quality was spotty, covering the whole gamut from embarrassingly absurd to the sublime.

New schools meant "novel"(untested/impossible) techniques, and *kata* became ridiculously ostentatious—visually appealing but removed from the reality of actual dueling and soldiery. Toward the end of the seventeenth century there were few, if any, Samurai still alive who had experienced battle. Although some schools retained a battle-oriented curriculum, many others provided esoteric techniques that were far from practical.

Schools competed to attract students by issuing teaching licenses and diplomas proving mastery of the school's curriculum.

BUDO CALLIGRAPHY: *Rinki-ohen* **"Going With the Flow"**

The ability to react freely as the situation requires. Even though the martial artist learns *kata* in precise terms, the point is to be able to adapt movements to suit the conditions and different types of enemy. *Rinki-ohen* is the capacity to go with the flow.

"The Cat's Eerie Skill"—A Parable

One of the more entertaining books in the genre of martial spiritualism is Issai Chozan's *Neko-no-Myojutsu* (1729). Chozan was a gifted student of Zen, Confucian and Chinese classics, as well as the martial arts. Translated as "The Cat's Eerie Skill," it is a well-known story concerning a large rat that defiantly torments local cats. Each cat tries to outdo the other and capture the bold rat, but none is successful. Then, an old cat decides to take up the challenge and he apprehends the rat with seemingly no effort. The other cats are amazed by his graceful display and inquire how he did it. The narrative then turns to the wise old cat educating his younger protégés, his discourse centering on the "natural way of the universe," and how one who can maintain control over his mind and access the very essence of his being will be able to triumph in all things.

First, a young black cat talked of how he trained himself by running through the rafters, and that he had never before failed to catch a rat until today. The old cat commented that he was too absorbed in developing technical skills and was pre-occupied with procedure. Next, a big cat with "tiger's whiskers"

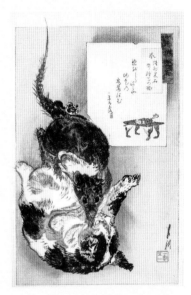

said that he believed *ki* to be the secret and that he had forged his internal energy to overpower opponents. But, for whatever reason, he failed to subdue the rat. The old cat replied that simply relying on the powers of *ki* will never be effective against an opponent who is not compliant. Next, an older gray cat told the group how he had focused his training on the "Way" and had learned to be victorious through non-confrontation. But the troublesome rat did not take the bait. The wise old cat pointed out that the gray cat's plan was a conscious ploy and therefore ineffectual. "We exist, therefore so does the enemy. If we have no form in our minds, nothing can oppose it and there will be no conflict, that is, there is no enemy. In the final analysis, the problem lies in the mind. If the mind is in a state of nothingness (*mushin*), there can be no foe."

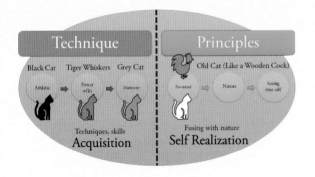

Left The process of spiritual growth outlined in the "Cat's Eerie Skill."

Above Either a small cat or a very big rat! It is only when the cat becomes like a lifeless *mokkei* (wooden-cock) that victory can be had.

The Sportification of Budo

Purists derided the "theatrical" martial arts and referred to them contemptuously as "flowery," with their fierce glares, surreal fighting stances, colorful vocalizations and stylized movements that served no purpose other than to look good. Nowadays, we refer to this kind of questionable Budo as a "McDojo."

"Flowerization," however, ultimately led to the "sportification" of martial arts, with the invention of protective training equipment and bamboo swords from the early eighteenth century. This enabled full-contact bouts as opposed to *kata*-centric training methods, which had come to resemble dance movements. There were those who stubbornly clung to the traditional method of *kata* practice, whereas others enjoyed engaging in full-contact training that was both safe and exhilarating. At first the two camps remained staunchly opposed, but by the end of the eighteenth century most *ryuha* had incorporated both approaches to differing degrees.

In addition to the rise of clan schools that taught young Samurai martial arts, we also see the establishment of commercial *dojo*, especially in Edo, and the codification of fencing techniques. This sportive style of swordplay (referred to as *gekiken*) attracted a number of townsmen who took immense pleasure in emulating Samurai practices. Ironically, non-Samurai played a significant role in popularizing this prototype of modern Kendo, and many of the most celebrated martial artists from the late eighteenth century onwards were, in fact, not of warrior stock.

Samurai had always idealized the simple concept of *itto*—to win with a single cut or thrust. This ideal is alive and well in Budo today and has its foundation in medieval *kata* in which the simplest yet most difficult technique was the "magic bullet." It could supposedly defeat all others when perfected. Mastering the ultimate killing technique was

Above An illustration of prototypical training armor. The warrior on the right uses a wooden *naginata* against two pike-wielding opponents. Note the padded pike tips.

Right Samurai swordsmen compete in bouts under the watchful eye of the domain's lord.

the Samurai's singular goal. The idea of *itto*—one cut to end all cuts—made a transition from *kata* into full-contact sparring. This is the idea behind the *ippon* or "one-point" that we compete fiercely to score in the modern competitive arena of Budo.

Zen and the Martial Arts

A common misconception about the martial arts is that they are inextricably linked to Zen Buddhism. Another misconception is that Zen was the "official religion" of the Samurai.

Actually, the Samurai believed in many religious traditions simultaneously.

Zen's arrival in Japan was facilitated in the late twelfth century through the efforts of the monks Eisai (1141–1215), who introduced the Lin-chi sect of Ch'an Buddhism (Rinzai) from China, and Dogen (1200–53), who did the same for the Ts'ao-tung sect (Soto).

Eisai believed that everybody could attain enlightenment through insight and personal experience and that it was triggered by some random event in life

when you just "suddenly get it." Rinzai Zen is known for the use of *koan*, or riddles that one ponders until some great epiphany jolts you to a higher plane of understanding, even if only temporarily. To meditate day and night over a *koan* like Hakuin's famous "What is the sound of one hand clapping?" returns your mind to the roots of consciousness and opens it up to new, unfettered ways of seeing things.

Soto Zen takes a different tack. Dogen was of the opinion that one cannot become enlightened by actually thinking about it. "Just sit ... drop off the body and mind." He was a staunch advocate of meditation—*zazen*. He was critical of the *koan* approach, thinking that solving a riddle amounted to little more than delusional enlightenment.

Overall, the essence of Zen is not predicated so much on philosophizing things but is more about a gradual process of coming to a realization that everything is nothing and nothing is everything. It points

KEY BUDO CONCEPTS:
Shikai 四戒 "Four Weaknesses of the Mind"

The *shikai* are the "four illnesses" of the mind: *kyo* (fear), *ku* (surprise), *gi* (doubt) and *waku* (hesitation). These are mental states that must be avoided in combat and why training is so important. In the case of *kyo* and *ku*—surprise and fear—you must remain calm and collected regardless of who you are up against. It is easy to become surprised or afraid if your opponent is famous, but to yield is to lose before the encounter even begins. *Gi* and *waku*—doubt and hesitation—also invite defeat. Are you being enticed into making a move? If you see an opening, is it really one? Or is it a trap? These are the conundrums that bring on doubt and hesitation. Not being sure of when and where to strike, or suddenly having a change of heart, are fatal weaknesses. Such indecision makes you vulnerable and will lead to certain defeat. You've got to trust your instincts and commit yourself fully come what may.

to the "original mind" or "true human nature" without the constraints of intellect, logic or egotistical attachment, including attachment to life itself.

Zen points to a path of emancipation from concerns with life and death, and this fitted well with the Samurai's violent culture. Monks such as Takuan Soho had a profound effect on the way the martial arts were philosophized by drawing comparisons with the "spiritual illness of attachment" that prevents one from reaching an enlightened state.

The same attachment to life was debilitating to the martial artist in the throes of combat. As soon as the combatant's mind is distracted by something, he is as good as dead. Zen and other religious terms were introduced into the lexicon of the martial arts to explain the complex psychological intricacies of combat.

Generally speaking, Zen appealed to the sensibilities of Samurai and martial artists precisely because it helped them add context to their precarious lifestyle. Samurai would seek counsel from monks to make sense of the universe, but Zen monks also sought the advice of Samurai for similar reasons.

More than a few Samurai became Zen monks after hanging up their swords. They were seen as different paths but with many complementary elements.

Shugyo 修行 Ascetic Training

A literal translation of the ideograms would render into something like "a perpetual, solemn and conscious physical and mental practice engaged in with passion and humility to acquire a great wisdom that transcends our delusional ignorance and prejudicial preconceptions, while having the strength and courage to proceed in a quest to access the enlightened human nature that defines humanness at every single moment at the crossroads of life and death." OK, so it's basically tough training that involves years of self-inflicted privation in the perpetual quest for perfection.

Shugyo is a term used in reference to the spiritual study of Buddhist monks, and it became an important part of Budo culture as indicated by the practice of *musha-shugyo*. An essential feature of the study of Budo is that there is no end. The practitioner endures hardship in order to temper the mind and body. In *shugyo*, it's not so much the destination that matters but the path taken to reach each milestone. There is no end because there is always another mountain to climb once the pinnacle of one is reached.

The original *musha-shugyo* in which itinerant warriors tested their dueling skills lasted for months or even years. The very act of living on the edge could lead to some kind of explosive revelation or spiritual liberation, or it could simply end in an unceremonious death with the swish of a sword. *Shugyo* in modern Budo is meant to promote discipline and foster inner strength to facilitate the same search for truth and to encourage people to make contributions to society at large.

KEY BUDO CONCEPTS: *Kokoro* 心 "Heart"

Kokoro means heart, spirit or mind. A pure person is described as having a "good *kokoro*." *Shin* is another reading for the *kanji* and you will see it attached to many teachings in Budo: *zanshin* (lingering mind), *heijoshin* (usual mind), *fudoshin* (immovable heart), *mushin* (no mind), *kogishin* (mind of doubt). Studying Budo requires the right mindset (*kokoro-gamae*), and the heart is further replenished through arduous training. The Budo practitioner must be self-assured and aware of his or her own strengths and shortcomings. That is to say, in order to advance in Budo the student is constantly reassessing his or her abilities and is compelled to find ways to overcome any deficiencies. Improving technical aptitude is inextricably linked with self-development, and ultimately self-determination. Techniques, and the way in which they are executed, are viewed as a representation of the Budoka's *kokoro*. This is why Budo abounds with traditional concepts that address the *kokoro*. Another common word is *kokoro-e*, which means the qualities of mind that devotees of Budo should strive to acquire.

MODERN-DAY SAMURAI

A sense of urgency arose toward the end of the Tokugawa period with the increasing frequency of foreign ships visiting Japan's shores. Samurai realized that they were outgunned and out of their depth against Western military powers. Martial training was stepped up, but nobody brings a stick to a cannon fight. Monumental changes had to be made in the way the military operated for the sake of national defense because conventional martial arts were deemed ineffectual. The Meiji period saw the reinvention of martial arts and a new epoch of educational Budo was born.

Japanese military arts had evolved into cultural pursuits rich in ritualistic symbolism and spiritualism, but these were not going to be enough to defend the country from foreign incursion. Enthusiasm for traditional martial arts came to an abrupt end in the years following the arrival of Commodore Perry's "Black Ships" to Japan in 1853. Many of the men responsible for the Shogunate's eventual downfall were famous fencers who used their training sojourns around the country to hatch seditious plots.

Following the Meiji Restoration (1868), the new imperial government set about quickly rectifying Japan's military shortcomings in the face of superior Western technology. The traditional martial arts fell out of favor due to their lack of practical application in the modern theater of war. Guns, cannons and a new conscript army were the order of the day, and *bujutsu* became a relic of an outdated feudal past that was best forgotten if Japan was to modernize successfully.

Once esteemed traditional martial arts masters soon ran out of work. Nobody wanted to learn anymore. Many *ryuha* closed down in the second half of the nineteenth century. Those who did continue practicing were scorned for wasting their time and not contributing to the productivity of the nation.

Above Fencers engaging in bouts open to the public. The *gekken-kogyo* shows provided unemployed swordsmen with enough income to get by.

Left Sakakibara Kenkichi's *gekken-kogyo* bridged the gap between antiquity and modernity and prevented the extinction of traditional martial arts.

Bringing It All Back

A few things managed to keep *bujutsu* afloat, if only long enough for the country to find new uses for tradition in an age of modernization. Of particular importance was Sakakibara Kenkichi (1830–94), a former retainer of the Tokugawa shogun and instructor of *kenjutsu* at the Shogunate's military academy (Kobusho). He set about rekindling interest in the martial arts through public demonstrations known as *gekken-kogyo*. The idea soon spread, and fencers received a portion of the gate takings from these traveling martial art extravaganzas. He based his model on the popular professional Sumo tournaments, which can now be seen on television six times a year in Japan.

Then a strange thing happened during the Satsuma Rebellion (1877). The Battotai (Bare Blade Brigade) was a government police unit made up of

Sakakibara Kenkichi (center) poses with members of his fencing troupe. Satake Kanryusai's (right) wife is kneeling at the front with her *naginata*.

The Battotai, an elite group in the Meiji government's police force, march to the front in the Satsuma Rebellion with swords as their only weapons.

Enbu is a term you will come across often in Budo. It means "demonstration." It usually consists of public displays of *kata* although demonstrations of modern Budo matches are also held. *Enbu* may be convened at gymnasiums and Budokan or sometimes in shrines as an offering to the deities. Although they are not competitions in the conventional sense—there are no winners or losers—they are terribly nerve-wracking affairs. The practitioner is expected to demonstrate the "best technique" he/she can with precision, power and feeling. You look like a complete idiot if you mess up and there is no going back. Perfection in performance is sought but rarely achieved. Preparation for *enbu* is meticulous. It is a matter of pride for you and your *dojo* and that keeps everybody on the straight and narrow and training hard. Essentially, it's a competition with the self.

100 former Samurai from the pro-Shogunate Aizu domain (the losing side in the Boshin War that culminated in the Meiji Restoration). Now, ironically, they were fighting for the imperial government, not against it, whereas public enemy number one enemy, Saigo Takamori, was now fighting against the imperial government, not for it. Being skilled swordsmen, the Aizu men in the Battotai contributed to a hard fought victory against Saigo's Satsuma rebels at the Battle of Tabaruzaka in Kumamoto from March 4 to 20, 1877. This is the conflict which is depicted in the movie *The Last Samurai*.

What was remarkable about this turn of events was that the Battotai men took only their swords, not guns, to the front. This was possibly out of repentance for their ill-fated allegiance to the Shogunate a decade earlier, or maybe they wanted to slice their nemesis the old-fashioned way.

Amazingly enough, the sword bearers triumphed over the heavily armed rebels, and their victory was eulogized in the media of the day. The incident proved to be a turning point for *bujutsu*, and a tremendous windfall for martial art experts just managing to hang on in the shadows. This battle ultimately became a bridge for near-obsolete *bujutsu* to pass into the modern world as Budo.

Kawaji Toshiyoshi (1829–79), a former Satsuma warrior himself, and commissioner of the newly formed national police, expressed his admiration for the Battotai and their exploits. He decreed that *bujutsu* be introduced into the police from 1880 and no longer be regarded as an antiquated remnant of a bygone era. Its practical value had been verified in modern warfare and it would provide an excellent means for training the nation's patrolmen, both physically and mentally. It would instil discipline and provide them with the necessary skills for self-defense.

The *gekken-kogyo* shows died out not long after as their popularity waned but they kept *bujutsu* alive long enough for the stars to find gainful employment as instructors in the police and the armed forces.

Reinventing Traditions
Although martial arts were adopted quickly in the police and armed forces, efforts to get *bujutsu* included in the national school curriculum proved more problematic. There were government officials in the 1870s who voiced inhibitions about totally "Westernizing" the Japanese education system. They advocated retaining a modicum of "Japaneseness" in the curriculum. This was especially the case with physi-cal education, which at the time was centered on Western gymnastics. Some raised the question of why it was not possible to construct a PE curriculum around traditional Japanese *bujutsu*. But first, *bujutsu* had to be modernized:

1. Safety had to be assured. (Modification of techniques, training facilities, equipment.)
2. Impartial evaluation standards for matches had to be formulated. (Objective quantifiable evaluation criteria.)
3. Traditional *ryuha* affiliations had to be discarded.
4. Connection to any particular religion had to be abandoned.
5. Needed to be accessible to all echelons of society.
6. Systematization, standardization and rationalization of instruction methods and rules.

The Ministry of Education remained cautious. To investigate the potential benefits and dangers of teaching *bujutsu* in schools, the MOE commissioned several surveys such as the 1883 assessment conducted by the National Institute of Gymnastics:

PROS:
1. An effective means of enhancing physical development.
2. Develops stamina.
3. Rouses the spirit and boosts morale.
4. Expurgates spinelessness and replaces it with vigor. (My favorite)
5. Arms the student with techniques for self-defense in times of danger.

CONS:
1. May cause unbalanced physical development.
2. Always an imminent danger present in training.
3. Difficult to determine the appropriate degree of exercise, especially as physically stronger kids must train together with weaker ones.
4. Could encourage violent behavior due to the rousing of the spirit.
5. Stimulates the will to fight which could manifest itself as an attitude of winning at all costs.

BUDO CALLIGRAPHY: *Kiai* "The Act of Focusing the Mind"

It also refers to the vocalizations one produces when attacking or assailing. Shouting serves to build one's own confidence and morale while intimidating the opponent.

6. Danger of encouraging a warped sense of competitiveness.
7. Difficult to teach large numbers of students in a unified way.
8. Requires a large area to conduct classes.
9. Even though *jujutsu* only necessitates *keiko-gi* (training wear) *kenjutsu* requires the use of armor and other special equipment which is expensive and difficult to keep hygienic.

Good, but no cigar. The MOE was not prepared to sanction Budo in schools just yet. Some innovative educators created "*bujutsu* calisthenics"—gym exercises with wooden swords and other weapons to try and get the martial

A Sumo tournament in the Meiji period. The format remains largely unchanged to this day, except the four pillars supporting the roof over the mound were removed when Sumo became a popular television fixture.

arts in some form or another in schools, but the initiative fizzled out as *bujutsu* proper finally started to make inroads.

Kodokan: Martial Innovation
Kano Jigoro was particularly active in adapting his Judo to overcome the problems identified by the government. Being a qualified educator, he had a firm grasp of the country's educational needs. Influenced by the ideals of Herbert Spencer regarding moral, intellectual and physical education, Kano provided a blueprint with Judo for the modernization of the other Budo arts.

He formed the Kodokan in 1882 where he taught a small group of young men academic subjects and his new style of *jujutsu*. Kano continually incorporated ideas to enhance the value of Judo to society. He compared various classical styles of *jujutsu* and their techniques and formulated a rational framework for safe sparring (*randori*), and retained dangerous techniques in *kata*.

KEY BUDO CONCEPTS: *Dan'i* 段位 "Dan Grades"

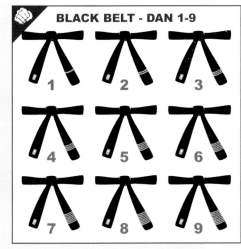

BLACK BELT - DAN 1-9

Kano Jigoro's Kodokan Judo was the first of the modern Budo to introduce Dan grades in 1883. Before that, Kano ranked his students with Ko, Otsu, Hei, which basically means A, B, C. In 1908, these became the Kyu grades—the ranks that led up to the first Dan. Kodokan initially had Dan grades up to 12. Kano borrowed the idea from the popular board games *go* and *shogi*, which utilized the ranking system during the Tokugawa period. A 9th Dan in *go* was considered to be a *meijin*—a master of the game of strategy.

Kendo was the second modern Budo to introduce grades when the Keishicho (police) adopted Kyu ranks in 1885. Upper 1st Kyu was the equivalent of 10th Dan in Kodokan Judo. Lower 1st Kyu was equivalent to 9th Dan. Both ranking styles were integrated from 1917 after Budo was permitted to be taught at schools. From this time, both Kendo and Judo employed Dan grades through the auspices of the two main colleges that nurtured professional Budo teachers—The Tokyo Higher Normal School and the Butokukai's Bujutsu Vocational School—but only up to 5th Dan. From 1923, all other modern Budo under the umbrella of the Butokukai—Kyudo, Sumo, Naginata, etc.—adopted the Dan system, too. It wasn't until 1937 that the Butokukai introduced 6th Dan and above for all of the Budo. Weapon arts such as Kendo, Naginata, Kyudo and Jukendo have never used colored belts to indicate rank.

In order to motivate his students, Kano introduced a rational ranking system of *kyu* and *dan*. He also formulated rules and conventions enabling safe sparring and matches (*randori*). The Kodokan became an incorporated society in 1909 which enabled effective dissemination.

Kano maintained that "Teaching of a Way is the primary motivation of Kodokan instruction, and learning technique facilitates this." He told his students that Judo could be divided into three levels—upper, middle and lower teachings. The "upper teaching" involved the study of how one utilizes energy for the benefit of others in society. The "middle teaching" centered on the personal well-being attained as a "by-product" of exercise. The "lower teaching" was simply training for combat or competition.

Lowest though it was, when he first created his school he had to show that Judo was practical to be considered credible. To this end, his students entered the Police Bujutsu Tournaments in the 1880s. Cleaning up the opposition, they thrust Kodokan Judo into the limelight.

Throughout his life, he continued to stress the educational value of Judo above all else. Promoting Judo as a means for social betterment, he published hundreds of articles and periodicals about how Judo could go a long way to remedying all manner of societal ills. He was also a proactive lecturer on the subject, and moved in influential circles in government and education. Incidentally, he was fluent in English and foresaw the value of spreading Judo overseas from early on.

A Martial Arts Gatekeeper

The formation of the Dai-Nihon Butokukai (The Greater Japan Society of Martial Virtue) in 1895 was undoubtedly a major turning-point in attempts to popularize the martial arts in schools and ensured their survival

Kano Jigoro sits in the Kodokan *dojo* overseeing his students going through their drills.

自
他
共
栄

BUDO CALLIGRAPHY:
Jita-kyoei "Mutual Prosperity For the Self and For Others."

Kano Jigoro promoted *jita-kyoei* as one of the core principles of Judo.

Left The Butokuden *dojo* in Kyoto. The Butokuden served as the Butokukai's HQ. It still stands to this day.

into the next century and beyond. The Sino-Japanese war (1894–95) led to a surge of nationalism in Japan, which in turn sparked a revival of interest in *bujutsu*. The year 1895 also marked the 1,100th anniversary of Kyoto becoming the capital of Japan.

According to legend, Emperor Kanmu constructed the Butokuden (Hall of Martial Virtue) to promote a martial spirit and encourage warriors to further advance their military prowess. Riding a growing wave of jingoism, the Butokukai Association was

established in Kyoto by a cooperative of businessmen, politicians and other prominent members of society with the endorsement of the Meiji Emperor. Its goals were to research, protect and promote time-honored martial arts as important cultural treasures. The organization was also instrumental in creating modern generic forms of Budo for school education.

The Butokuden *dojo* was built in 1899 near the grounds of the newly constructed Heian Shrine in Kyoto as the Butokukai headquarters. The organization held events, such as an annual *bujutsu* gala, and in 1905 a division was established to train instructors.

Still, there were numerous problems that needed to be overcome before nationwide dissemination could be realized. In an attempt to unify the many *bujutsu* traditions and their techniques into something that transcended affiliation to a specific *ryuha*, the Butokukai developed standardized *kata* for *kenjutsu*, *jujutsu* and other disciplines by cherry picking techniques from the classical schools. This contributed greatly to the spread of *bujutsu* by providing unified content for teaching.

Following the Sino-Japanese war and the Russo-Japanese war (1904–05), Japan, like many other countries around the world, pushed ideologies of "self-cultivation" and physical well-being to augment patriotism. When the National Curriculum was amended in 1911 by

KEY BUDO CONCEPTS: *Sho-go* 称号 "Teaching Titles"

Shogo are special teaching titles. The Butokukai was the first organization to introduce these in 1895. They conferred the title of "Seirensho" to Soke (headmasters) of classical *bujutsu* schools to recognize their position and efforts in preserving their arts. In 1902, the Butokukai introduced the *shogo* titles of Kyoshi and Hanshi as well. An instructor needed to have the title of Kyoshi to be allowed to teach at Butokukai branch *dojo*, so it was an affirmation of expertise and legitimacy. Hanshi was the highest level of *shogo* and recipients were given a stipend to live off until 1921. It was the supreme teaching license in the Butokukai.

So, originally there were the three *shogo* teaching titles of Seirensho, Kyoshi and Hanshi. Seirensho was replaced with the title of Renshi in 1934, and it is these three that remain in use in most of the Budo arts today. (Except for Judo, which did away with the system after the war.) Nowadays, Dan is usually thought of as representing technical ability and *shogo* titles as representing teaching ability and contributions made in promoting the art. For example, Kendo explains the requirements for each *shogo* as follows:

- *Renshi* must be accomplished in the principles of Kendo and have distinguished powers of discernment.
- *Kyoshi* must be expert in the principles of Kendo and have superior powers of discernment.
- *Hanshi* must have mastered the principles of Kendo, show maturity in character with extraordinary powers of discernment, and be a person of unimpeachable moral demeanor

Each Budo has different rules and standards for the awarding of both Dan and *shogo*.

the MOE, *bujutsu* was officially allowed to be taught as an elective subject in schools. This only really came into effect from 1913 as it took time to prepare consistent teaching content and convenants. Membership in the Butokukai in 1911 had reached several million, and there were branches located throughout the country. Each branch built a *dojo* modeled after the Butokuden in Kyoto. This was a golden era for Budo.

From Bujutsu to Budo

Interestingly, it wasn't until around this time that the word *bujutsu* was replaced with "Budo." The change was instigated by Nishikubo Hiromichi, a Kendo master who was also principal of the Butokukai's Teacher Training School. Possibly motivated by Kano Jigoro, he replaced the *-jutsu* with *-do* in 1919 to emphasize educational and moral objectives. The government followed suit in its official documents in 1926.

The Dying Martial Arts

Some modern Budo practitioners also study Kobudo, the classical martial arts, although we are a minority. The Kobudo I study are Kashima Shinden Jikishin Kage-ryu *kenjutsu*, Hoki-ryu *iaijutsu* and Tendo-ryu *naginata-jutsu*. I am fascinated by the esoteric teachings that underpin the *kata* and I find that Kobudo illuminates the philosophical and technical roots of modern Budo.

The Kobudo arts are represented by two main organizations in Japan: The Japanese Classical Martial Arts Society and the Society for the Promotion of Classical Japanese Martial Arts. Over the years, membership organizations have decreased steadily as *ryuha* continue to die out. Popular manga such as *Vagabond*, the story of Miyamoto Musashi, have contributed to greater awareness of the old styles among youth, but by and large young Japanese are not interested in joining a classical school of *bujutsu*. To them, they seem antiquated and irrelevant. Few see any point in devoting time to anything with no sporting component.

There are several large public Kobudo demonstrations held throughout the year. Adherents from different schools demonstrate their forms, but

Girls practicing Naginata in a school courtyard in the late 1930s. Women rarely did Kendo. The options available to them were Naginata, Kyudo and, in some cases, Judo.

KEY BUDO CONCEPTS: *Ki* 気 "Life Force"

"It's an energy field created by all living things. It surrounds us and penetrates us. It binds the galaxy together," said Obi-Wan Kenobi of the "Force." So, what is *ki* in the context of Budo? It's sort of the same thing. *Ki* is the fundamental energy that exists in all living things. It is the source of the kinetic energy that facilitates perception, sensations and instincts. Originally a Chinese concept (*chi* or *qi*), clues to its meaning can be ascertained by looking at its *kanji*. Although simplified to 気 now, its older ideogram was 氣, made up of 气 = air, breath, etc. and 米 = rice. This connotes the steam rising from rice as it cooks, rice being the staple diet from whence one gets energy. *Ki* is such an important concept in the martial arts that the word itself has become international. Rendered into English, it would be "vital life energy" or "life force."

Ancient Chinese philosophers such as Mencius taught that *ki* was the energy required to act and this was controlled by one's will. *Ki* was something that could be nurtured to extend beyond the scope of the physical body. Training the body and mind in Budo is actually annealing one's *ki*. It makes the functioning of mental and physical faculties harmonious. This means that it can be used for evil as well as good and is why *ki* is associated with morality and emotion. In popular terms, bad *ki* is the "Dark Side." Of course, *ki* is not just a Budo thing. The simple act of getting out of bed in the morning requires an internal explosion of *ki*, more for some than others. There are many words which indicate its pervasiveness in Japanese culture. For example, weather (*tenki*) is the "*ki* of the heavens."

KEY BUDO CONCEPTS:
Shu-ha-ri 守破離
"Acquiring, Breaking, Detaching"

The procedure for learning the syllabus of a martial tradition is different in each school or *dojo* but there are universal principles that apply. One common model for the learning process is found in the concept of *shu-ha-ri*. This is also used in non-martial arts such as ikebana and the tea ceremony and denotes the route taken to reach perfection. Generally speaking, in order to master the teachings of an art, the master's instruction must first be strictly and obediently adhered to. This is the first step called *shu*, which literally means to "protect" or "abide by." In other words, the *kata* is practiced and memorized exactly as the master teaches it. The student is essentially copying the master's movements, right down to the position of the pinkie. There is no room for personal interpretation. When students have absorbed all they can from the master they must develop their own take on the techniques. They "break away" (*ha*) from their *ryuha* in search of a different perspective. In the old days, this would have been achieved through *musha-shugyo*. After testing and enhancing their basic knowledge, and identifying strengths and fallibilities, the student progresses to a higher level of understanding and confidence. This is when the student completely "breaks away" (*ri*) and creates his own path. Reaching this ultimate state of martial "enlightenment" is when a new *ryuha* is formed.

College students studying Naginata in the early 1940s. Although taught in schools to foster womanly virtues, towards the end of World War II Naginata was encouraged as a last line of defense should the enemy invade the islands of Japan.

you won't see too many people under 40 on the stage, let alone children. Kobudo is studied mainly by old men and women, and when they go, so too will many of the smaller schools with no new blood to carry on the systems. The whole purpose of *ryu*, which means to flow, is to keep relevant with the times. If it is not relevant, then it is no use, and this is very much the perception today. It is a sad state of affairs because I believe people are looking for relevance in the wrong places.

There are classical Kobudo schools which have managed to consolidate a strong multi-generational following and these will surely continue to prosper. Others, however, might simply disappear at the drop of a sword, together with their centuries-old knowledge.

Cowboy-ryu

Even in Japan, you will come across McDojos. Just because it's in Japan, doesn't mean to say that it's authentic. History abounds with questionable Samurai with no combat experience who woke up one beautiful morning and decided to make their own cult martial art. Ironically, if they stand the test of time, they come to be considered genuine representations of traditional *bujutsu*, even though they may not have started out that way.

The success of a school is very much a matter of timing and circumstance, and who you know. This still happens today, but who is to say what is real and what is not? Kobudo enthusiasts will often decry modern Budo as being a false representation of the true martial spirit. Then again, Kobudo devotees may be criticized by modern Budo practitioners for doing something that

Beware of charlatans claiming to be "protectors of the true Samurai Way." Budo cowboys are everywhere.

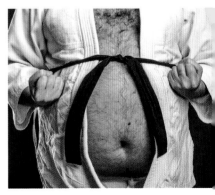

KEY BUDO CONCEPTS:
Jiri-itchi 事理一致 "Coalescence of Technique and Theory"

Ji refers to the techniques (*waza*) or methodology for learning them. *Ri* is more difficult to explain but is generally translated as theory. This also means the psychological aspects and principles of the art. So, *jiri-itchi* is a teaching that advocates the importance of learning the techniques and the principles behind them as two wheels of a cart. In other words, realizing the interaction of mind and body through mastering the techniques.

Jiri-itchi reminds the Budo practitioner that considerable contemplation and physical training are needed to achieve a coalescence of motion and logic, and that both of these important aspects are complementary. It is what links technical training with the cultivation of the mind. And a cultivated mind leads to better techniques. You cannot continue Budo into your old age if all you have acquired is technical athleticism. This is important to start with, but continuation beyond the years of your physical peak requires an understanding of the deeper principles and theories that underpin the movements.

has no basis for determining true skill in the thick of the fray—in other words, "pretend Samurai" who do a lot of *kata* and a lot of talking, but no real fighting.

Indeed, for a country that holds harmony in high esteem, the Budo world can be quite a fractious environment. Even now, incessant squabbling over matters of authentic Sokeship (head of the tradition) plague many of these small Budo organizations.

So, if it's like this in Japan, what's it like outside the country? One concern in Japan is the emergence of sundry Kobudo schools overseas. Some are actually authorized by the *ryuha* and the current Soke in Japan, but the lion's share are totally fabricated eyesores, underwritten by bogus claims of historical legitimacy. Typically, the representative masquerades as a sanctioned Professor 12th Dan Grand Poobah Master of "such-and-such-ryu's ancient traditions," but actually has no association whatsoever with the *ryuha* in Japan, if it even exists here.

At least with modern Budo, the federations oversee a generic version of their discipline. Although methods for training will differ between each *dojo*, the techniques and rules will be the same. This is not the case with Kobudo. There will be splinter groups splintering off splinter groups. They all have their own take on things and are less accepting of other styles.

So, how do you know what is the real deal and what isn't? I can't speak for any country other than Japan, but the best way to navigate around the crapton of cowboys is to contact the national federation of a modern Budo affiliated with the Japanese Budo Association or the Japanese Kobudo Association for classical martial arts. That is not to say that nobody else is

精力善用

BUDO CALLIGRAPHY:
Seiryoku Zenyo
"Efficient Use of Energy"

One of the core ideals articulated by Kano Jigoro in Judo. Using one's energies and strengths rationally for maximum effect.

not legitimate! You have to be the judge of that yourself, but these are good places to start.

Signs that indicate a purveyor of Bullshido are exorbitant monthly fees, *sensei* who wear gold chains or tinted glasses during training, and students who act and look like arrogant thugs. Rather than being committed to teaching Budo, they are usually concerned with making a profit or living a Samurai fantasy where they can be top dog.

CHAPTER 4

MARTIAL ARTS IN JAPAN TODAY

Budo disciplines are seen as conduits for self-cultivation and instilling discipline. They are also popular in school clubs and in the community as exciting competitive sports. There are more than nine Budo arts in Japan, especially if you include the hundreds of classical schools of Kobudo in the mix. The nine that I introduce here, however, are the "modern Budo" disciplines that come under the umbrella of the Japanese Budo Association. In other words, these are "mainstream" Budo arts that have government recognized central governing bodies. Budo really is something that can be practiced for the entirety of your life, from the moment you can stand up until the second you fall over dead from old age. I don't know any football players still mixing it up with teenage athletes when they are in their eighties and nineties but this is commonplace in Budo! There are distinct stages with regards to the competitive side. Younger practitioners will concentrate on learning techniques and strategies to win, but as the practitioner ages and gradually loses the competitive desire s/he will focus more on beauty in form and dignity of mind than athletic dexterity. You compete against yourself rather than your opponent. Basically, Budo is for everyone.

THE NINE MODERN BUDO ARTS

It is important to note here the difference between pre-modern and modern Japanese martial arts. The various modern Budo disciplines were developed during and after the Meiji period (1868–1912). Those already in existence before this are now referred to as *kobudo* (old = classical Budo), *koryu* (old styles) or simply as *bujutsu*. Although modern Budo traces its philosophical and technical roots back to the classical traditions, the current forms and rules, protocols of etiquette, pedagogical methodologies and objectives have all been modified for wider and safer participation. The often heard term "Budo seishin" (spirit of Budo) alludes to an understanding of martial arts as premised on peace and respect. Once systems for killing, Budo is now an instrument for education.

A female Karate exponent performs a solo *kata* during a competition. Karate will be included as an official event at the 2020 Olympic Games in Tokyo for the first time. Both *kata* and *kumite* will be contested.

Karate (Empty Hand Fighting)

Karatedo (空手道), usually just called Karate, is by far the most popular Japanese Budo discipline internationally. The Japanese Ministry of Foreign Affairs claims there are 50 million Karate practitioners worldwide! The World Karate Federation is even more audacious in claiming over 100 million. Clearly nobody really knows, but even a conservative estimate of 10 million means Karate is a major sport on the world stage. Interestingly though, with only around 300,000 practitioners in Japan itself, it is a minority Budo here and has been so for much of its short history on the mainland. This may soon change, however, as Karate will be included in the 2020 Tokyo Olympiad.

Karate developed in Okinawa from fighting techniques introduced by Chinese immigrants and traders back in the fourteenth century. It is usually said that when the Satsuma clan usurped the Ryukyu Islands in 1609, weapons were confiscated from the locals and techniques of hand-to-hand combat known as *te* remained underground until Japan modernized at the end of the nineteenth century. The idea that Karate was developed by peasants as a form of self-defense is simplistic and mostly incorrect. Commoners, however, were known to have ventured to China to study fighting arts there. If anything, it was the Okinawan aristocracy who excelled in this combat form.

Incidentally, not all Okinawan martial arts were weaponless. Even today there are adherents of what is generically called Okinawa or Ryukyu Kobudo which specialize in using all sorts of weird and whacky weapons.

From the early 1900s, public demonstrations of Karate were held in Naha and classes were offered at some public schools by Itosu Anko (1831–1915), one of the modernizers who adapted the traditional forms for educational purposes. Other notable practitioners include Matsumura Sokon, Higoanna Kanryo and Matsumora Kosaku, who are collectively referred to as the "Three Okinawan boxing saints" of the late nineteenth century. Karate was virtually unknown in mainland Japan until 1922 when the legendary Funakoshi

---

KEY BUDO CONCEPTS: *Budo no Rinen* 武道の理念 "The Philosophy of Budo"

Established on October 10, 2008 by the Japanese Budo Association, "The Philosophy of Budo" is a document that seeks to elucidate common ground between modern Budo in terms of cultural identity and social significance. It is basically a definition of modern Budo and its fundamental philosophy. "Budo, the martial ways of Japan, have their origins in the traditions of Bushido—the Way of the Warrior. Budo is a time-honored form of physical culture comprising of Judo, Kendo, Kyudo, Sumo, Karatedo, Aikido, Shorinji Kempo, Naginata and Jukendo. Practitioners study the skills while striving to unify mind, technique and body; develop his or her character; enhance their sense of morality; and to cultivate a respectful and courteous demeanor. Practiced steadfastly, these admirable traits become intrinsic to the character of the practitioner. The Budo arts serve as a path to self-perfection. This elevation of the human spirit will contribute to social prosperity and harmony, and ultimately, benefit the people of the world."

Gichin (1868–1957), was invited to demonstrate the art. His activities were supported by the founder of Judo, Kano Jigoro, who gave him floor space at the Kodokan to teach. Karate subsequently adopted white uniforms and colored belt ranks just like Judo.

Karate was accepted by the Dai-Nihon Butokukai in 1933, meaning it was officially assimilated into the pantheon of "Japanese Budo," and its ideograms were changed from "Chinese (*kara* = 唐) hand (*te* = 手)" to "empty (*kara* = 空) hand," with *do* added like all the others to highlight its educational component and "Japaneseness." Later on, *kumite* (sparring) became widespread and this facilitated Karate's rapid development into a competitive sport, especially among college students.

Other Okinawans started promoting their own styles of Karate on the mainland. Shotokan, Goju-ryu, Wado-ryu and Shito-ryu remain the four most significant styles in the governing Japan Karate Association. Of course, there are many other styles of Karate, such as Kyokushinkai, that do not belong to the JKA, and there is also considerable diversity within the schools themselves. Some focus more on *kata* training, others on non-contact *sundome* sparring with kicks and punches. Others feature full-contact fighting and the smashing of baseball bats. In accordance with the old saying *Karate ni sente nashi* ("the first move is never made in Karate"), the techniques are not promoted as a means to instigate aggression but to mitigate it.

Kendo (Fencing)

Kendo (剣道) doesn't have any obvious benefits for self-defense (nobody carries swords around anymore), and the rules are complex. It isn't just a matter of hitting the opponent, it has to be done the right way. It is hard to gauge personal progress, but it is a discipline in which anyone can participate irrespective of gender, age or size. In terms of numbers, Kendo is the most popular Budo

in Japan with 1.5 million practitioners. Kendo, meaning the "Way of the Sword," is the quintessential Samurai martial art, which looks like something out of *Star Wars*. Of course, it is the other way around. Samurai started using bamboo swords (*shinai*) and protective equipment from the eighteenth century to engage in full-contact training. By the end of the Tokugawa period, fencing was widely practiced not only among warriors but by commoners as well. That was because, just like *Star Wars*, it was damned exciting.

Practitioners dress in the traditional *hakama* (split skirt) and *kendo-gi* (training top) and use *shinai* bamboo swords to try to strike four specific target areas on the opponent's armor. The targets must be called out in a loud voice (*kiai*) as they are struck accurately with a strong spirit and upright posture. The targets are the *men* (head), *kote* (wrists), *do* (torso) and *tsuki* (a thrust to the throat). There are off-the-mark attacks and counter-attacks. The standard fighting stance is the middle *chudan-no-kamae* but some people prefer the overhead *jodan* stance and a small number also fight with two swords (*nito*) in the style of Miyamoto Musashi.

The competitor who scores two points first is the winner. Kendo places a lot of emphasis on showing respect to one's opponents. Anybody who celebrates a point will have it nullified as this is considered a gross breach of etiquette.

Above A Kendo practitioner attacks his opponent's head during a match at the Butokuden.

Left The World Kendo Championships are held once every three years. The two heavyweights are Japan and Korea and matches between these two countries are always fierce.

Judo (The Gentle Martial Art)

Judo (柔道) was created by Kano Jigoro in 1882. Judo was the first (and so far only) of Japan's Budo disciplines to feature at the Olympics. It debuted at the Tokyo Olympic Games in 1964 and is immensely popular around the world with 200 affiliates in the International Judo Federation. There are two representative bodies for Judo in Japan: The All Japan Judo Federation and the Kodokan. Both are connected but the Kodokan is considered the sentinel of Kano's educational ideals, while the AJJF is generally seen as the organizing body for Judo competitions.

After training for several years in the classical styles of *jujutsu*, Kano developed the theories of *tsukuri* and *kake*. *Tsukuri* is the action of setting up a throw through breaking an opponent's balance (*kuzushi*). *Kake* is executing the technique after *kuzushi*. Judo's technical corpus comprises throws (*nage-waza*) and grappling techniques with holds and locks (*katame-waza*) and ground techniques (*ne-waza*). The objective is to either throw the opponent or get them to the ground and pin them down for a set amount of time, or until they tap out of a choke or joint lock. Kano encouraged the competitive side of Judo but promoted it more as a way of life for strengthening mind and body, developing intellect and cultivating respect and morality. There are no punches or kicks in competitive Judo, although such techniques are preserved in the *kata*.

The rules can be a little confusing, but a throw that puts an opponent firmly on his/her back will be awarded *ippon* and the match will be over. If the opponent ends up on his side or back with not enough force to be called *ippon*, the thrower will be awarded *waza-ari*. Two *waza-ari* in the match equals an *ippon*. A lesser throw that puts the opponent onto his side is called a *yuko*, but these are only taken into account if the match is tied at the end of duration time. An *ippon* can also be scored by pinning an opponent on his or her back with a ground technique for 20 seconds or through a forced submission signaled by tapping out.

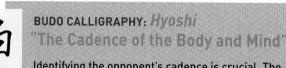

BUDO CALLIGRAPHY: *Hyoshi*
"The Cadence of the Body and Mind"

Identifying the opponent's cadence is crucial. The split-second pause between each beat of the heart and mind is an opening there for the taking. Hiding one's own "beat" is also important for this reason.

KEY BUDO CONCEPTS: *Chushin* 中心 "Center"

Chushin is a term fundamental to all Budo disciplines. It means "center" and taking it is the key to offense and defense. So, where is it exactly? Is it a point or an axis? It actually refers to both. "The center" is a point in your body, whereas "taking the center" means controlling the axis of your opponent. Most Budoka will tell you that their "center" is located in the *seika-tanden*, the point just below the navel in the middle of the body. I call this the T-spot. This is the center of balance and center of gravity, the focal point of breathing, the root of one's inner compass and the spring from whence one's *ki* flows. *Seika* means "below the navel" and *tanden* is literally "red rice paddy," the rosy source of energy. In Budo this represents the center of your universe, where balance is maintained physiologically and psychologically and the point from which all techniques are executed.

"Top heaviness" in strength and form is a feature of many sports and is good for generating speed. For example, think of a tennis player hunched over waiting to receive a serve. The center of movement in this case is positioned above the navel. But in Budo, equilibrium is sought through straightening the posture, relaxing the upper body and holding tension in the belly for stability and explosive power. Posture makes the difference between tapping an opponent and cutting him to the bone. Most beginners start top heavy and use brute strength, but as they improve, they become more focused or "centered" in their movement and demeanor.

"Taking the center" includes pressuring the opponent's center point and broadly refers to controlling the vertical central axis, which also equates to protecting your own. When you have control of the center, your techniques reach the target quicker with less effort, whereas the opponent's attacks can be deflected and exposed. To use another tennis analogy, imagine one player standing in the center of the court running the other player ragged by effortlessly hitting alternately to each side of the court. When you see Kendoka facing off with bamboo sword tips tapping together, they are actually engaged in a process of trying to assert dominance over each other's centers. As soon as one tip drops away from the center line, this reveals an opening that can be struck. But then again, it could be a trap to draw the opponent in. Whatever the case, "taking the center" and "moving from one's center" is central in all Budo."

Above An Aikido master nonchalantly throws two assailants at once.

Right Judo students scrap it out on the mats in a *randori* session.

Left Ueshiba Moriteru demonstrates Aikido techniques at the Aikikai Hombu in Tokyo.

Aikido (Unifying the Life Force)

Perhaps the most esoteric of the modern Budo arts is Aikido (合気道). Aikido is distinctive from the other mainstream Budo in that it adopts the hereditary transmission model for the head of the organization. Currently, the founder Ueshiba Morihei's grandson, Ueshiba Moriteru, is the third Doshu, meaning "master of the way." At the heart of Aikido is the concept of *ki* or life force, which was described by the founder as "love." The Aikikai Foundation is the parent organization for the development of Aikido and is sanctioned as the representative Aikido group in the Japanese Budo Association. Nevertheless, there are other Aikido groups that stem from students of the founder. For example, the Shodokan founded by

Tomiki Kenji in 1967 is unique in that it promotes "sport Aikido." Shioda Gozo (1915–94) created the Yoshinkan style considered to be more in line with the rigorous techniques employed by Ueshiba Morihei in his earlier days.

Ueshiba once stated that "True Budo is not the act of using one's strength to combat an opponent. It is a quest to perfect one's character." In this sense, Aikido is more about joining forces (*aiki*) to improve together rather than competing to determine supremacy. Practitioners engage in what looks like a flowing dance where the objective is a balanced synchronization of body and mind and harmonious interaction. That is why there are no competitions in Aikido, only demonstrations and training. The techniques involve linear movements going forward into your partner (*irimi*) and pivoting movements (*tenkan*) to execute throws, pinning techniques and combinations. These are further divided into standing techniques, seated techniques and variations against armed or multiple opponents. The flowing, effortless movements make Aikido beautiful to watch.

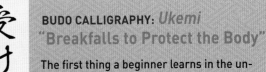

BUDO CALLIGRAPHY: *Ukemi*
"Breakfalls to Protect the Body"

The first thing a beginner learns in the unarmed martial arts. It is the skill required to fall safely by protecting the head and mitigating the force of hitting the ground.

That's gotta hurt! Shorinji Kempo is a dynamic martial art that thankfully utilizes protective equipment when practicing full-contact kicks and punches.

SHORINJIKEMPO

Shorinji Kempo (Shaolin Kungfu)

The newest of the nine Budo arts is Shorinji Kempo (少林寺拳法), founded in 1947 by So Doshin (Nakano Michiomi, 1911–80). Even though it is included in the nine Budo, it is distinct from the others in that its roots are in China. Advanced practitioners wear monk-like uniforms and everybody greets each other using the *gassho-rei* with both palms put together and raised in front of the face—a Buddhist gesture of piety—as opposed to bowing.

Doshin studied Shaolin fighting techniques in China before and during World War II. Upon returning to Japan, he codified the techniques—kicks, strikes, throws and holds—and added a Zen-based philosophical and educational dimension.

The techniques can be broadly separated into *goho* (hard method) and *juho* (soft method). *Goho* includes receiving strikes and kicks by deflecting and countering. *Juho* techniques are joint manipulations, reverse throws and holds employed when an aggressor grabs your arms or clothing. There are also teachings called *seho*, which focus on the body's pressure points.

Priesthood qualifications for Kongo Zen are offered by the federation as at the heart of the discipline are spiritual teachings. In fact, Shorinji Kempo is legally a religious entity in Japan. The principles of training are expressed as *kenzen ichinyo* (*ken* and Zen as one and the same)—*ken* (fist) points to mastery of the physical techniques and Zen to the spiritual. The swastika, or *manji* in Japanese, was the original emblem for Shorinji Kempo because of its Dharma affiliation. Symbolic of Kongo Zen teachings, the swastika signifies "love" (left-facing) and "strength" (right-facing), but due to the symbol's repugnant association with Nazism, a new insignia was introduced in 2005, comprising a double circle inside two interwoven *manji*.

Kyudo (The Art of Archery)

The elegant and uniquely shaped Japanese bow, with its grip located one-third the distance from the bottom, is 2.2 m (7.2 ft). It is made by combining two outer slats of bamboo with split bamboo in the middle and then covered with lacquer. Kyudo (弓道) differs from other Budo arts in that the opponent is not another person but a tiny little target. Target size and distance also vary. In close-distance competitions the target is

---

KEY BUDO CONCEPTS: *Osu* 押忍 "Push On"

If the international population of Karate truly is 100 million, then "oss" (*osu*) might very well be the most frequently used Japanese word outside the country. What does it mean? In the Karate *dojo* it's used as a "Hello," "Good morning," "Good evening," "Goodbye," "Please," "Thank you," "Excuse me," "You're excused," "Yes," "No," "I get it," "I don't get it," "Make sure you kick ass," "Ok, I'll be sure to kick ass." It all depends on the context. Given its many meanings, you might think this is the perfect word—simple yet deep. The actual etymology is a point of contention. One explanation suggests that it first appeared in the Imperial Japanese Naval Academy in the early twentieth century. Another theory suggests that it originated in Kyokushinkai Karate founded by Mas Oyama with his mantra of *osu no seishin*—the "spirit of *osu*." The two *kanji* used to write *osu* are 押 = "push," and 忍 = "persevere." In other words, to "push through hardship."

There are other more mundane explanations of the term. Japanese people have a tendency to shorten words. For example, *ohayo gozaimasu* (good morning) or *onegai shimasu* (please) are often abbreviated to *o-ssu*. This is not necessarily rude, but you wouldn't say this to superiors unless it is accompanied by a sincere bow of the head. In this case, it would be interpreted as meaning that you are bursting inside to say the greeting quickly as a sign of utmost respect. *Arigato gozaimasu* (thank you) is another word often shortened in this way, especially in Budo circles. It sounds like "ass" with a Scottish accent. Similarly, *kon'nichiwa* (hello) is often expressed as "ncha-!"

Left and below The "eight stages of shooting" in Kyudo are footing, forming the torso, readying the bow, raising the bow, drawing apart, full draw, release, remaining spirit.

bow creaks as it is drawn and the pressure builds. The arrow must be released with correct posture: back straight, chest out, maintaining equilibrium with power centered in the lower abdomen. The build-up is intense and the arrow is released when a unity of self, bow and target has been achieved. After the release, the body remains in a concentrated state of *zanshin* (continuous physical and mental alertness) and the right hand flicks back, making the body like a cross. The quality of the release can be sensed by the twanging sound made by the bowstring.

Kyudo is popular among men and women of all ages in Japan. Competitions are subdued affairs, and just from looking at the faces of the archers it's impossible to tell whether or not the arrow hit the target.

The higher ideal aspired to in Kyudo is described as *shin-zen-bi* (truth, goodness, beauty). The archer seeks to correct him or herself in mind and posture before, during and after shooting the arrow. If the arrow doesn't hit its mark, it must be acknowledged that the cause of failure is in the self. Goodness of "self" corresponds to goodness of the arrow's flight. Beauty is sought in each and every shot, and in all of the meticulously followed eight stages (*hassetsu*) of the shooting procedure.

Kyudo uses an eccentric bow. Two-thirds of its length is above the grip and one-third below. All lines lead to the T-spot in the *hara*.

36 cm (14 in) in diameter at a distance of 28 m (91 ft). In long-distance competitions, the target is 1 m (3.2 ft) in diameter and situated further away at 60 m (197 ft). Shooting protocols are stringent and rules of etiquette and respect must be carefully followed. From start to finish, the shooting process is divided into eight stages. Instead of being concerned with whether or not the arrow hits the mark, practitioners are encouraged to appreciate each shooting sequence at a time. It is surprisingly exciting to watch.

The arrow is held with the right hand and the bow with the left. The bowstring is pulled back fully to the right shoulder with the right hand. The

Sumo (Japanese Wrestling)

Sumo (相撲) has two distinct categories: the professional sport of Ozumo governed by the Japan Sumo Association, and amateur Sumo, which is administered by the JBA-affiliated Japan Sumo Federation. Sumo is referred to as Japan's "national sport" because of its ancient ties with the Shinto religion and

Above The *tachiai* is the all-important initial charge at the beginning of a Sumo bout.

Right When refereeing, senior *gyoji* wear beautiful medieval-style silk costumes.

Far right Feeling like a Hobbit, the author shares a meal of *chanko* stew with a couple of professional *rikishi*.

Naginata versus Kendo matches are always a crowd favorite. Naginata tends to win most of the time.

the founding myths of Japan. It also has a strong connection with agrarian rites and with medieval Samurai culture. During the Tokugawa period, Sumo became a form of entertainment (not a martial art) enjoyed by townsmen. It evolved into a modern amateur sport at the end of the Meiji period, finding a keen following among schoolboys and university students, just like the sport of wrestling in the West.

Amateur Sumo is sometimes called Sumo-do. In contrast to the seemingly feudal world of professional Sumo, the amateur version has weight divisions, a Dan ranking system and does not include the many Shinto-based rituals such as salt throwing, water spitting and bow slinging. Rituals such as *chirichozu*, in which the hands are opened out and shown to the opponent symbolizing the intention to grapple fairly and squarely without the use of weapons, are common to both.

Originally, Sumo never had height or weight divisions, so wrestlers devised techniques to overcome the brute strength of bigger opponents. After the introduction of the *dohyo* mound during the Tokugawa period, techniques such as *yori* (pushing), *oshi* (shoving) and *tsuri* (lifting) became the mainstay. It is said that there are 48 basic Sumo techniques but this number is merely figurative as over 100 techniques can be identified in Sumo today.

Each bout starts with the face-off (*tachiai*), which is a crucial factor in determining the result. In the *tachiai*, it is considered good form to collide with the opponent head on with all one's might. Apparently, the force created in the *tachiai* by two wrestlers each weighing 100 kg (221 lb) is over 1 ton (2,000 lb)! To avoid being

knocked off the *dohyo* and into the outer seating for a home run, lighter wrestlers angle their bodies slightly on impact, or vary the timing to deflect the force. Strategy is a very important aspect of the sport. Although it seems like two massive meat tanks smashing into each other, it's much subtler than that.

Amateur Sumo is on a mission to internationalize and become an Olympic event. This has resulted in the recent acceptance of women into the sport, a controversial change that will never happen in professional Sumo. Women also have to don the *mawashi*, a belt that looks like a giant thong, but worn over leggings!

Naginata (Glaive Combat)

Although commonly encountered on early medieval battlefields, the *naginata* (薙刀) eventually became obsolete around the fifteenth century in favor of long pointy pikes called *yari*. During the Tokugawa period, the weapon was studied by women as a "hidden art" for self-defense. As such, it survives today as a Budo discipline practiced and run by women. Boys traditionally did Kendo and girls Naginata, but this attitude has softened a little in the last few decades.

The *naginata* used in the modern sport version consists of a bamboo blade taped onto an oak shaft measuring 210–225 cm (83–89 in) in length. Practitioners wear armor similar to Kendo with a protective mask (*men*), body protector (*do*), gauntlets (*kote*) and the addition of shin guards (*sune-ate*). Competitors try to strike each other on these target areas or thrust to the throat (*tsuki*). The target must be struck with precision and with a coalescence of body, mind and *naginata*.

Being a long weapon, the *naginata* is held in a side-on stance and is manipulated on both sides of the body. Strikes are made with *furiage* (swinging the weapon overhead), *mochikae* (changing the grip and sides that the *naginata* is held on), *furikaeshi* (twirling the *naginata* overhead), *kurikomi* and *kuridashi* (pulling the *naginata* in or pushing it out to adjust the distance).

Apart from full-contact sparring, there is a competitive category called *engi-kyogi*. Pairs are judged on their performance of basic attack sequences and counter techniques (*shikake-oji*) or by performing the All Japan Naginata Federation *kata*. Nowadays, practitioners mostly train in the sporting version that was developed in the postwar period. Some study a classical style as well. *Naginata* is reputedly practiced by over 40,000 people in Japan, most of whom are women.

Jukendo (Bayonet Combat)

The prototype of Jukendo (銃剣道), the "Way of the Bayonet," was first demonstrated in Japan in 1841 by the

Above Jukendo has several sets of *kata* utilizing various weapons. Above is *mokuju* versus *mokuju*.

Left People of all ages can train together.

KEY BUDO CONCEPTS: *Ningen-keisei* 人間形成 "Personal Cultivation"

A literal translation of *ningen-keisei* would be something like "formation of the human," that is, how to become a better person. This entails both physical and moral development. The Budo practitioner is expected to make him or herself stronger in body and mind through training, and ultimately use this strength to be of service to others. Personal cultivation means striving for excellence in the technical and mental aspects of the art with single-minded determination, not by taking shortcuts or skirting around the hard stuff. Budoka have to endure hardship and failure along the way, but the never ending journey of persevering and overcoming all hurdles, great and small, will make you one resilient, respectful and replete. That is what is meant by *ningen-keisei*. Of course, there is no such thing as perfection and one does not become a better person simply through training in a martial art. If you truly want to become a winsome individual, Budo does provide a physical and philosophical framework that is useful in your quest for improvement. But self-improvement must be aimed for and requires guidance. A *sensei* you can respect and look up to is crucial to keep you on track and open your eyes to Budo's life-changing potential.

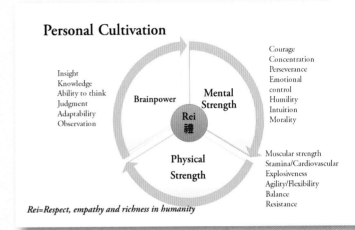

Personal Cultivation

Brainpower — Insight, Knowledge, Ability to think, Judgment, Adaptability, Observation

Mental Strength — Courage, Concentration, Perseverance, Emotional control, Humility, Intuition, Morality

Physical Strength — Muscular strength, Stamina/Cardiovascular, Explosiveness, Agility/Flexibility, Balance, Resistance

Rei 禮

Rei=Respect, empathy and richness in humanity

---

musketeer Takashima Shuhan (1798–1866). He learned the techniques through contact with the Dutch in Nagasaki. It was not until after the Meiji Restoration (1868) that the bayonet became an established combat skill in the Japanese military although it is often associated with classical schools of the pike (*sojutsu*). A French instructor, François Ducros, first introduced Western-style fencing and bayonet practice into the Toyama Military Academy's curriculum in 1874. *Jukenjutsu*, as it was called, was recognized by the Dai-Nihon Butokukai in 1925 and its name changed to Jukendo in 1941. As recently as 1998, the All Japan Jukendo Federation introduced traditional navy blue *hakama* and training tops (like those worn in Kendo). Until then, the conventional uniform consisted of white shirts and trousers reminiscent of military physical exercise uniforms. The armor is also similar to Kendo, with the addition of a large pad covering the left shoulder and heart.

There are only two targets: the heart and the throat, although the wrist also counts if it is used to block a thrust. The weapon is called a *mokuju* and resembles a rifle with a long tip and a rubber cap on the end to soften the blow. Thrusts are made with strong *kiai* (spirit) and forward momentum of the whole body, followed by a swift withdrawal from the point of contact.

It sounds and looks dangerous but it is surprisingly safe. Although the techniques seem easy—straightforward thrusts—getting the right form, keeping composure amidst a flurry of stabs, judging the distance and subtly moving the tip of the *mokuju* to create openings is quite challenging. The speed at which the tip reaches the target from start to finish in the hands of an average practitioner ranges from 0.30 seconds to 0.19 seconds—fast and furious.

The Jukendo Federation is still battling to overcome lingering images of militarism. Despite the obstacles it faces, Jukendo is currently looking at creating an international federation. Incidentally, the vast majority of its 80,000 or so practitioners are members of Japan's Self-Defense Forces. As the SDF has diversified in recent years, however, the number of personnel training in Jukendo is decreasing as Karate becomes more predominant.

Through training in Iaido, Samurai learned to parry and riposte against a single or multiple imaginary opponents while seated, standing or walking. There are many different schools still in existence today, and Iaido is popular in university clubs.

OTHER MODERN BUDO

Iaido (Sword Forms)

Iaido (居合道 *iaijutsu*), the "Art of Drawing the Sword," traces its roots back to the Muromachi period (1336–1573). A Samurai trained in how to wield his 76 cm (30 in) razor-sharp blade by unsheathing it in a flash against imaginary foe(s), following up with a kill cut and finishing by shaking the phantom blood off the blade before returning it to the scabbard. Victory or defeat is supposedly decided the instant the blade is unleashed. *Iai*, which literally means "meeting on the spot," was never studied alone. It complemented *kenjutsu* (swordsmanship practiced against a partner). It could be described as shadow boxing for sword fighters but keeping within the confines of *kata* rather than random cutting.

Nowadays, Iaido is often practiced as a stand-alone discipline. There are various federations in existence but the biggest group is affiliated with the All Japan Kendo Federation. In a match, two competitors use live blades (if 4th Dan or above) or blunt replica swords to perform prescribed *kata* from the AJKF's set of 12 forms and from the classical style that they study. Three judges evaluate the performance looking at accuracy of cutting, etiquette, precision, attitude and the realistic kill scowl on their faces.

Jodo (Staff Fighting)

Jodo (杖道) is the "Way of the 128 cm (4 ft) long, 2.4 cm (0.9 in) diameter

Jodo is strongly focused on defense against the sword. It is a purely *kata*-based Budo.

Left Tankendo is not very well-known in Japan but is probably one of the easier Budo disciplines to learn.
Below Two students engaged in a heated Nihon Kempo match.

staff." The *jo* is probably the simplest weapon in the entire world but can be lethal in the right hands. According to standard Budo philosophy, the *jo* is not supposed to be used as a weapon of attack but to subdue and incapacitate an aggressor, usually armed with a sword. The first *jo* school emerged in the seventeenth century. The Shinto Muso-ryu was created by the legendary Muso Kennosuke. Jodo matches are now conducted between two pairs performing *kata*. Winners are judged on fullness of spirit, correct posture, preciseness and strength of the techniques, control of distance, etiquette, synchronicity and, of course, the mandatory realistic combat expressions. Like Iaido, Jodo as a stand-alone Budo is also a subdivision of the All Japan Kendo Federation, but there are various Kobudo schools that specialize in or include *jo* techniques as well.

Tankendo (Short Sword)

Falling under the auspices of the All Japan Jukendo Federation is a subsidiary sport called Tankendo (短剣道 "Way of the Short Sword"). Very similar to Kendo in terms of equipment, Tankendo uses a one-handed short sword—a detached bayonet. Stabs to the body and throat make up the bulk of the offensive techniques,

but *men* and *kote* strikes are also valid. There are a number of fascinating *kata* against rifles, swords and short swords. Tankendo can be studied as a stand-alone Budo but is usually practiced together with Jukendo.

Nihon Kempo (Japanese Fist)

Nihon or Nippon Kempo (日本拳法) is similar to Karate and involves full or semi-contact matches using protective equipment. It was developed in 1932 by Sawayama Muneomi and has a wide range of strikes, kicks, blocks, take-downs and ground techniques. The armor consists of a helmet, breastplate, gloves and groin protector. Matches are energetic and exciting to watch.

Very much a minority Budo in Japan, Nihon Kempo is not one of the nine members of the Japanese Budo Association but it is popular at Kansai University where I teach. Actually, the founder was a graduate of Kansai University! So Doshin, the progenitor of Shorinji Kempo, also studied it briefly. The police are known to practice it in addition to their own special, particularly vicious martial art called *taiho-jutsu*.

冴え

BUDO CALLIGRAPHY:
Sae "Clarity"

Crispness or sharpness in technique, movement and intuition.

THE FIFTEEN BEST JAPANESE SAMURAI FILMS OF ALL TIMES

Well, the fifteen best according to my personal tastes. The swordsmanship that you see in movies is very different to the classical *kenjutsu* and modern Kendo that I practiced in the *dojo*. The fight scenes are totally unrealistic, but I watch martial art movies for the action and entertainment, not the reality.

1. ***Seven Samurai*** (七人の侍 **Shichinin no Samurai, 1954)** The most incredible Samurai good versus evil movie of all time. At five hours it is epic, with the last fight scene in full swing for a whole hour. An Akira Kurosawa masterpiece.
2. ***After the Rain*** (雨あがる **Ame Agaru, 1999)** A beautiful story written by Akira Kurosawa about a kindly Ronin stuck in a hut with his wife and other travelers because torrential rain has made the river uncrossable. He uses his sword skills to earn money and puts on a feast for everybody. Nobody is killed in this movie!
3. ***Sword of Doom*** (大菩薩峠 **Dai-bosatsu Toge, 1966)** If the *katana* is the "soul of the Samurai," what does it say about his soul when his sword is a bloodthirsty tool of destruction? Ryunosuke is the "hero" of the movie, a violent man with no empathy and some nasty demons.
4. ***Samurai Assassin*** (侍 **Samurai, 1965)** A group of lords hire Samurai mercenaries to carry out the assassination of Ii Naosuke. Set in the period immediately before the Meiji Restoration, this movie is intriguing, dark and violent.
5. ***Harakiri*** (切腹 **Seppuku, 1962)** A window into the stark, cruel and ephemeral existence of the Samurai. Contains an intense and disturbing *seppuku* scene committed with a bamboo sword.
6. **Samurai Trilogy** (宮本武蔵 ***Miyamoto Musashi*, 1954;** 一乗寺の決闘 ***Duel at Ichijoji Temple*, 1955;** 決闘巌流島 ***Duel at Ganryu Island*, 1956)** A series of three films that star the greatest Samurai actor of all time, the legendary Toshiro Mifune, as the greatest swordsman of all time, Miyamoto Musashi. These three films are true classics!
7. ***Yojimbo*** (用心棒, **1961)** Another phenomenal Kurosawa film, *Yojimbo* is the bizarre and compelling tale of a mercenary played by Toshiro Mifune who "tidies up" a dirty little town ruled by crime lords.
8. ***Shogun Assassin*** (**Kozure Okami** 子連れ狼, **1980)** One in a series of movies about the "Lone Wolf" and his child (Cub) whom he pushes throughout the Japanese countryside in a pram whilst killing hundreds of bad guys. Quentin Tarantino's *Kill Bill* was influenced by this movie, so you can just imagine how gory it is.
9. ***Zatoichi*** (座頭市, **2003)** The original *Zatoichi* series consists of 26 films about a blind but freakishly lethal swordsman/masseur. Rutger Hauer's *Blind Fury* was based on No. 17. A more recent version released in 2003 stars Takeshi Kitano. Dark but [bloody] colorful at the same time.
10. ***13 Assassins*** (十三人の刺客: **Jusannin no Shikaku, 2010)** Based on a true story about a group of Samurai who plot to kill an unpopular Shogun for the greater good. There were thirteen of them.
11. ***The Twilight Samurai*** (たそがれ清兵衛: **Tasogare Seibei, 2002)** A moving story about an easygoing widowed Samurai who only wants to look after his two lovely daughters and senile mother. If life was that easy there wouldn't be a movie. Heartwrenching stuff.
12. ***When the First Sword was Drawn*** (壬生義士伝 **Mibu Gishi Den, 2003)** A story told in flashbacks by two Samurai who belong to the infamous Shinsengumi (Shogun's special police force). The fight scenes are second to none and the underlying themes of loyalty, honor and self-sacrifice to do the right thing are profound.
13. ***Samurai Fiction*** (SF サムライ・フィクション **Esu Efu Samurai Fikushon, 1998)** Let's lighten up a bit. A Samurai comedy filmed in black and white, with flashes of red you know when. Excellent soundtrack by Japanese rock star Hotei Tomoyasu accompanies Inukai Heishiro's quest to retrieve his clan's stolen treasure, a sword presented to them by the Shogun. Hotei Tomoyasu plays the music and the role of the thief.
14. ***The Hidden Blade*** (隠し剣 鬼の爪 **Kakushi ken: Oni no tsume, 2004)** A brilliant Yamada Yoji film. A young Samurai called Katagiri just wants to fantasize about the love of his life, a servant in his household, but ends up having to seek and kill his old friend who is plotting to overthrow the Shogunate. Awesome fight scenes and a good look at the turbulent Bakumatsu era.
15. ***Taboo*** (ご法度 **Gohatto, 1999)** Based on the Shinsengumi and bromance, the plot deals with homosexuality among Samurai and the jealousy it caused. This film is one of the few that highlights the rampant man-love aspect of Samurai culture not widely known about outside Japan.

EIGHT MODERN BUDO MASTERS

What is it that makes a Budo practitioner a true master of their art? It's not just technical ability and charisma, although these are important. It requires a lifetime of dedication and discipline. There are hundreds of people who could be included in this section but I chose a handful of masters who are widely acknowledged for their significant impact on the way modern Budo developed in the twentieth century.

Kano Jigoro (1860–1938)

On his way back from a tour of European education facilities in 1891, a little Japanese man by the name of Kano Jigoro was challenged to a fight by a famous Russian wrestler onboard a boat. To the bemusement of onlookers, Kano effortlessly flipped the big Russian on his back while simultaneously protecting his head from smashing into the deck. "What a righteous guy!"

Kano was born in 1860, a riotous time in Japan when violence was commonplace. He later explained how he came to study *jujutsu*.

> "Weaklings were invariably beaten up. I had no problems as far as academia went but I wasn't so confident with my physique. I then heard about *jujutsu*. I figured that through learning this art, even someone as puny as me could become a match for any opponent. I did not possess the high ideals I hold today and simply wanted to learn the skills needed to beat others."

Training in the *jujutsu* schools of Tenjin Shin'yo-ryu and Kito-ryu, Kano discovered that his physical and mental strength vastly improved, not to mention his ability to fight off the bullies who teased him for his superior intellect and inferior size. He also realized that with a bit of fine tuning, combat principles could be employed to enhance intellectual, moral and physical education. To this end, he systematized the techniques into logical categories for teaching and learning them safely through sparring (*randori*). He did away with lethal techniques in sparring but preserved them in the *kata* forms.

> "From the very beginning, I categorized Judo into three parts: *rentai-ho*, *shobu-ho* and *shushin-ho*. *Rentai-ho* refers to Judo as a physical exercise, while *shobu-ho* is Judo as a martial art. *Shushin-ho* is the cultivation of wisdom and virtue as well as

Above right A young Kano Jigoro looking decidedly constipated. Perhaps this pose is meant to show off his muscle definition.

Right Kano demonstrates Judo techniques with the legendary Mifune Kyuzo (left).

the study and application of the principles of Judo in our daily lives. I designed it so that practitioners could develop their bodies in an ideal manner, would be competitive in matches and expand their wisdom and virtue by incorporating the spirit of Judo into their daily lives."

He created competition and refereeing protocols and pioneered the now pervasive Dan ranking system, 10th Dan being the highest. Students who passed the 1st Dan rank (*shodan*) were permitted to wear a black *obi* to stand out from the crowd.

Kano made good use of his status as a prominent educator to popularize Judo in Japan and around the world. Taking ten overseas trips throughout his career, he never let an opportunity slip by to wow crowds of curious Westerners with displays of his Judo "tricks." He explained the principles of Judo to foreign audiences with evangelistic fervor in his trademark "headmaster's English."

Kano also sent some of his top students abroad to spread the word. Yamashita Yoshitsugu, for example, went to the United States and instructed President Theodore Roosevelt in the White House in 1904.

Guided by his friend Baron Pierre de Coubertin's ideals of Olympism, Kano advocated the virtues of sport as a vehicle for self-discipline and service to society. The Judo ethos as defined by Kano ultimately became *seiryoku-zen'yo* (the use of energy to maximum efficiency) and *jita-kyoei* (mutual prosperity for self and others). In other words, train hard to become a good Judoka, a first-rate citizen who can work for the benefit of everybody.

He founded the Japan Amateur Athletic Association (today's Japan Sports Association), and in his capacity as the first Asian director of the IOC he accompanied the first two Japanese Olympians to the Stockholm Games (1912). Kano became known as Japan's "father of sports," and with some deft political footwork he managed to convince the IOC to hold the 1940 Olympic Games in Tokyo.

The plan was eventually vetoed by militaristic elements in the government. Kano died just before this decision was made, on May 4, 1938, on the return journey from Cairo to Japan via America.

Incidentally, the boat he sailed on was the *Hikawa-maru*. It is now permanently berthed as a floating museum in Yokohama's Yamashita Park. Before Japan's entry into World War II, this ship was used to transport hundreds of Jews fleeing to North America to escape Nazi persecution in Europe.

Yamaoka Tesshu (1836–88)

A young swordsman called Yamaoka Tesshu visited the priest Dokuon to pick his brains and boast of his growing understanding of Zen. He rather pompously announced to the priest, "The mind, Buddha and sentient beings, after all, do not exist. The true nature of phenomena is emptiness, is it not?" Dokuon was smoking his pipe at the time and summarily smacked Tesshu on the noggin with it, angering the young upstart. Said the priest, "If nothing exists, Tesshu, why are you so angry dude?" "…?"

Tesshu was a dogged self-improver and is now considered Japan's last great *kengo*. He started his apprenticeship in swordsmanship at the age of nine. He went to Edo in 1852 after his parents died and joined Chiba Shusaku's famous *dojo* to learn Hokushin Itto-ryu. He also took lessons from other prominent instructors of the day, such as Saito Yakuro and Momonoi Shunzo.

Fiercely competitive, he soon gained a reputation for being a rambunctious scrapper, but his road to stardom was hard. His defeat to Asari Matashichiro in a fencing bout proved to be his biggest stumbling block.

> "I engaged him countless times after our first encounter, but could never put down this almighty adversary no matter what I tried…. When I closed my eyes and focused, I saw images of Asari with sword in hand standing before me like a mountain. It was impossible for me to strike him or drive the vision away."

Yamaoka Tesshu was a famous calligrapher, Zen master and formidable swordsman. His students influenced the development of modern Kendo.

The image of Asari finally disappeared from his mind when he solved a Zen riddle about the real meaning of "nothingness" (*mu*). The two faced off again, and sensing Tesshu's enlightened state, Asari withdrew and taught him the secret technique of *musoken* (the sword of no form). This was in 1880, and his newfound spiritual liberation was reflected in his highly prized works of calligraphy.

> "On March 30, 1880, with my deep understanding of swordsmanship and Zen, I came to grasp the essence of calligraphy and the brush. Although I understand the secrets, I am unable to explain them in words."

Tesshu started his own school called the Itto Shoden Muto-ryu (School of No-Sword). He opened the Shunpukan *dojo* and many came to study under him even though the severity of his training was legendary. For example, the infamous *tachikiri* marathon of matches is Budo at its cruellest. One of his students relayed his experience of fighting hundreds of consecutive bouts without respite. On the final day, he had to be carried into the *dojo*. But then….

> "After a while I noticed one member come in and approach the master Tesshu to ask his permission to take part in the exercises. The master permitted him right away. I looked at him and at once realized that he was the one noted for his rascality, who would thrust his bamboo sword to the naked throat behind the protecting gorget and keep it up even after he was already struck over his head by his victorious opponent. I approached him now fully conscious of my fresh inner surge and lifting up the sword over my head was ready to strike him with one blow of it. At this moment came the master's emphatic command to stop and I dropped my sword."

The shattered disciple had accessed a higher realm in swordsmanship. He had completely forgotten his bodily self.

Not only was Tesshu an intimidating fencer, he was a key figure in Japan's modernization. In the spring of 1868, when imperial loyalists marched to Edo castle to topple the Shogunate, Yamaoka Tesshu was tasked with negotiating with their leader, Saigo Takamori. His diplomacy helped prevent considerable bloodshed. Although a staunch servant of the Shogunate, he was equally steadfast in his loyalty to the Meiji Emperor after the Restoration of 1868. He is remembered to this day as a man of high principle and otherworldly skills in swordsmanship and calligraphy.

Tesshu died in 1888 of stomach cancer. Apparently, he habitually took sips of highly carcinogenic charcoal ink before writing calligraphy. This was the probable cause. It is rumored that he died while meditating.

Tesshu was an "old-school" swordsman, and although not directly involved in the movement to include martial arts in the education system, many of his influential disciples, such as Takano Sasaburo, were very much at the forefront of the development of modern Kendo.

Ueshiba Morihei (1883–1969)

In 1923, Ueshiba Morihei accompanied his spiritual guru, Deguchi Onisaburo (leader of the Shinto-based religion Omoto-kyo), as his bodyguard on a trip to Mongolia. As they made their way through the mountainous terrain, their entourage was set upon by bandits. Bullets rained down on them from all directions but Morihei remained remarkably calm. Somehow he managed to evade the bullets by twisting and turning his body.

It must have looked like some kind of funky disco dance, but Morihei later described his reaction as being based on the principle of *sumikiri*—total clarity of body and mind. Such were the finely honed skills and sensibilities of the founder of Aikido.

Morihei was born in Wakayama prefecture in 1883. He began studying *jujutsu* when he was 13. In 1915, he became a student of the legendary Takeda Sokaku (1859–1943), reviver of the Daito-ryu tradition, when working on the northern island of Hokkaido. He revered Takeda, a hard man who took no prisoners, but eventually developed a different view of the true spirit of Budo. Morihei sought a more peaceful resolution to conflict.

Ueshiba Morihei (right) demonstrates the beauty of Aikido in front of students. He studied many martial arts during his lifetime, such as Kito-ryu and Shinkage-ryu. Takeda Sokaku of Daito-ryu Aiki-jujutsu had the biggest influence on his martial art development, although their relationship became strained later on.

Morihei met Deguchi Onisaburo for the first time in 1919. Deguchi apparently had miraculous healing powers and the encounter sparked Morihei's fascination with spirituality. Deguchi considered himself to be an incarnation of the Maitreya Bodhisattva and had aspirations to unite the world with his religious teachings. Moved by Deguchi's pacifistic moral beliefs, Morihei started his own *dojo* and taught his martial art which he called Aiki-bujutsu. In 1925, Morihei had an epiphany:

> "The moment I was awoken to the idea that the source of Budo is the spirit of divine love and protection for everything, I couldn't stop the tears flowing down my cheeks. Since that awakening, I have come to consider the whole world to be my home. I feel the sun, moon, the stars are all mine. Desire for status, honor and worldly goods has completely disappeared. I realized that Budo is not about destroying other human beings with one's strength or weapons, or annihilating the world by force of arms. True Budo is channeling the universal energy (*ki*) to protect world peace, to engender all things fittingly, nurture them and save them from harm. In other words, Budo training is to protect all things and cultivate the power of unconditional divine love within."

He accepted requests to teach certain individuals but was not inclined to give instruction to the general public lest his art be used in violent ways. He changed the name of his art to Aikido in 1942 when his organization was brought under the auspices of the government-run Butokukai.

> "It is a grave mistake to think that Budo is about being stronger than your opponent and that you have to defeat him. In true Budo, there is no partner. There is no enemy. True Budo is to become one with the universe. It is to be united with the universe's center. In Aikido, we do not train to become strong or to beat opponents but to make a small contribution to peace for all people in the world. To that purpose we must strive to harmonize with the center of the universe."

At the crux of Morihei's Aikido teachings is the concept of *ki*, or the life force that flows in each living being. Aikido translates as the "Way of Harmony with Ki" and this harmony, *ai-ki*, is none other than "love" itself. He explained this here:

> "To purge the self of maliciousness; to find harmony with the natural order of the universe; and to be at one with the universe.... That is to make the mind of the universe your own mind. What is the mind of the universe? It is the great love found in every corner of the universe, both in the past and the present.... True Budo is the movement of love. It is not to kill or fight but to let all things live, grow and flourish."

As Morihei said, the point is not to "fix the other person" but to "repair the self." This was Ueshiba's highest principle and is precisely the function of *ai-ki*.

Funakoshi Gichin (1868–1957)

Like Kano Jigoro, Funakoshi Gichin was born into a well-to-do family and was a physically weak young lad. Like Ueshiba Morihei, Funakoshi was a pacifist who preferred to avoid conflict if at all possible. In his autobiography, he admits to using his Karate skills once in his life when he was mugged. Instead of round-housing the thief with a powerful kick to the head, he sidestepped the initial attack and grabbed hold of the assailant's gonads. He held the hap-

less mugger in that painful nut-cracking grip until the police arrived, but always regretted that he had been unable to avert the situation from the outset.

Funakoshi was born in Okinawa. He studied Karate under Itosu Anko and Azato Anko. A school teacher by profession, he started his own Karate *dojo* at the age of 33. Much of his time was spent writing poetry and enjoying nature. His pen name was Shoto, which translates as "waving pine," hence the name of his style, Shotokan.

His first trip to mainland Japan was in 1921–22 when he was invited to demonstrate this mysterious and hitherto obscure fighting art of Okinawa. Interested onlookers quickly sought Funakoshi's guidance in setting up classes in Tokyo. At first he focused on teaching intellectuals and professionals such as lawyers. Apparently, he thought their physical prowess paled in comparison to the sharpness of their minds.

As the word spread, Karate started to gain a dedicated following in universities. Following in Funakoshi's footsteps, other Okinawans such as Mabuni Kenwa (founder of Shito-ryu) and Miyagi Chojun (founder of Goju-ryu) began teaching at universities and clubs around the Kansai region.

Kano Jigoro took Funakoshi under his wing and even requested personal lessons at the Kodokan. One of Funakoshi's early students at Takushoku University was the Karate legend Kanazawa Hirokazu. I translated his autobiography a few years back, and in it Kanazawa mentions Funakoshi's gratitude to Kano.

BUDO CALLIGRAPHY:
Shoshinsha "Novice"

In Budo, it is said that one must never forget what it's like to be a beginner. This keeps you humble and more inclined to improve.

"He was given an opportunity to demonstrate Karate at the famous Judo center, the Kodokan in Tokyo, with special permission from the founder, Kano Jigoro. The demonstration was well received and helped Karate's promotion greatly. Master Funakoshi always felt indebted to Kano Shihan, and every time he passed the Kodokan in a taxi he would remove his hat and bow deeply in gratitude. It is true to say that Kano Shihan also respected Master Funakoshi and asked for personal instruction in Karate *kata*."

In 1947, the Japan Karate Association named Funakoshi Gichin the country's top master of Karate.

Funakoshi was adamant that Karate should not be used in a fight. It was too dangerous for that. He was even opposed to his students training in *kumite*, preferring to focus on *kata*. This was not a popular stance among college students who revelled in the thrill of competitive fighting, but according to an old adage taught to him by Matsumura Sokon, "When two tigers fight, one will get hurt. The other will be killed."

His "Twenty Dojo Precepts" form the basis for the five official JKA ideological concepts today: 1. Never forget that Karate begins and ends with a bow of respect. 2. There is no first attack in Karate. 3. Know yourself first then you can know others. 4. The art of developing the mind is more important than the art of applying techniques. 5. In combat you must discern between vulnerable and invulnerable points.

Although his Tokyo *dojo* was destroyed in the Allied bombings, GI interest in Karate after the war was huge. Funakoshi never went overseas himself, but following many impassioned requests he sent his best students to teach the art around the world from 1953.

Karate is by far the most prevalent Japanese Budo internationally. Some Okinawans beg to differ, but Funakoshi is now widely acknowledged as the "father of Karate." It was he who initiated the first wave of dissemination in Japan and led by example through a life of virtue, humility and respect, consciously avoiding confrontation.

So Doshin (1911–80)

So Doshin visited the White Robe Hall at the Shaolin Temple and saw the famous Qing Dynasty mural of monks practicing martial arts. The painting contains pictures of dark-skinned monks fighting arts with monks of lighter color. They were Indians training with their Chinese brethren. It was apparently an inspiration to So Doshin, the founder of Shorinji Kempo.

He was born in Okayama prefecture on February 10, 1911 as Mitsutsuji Michio. Joining the army in 1928, he traveled around Manchuria and China in "behind the scenes work." He entered the tutelage of Liang Chen, under whom he studied Buddhism and the Chinese martial arts. Liang Chen was an instructor in the Northern Shaolin White Lotus Fist Society, which traces its roots back to the Shaolin Temple.

So Doshin was later introduced to Liang Chen's teacher, Taizong Wen, who had been a monk in the Shaolin Temple and had inherited the art of Yihemen Quan (the fist of righteousness and harmony) from Longbai Huang, the 19th headmaster. According to Shorinji Kempo's official history, So Doshin was made the 21st headmaster of the tradition by his mentor in 1936.

So Doshin was living in Manchuria during the Soviet invasion of 1945. He was able to escape the carnage through the help of his Chinese friends. Returning to Japan in 1946, he was dismayed to find the country in a terrible state. Buddhism seemed corrupted and youth were lethargic and lost.

"In order to escape from painful reality, they threw themselves into frivolous activities or readily accepted destructive foreign ideologies. Many lost sight of themselves as Japanese. Japanese pride had been erased because of defeat and the people had become completely despondent. Not knowing what to do, they neglected their children and indulged in gambling and the like, living without hope. Some tried to find solace in suspicious new religious groups that preached Buddha's teachings, but this just intensified their confusion. So many people were in a state of total despair."

He resolved to impart his values to help restore some order. No one was interested in what he had to say but a message from Boddhidharma in a dream convinced him to gather students through teaching the martial arts. Once he had their attention in the *dojo*, he lectured about morality based on the concepts of *jiko-kakuritsu* (self-establishment) and *jita-kyoraku* (half for your own happiness, half for the happiness of others).

So Doshin expressed the core teachings of his art through the terms *kenzen ichinyo* (unity of the fist and Zen) and *rikiai funi* (strength and benevolence stand together). His mantra was:

"The person, the person, the person; everything depends on the quality of the person.... By doing evil, I contaminate myself. By not doing evil, I purify myself."

So Doshin codified the arts he learnt in Japan and China and added a theoretical and spiritual dimension. He called his school Shorinji Kempo. As his reputation spread, more people came to him to learn. Although martial arts were forbidden in Japan in the immediate postwar period, authorities turned a blind eye to his activities as he was helping to keep the peace.

Students flocked to his organization and Shorinji Kempo spread in Japan and abroad, particularly in Indonesia. There is a 1975 dramatized movie of So Doshin's story entitled *Shorinji Kempo* starring Sonny Chiba. The English version is somewhat inappropriately called *The Killing Machine*.

So Doshin was invited by the Chinese government to demonstrate Yihemen

So Doshin (right) practices with a student at the Shorinji Kempo headquarters in Tadotsu.

Quan at the Shaolin Temple in 1979. He died before he could go. The World Shorinji Kempo Organization is currently headed by his daughter, So Yuki.

Sakakida Yaeko (1912–2004)

"If you gonna drops bombs, come down here and get a taste of my *naginata*, you cowards. C'mon! Bring it and fight like men!" This brazen challenge was from a young Sakakida Yaeko and directed at the B29s flying overhead as she whirled her *naginata* skyward.

During the war years, several Naginata instructors worked with the Butokukai and Ministry of Education to create standardized forms for teaching to Japanese schoolgirls. A totally new set of *kata* utilizing *naginata* versus *naginata* (as opposed to *naginata* versus sword) was planned as an initiative for more effective propagation of the art.

Traditionalists were opposed to ideas championed by Sakakida Yaeko, a graduate of the Butokukai's Budo Vocational School. Sakakida was renowned for her feisty nature and was considered to be quite the maverick. Nevertheless, her accomplishments and dedication to the promotion of Naginata were second to none. Her biggest gripe with Naginata before and during the war years was the difficulty in teaching it to large groups of students at once, and that they also had to learn sword usage in the *kata*.

"With Kendo, anybody with a *shinai* (bamboo sword) could travel wherever they wanted to and train with others. In Naginata, all we could do was *ichi, ni, san, ieiii*! and thrust at air. I couldn't stop wondering if there was not some way for *naginata* to fight against *naginata*."

She realized that just practicing *kata* and thrusting at nothing was never going to keep girls interested. Another problem was that students would be taught different styles of Naginata—Jikishin Kage-ryu at elementary school and then Tendo-ryu at high school—which was confusing and frustrating for pupils and instructors alike. Sakakida decided a new modern form of Naginata had to be created to supplement the old styles. She contacted the MOE and presented her ideas in 1943.

"There was a fellow named Onitsuka from the army, a colonel I think. He spoke. 'What's the story with Naginata these days. Wouldn't it be better to teach girls how to fight with a bamboo spear?' I exploded when I heard him say that! I felt the blood surging through my veins, and snapped back at this colonel Onitsuka. 'I beg your pardon!' I heard afterwards that I even thumped the desk and had a frightful scowl on my face. 'Are you insinuating that we should make Naginata training and spear training the same? I will have you know that Naginata is authorized by the government for girls' education and it's not meant to be taught as a way to kill people! If it gets to the stage where Naginata has to go to war, then Japan is already screwed!'"

She had already tried that approach against the B29s and it didn't stop the bombs. Sakakida continued her research

and was assisted by influential individuals in politics and the Budo world, such as the Minister of State and notable Kendo master Sasamori Junzo.

"After lots of hard work, at last a standardized form of Naginata was introduced into the elementary school curriculum for year five girls and in Budo classes at normal schools. The MOE authorized the new forms, the first to pit *naginata* versus *naginata*. From there it was a matter of teaching them nationwide. While traipsing all over the country to hold seminars from Kyushu to Tohoku, Japan lost the war. Then there was a long period where we could train no more."

Sakakida's newly devised Naginata was shelved and would not see the light of day for another ten years. Budo was banned in the immediate postwar period. But when it was allowed once again in the 1950s, Naginata experts came together to establish a unified sporting version of the art. Sakakida's innovations were brought to the table once again.

Young schoolgirls practicing Jikishin Kage-ryu. A great rivalry existed between this style and Tendo-ryu in girls' education.

"I solicited opinions from numerous teachers and eventually created what is now known as *atarashii* [new] Naginata…. It was quite revolutionary. The forms were not referred to as *kata* but called *shikake-oji* (attack-counterattack). It consisted of eight predetermined patterns which featured an array of techniques. Even the equipment was changed, and the *naginata* blade was modified by joining two slats of bamboo. This meant that Naginata practitioners could go anywhere in the country and compete or train with others, just like Kendo."

This was the genesis of the style of Naginata practiced today. The last time I saw Sakakida-sensei she was 92 and in full armor beating up a famous 8th Dan Kendo teacher at the Butokuden *dojo* in Kyoto. She was a remarkable woman who still frightens the life out of me when I think of her.

Awa Kenzo (1880–1939)

A German philosopher by the name of Eugen Herrigel (1885–1955) came to Japan in the 1930s and started learning the art of Kyudo to augment his understanding of Zen. When his teacher told him, "Don't aim the bow, just go with the flow," Herrigel was flummoxed. "How can I hit the target if I don't aim for it?" "Sheesh, the best way to teach this foreigner," thought his teacher, "is to just show him." Herrigel recorded his mystical experience in his classic book *Zen in the Art of Archery*:

> "Since the master was standing directly in the light, he was dazzlingly illuminated. The target, however, was in complete darkness. The single, faintly glowing point of the incense was so small it was practically impossible to make out the light it shed. The master had said not a word for some time. Silently he took up his bow and two arrows. He shot the first arrow. From the sound I knew it hit the target. The second arrow also made a sound as it hit the target. The master motioned to me to verify the condition of the two arrows that had been shot. The first arrow was cleanly lodged in the center of the target. The second arrow had struck the neck of the first one and split it in two."

The master in question was a mysterious fellow by the name of Awa Kenzo, and thanks in part to the writings of

Two pracititioners demonstrate *atarashii* Naginata. This photo is from Sakakida's ground-breaking Naginata textbook published in the early 1950s when Naginata was introduced back into schools.

Herrigel, Awa became a spiritual sage of sorts in the modern art of Kyudo. Actually, splitting arrows is a bit of a no-no in Kyudo because it means damaging your own equipment. It's not something Awa would have been proud of and he even admitted to one of his students that it was a fluke occurrence. Nevertheless, Herrigel was gobsmacked. His rational Western mind couldn't reconcile what had happened and it stimulated his hunger to understand Zen.

One of the pioneers of Kyudo in its modern form was Honda Toshizane, a former retainer of the Shogunate. Obsolete in an age of cannons and guns, Honda devised modern protocols for traditional archery in the hope that it would become a popular pastime for the masses. Awa Kenzo was Honda's student but it is Awa who became known

as the "God of the Way of Archery" through his teachings on its profound, spiritual aspects.

Few people realize, however, that he had never studied Zen before. Although he used Buddhist terminology, incorporated Zen breathing techniques and regarded the spirituality of Kyudo as something akin to Zen, he was certainly not advocating that Zen was the be-all and end-all in archery.

Influenced by the educational ideals of Kano Jigoro, Awa had an epiphany in the 1920s that he expressed as a "great explosion." He sensed that there was a greater goal in archery than just hitting the target, a skill in which he had no peer. He began to call archery *shado* (the "Way of Shooting") rather than *kyujutsu* and stated its main objective as "austere training in which one excels

KEY BUDO CONCEPTS: *Sutemi* 捨て身 "Total Commitment"

Sutemi is the requisite mental attitude in all Budo in which the practitioner commits body and soul into the attack with no concern for the outcome. The Samurai applied himself in the study of martial arts not only to master the techniques of killing but also to develop his "spiritual armor." The teachings of systemized martial art schools were simultaneously abstruse, mystical and practical in nature. It was kill or be killed. All or nothing. Although nobody fights with bows and arrows, swords or spears anymore, philosophical and spiritual underpinnings of "all or nothing" remain an important feature in all Budo. Budo is a precious legacy left by Samurai warriors and provides modern practitioners with fantastic insights into the beauty of life and how to live to one's full potential. This ideal paradoxically is based on the *sutemi* notion of self-annihilation. Wow. That's a bit heavy. The point is, just don't do anything half-hearted and don't be afraid.

Awa Kenzo was an archer par excellence. He was known as an absolute disciplinarian when it came to teaching.

KEY BUDO CONCEPTS: *Rei* 禮 "Respect"

Once I was riding the train home from an Iaido practice in Osaka. A seriously sozzled salaryman saw that I was carrying a sword bag. He found it somewhat perplexing that a foreigner could possibly be studying such an icon of traditional Japanese culture. He started a tirade in jumbled Japlish to reconcile his unbelieving eyes. "Do you know *rei*? How can *gaijin* know *rei*? You can't know *rei!*" Meaning that a foreigner could not possibly understand the true spirit underpinning Budo. I tried to diffuse the situation as the train was too crowded to move. "Yeah, I know Ray. Ray's a good guy. He says hello." Fortunately, the drunk disbeliever got off at the next stop. A common saying in all Budo disciplines is that it "always begins and ends with *rei*." The ideogram for *rei* is made up of two radicals: 示 "to

show" and 豊 "richness [in humanity]." *Rei* has two meanings: it is a seated or standing bow, and it is also the mindset of courtesy and respect. Simple manners such as greetings and various points of etiquette are accentuated in the *dojo* setting. You are bowing all of the time to people and things, and matters of deportment and attitude take precedence over pretty much everything else. The reason why *rei* is so important is because what you are doing in the *dojo* is dangerous. Anything can happen at any time, and injuries, bangs and bruises are a fact of life. Good manners are a safeguard against getting carried away and circumvent raw emotions running rampant in retaliation.

    Rei is a safety control on one level but is also a feeling of empathy toward peers that becomes a genuine part of your character over time. This is important in the *dojo* and also in the competitive arena. You always start with a bow of *onegai-shimasu* = "I appreciate that I have this opportunity to train/compete with you and I promise I will do my best." The bout finishes with a bow of *arigato gozaimashita* = "Thank you very much for training/competing with me. I learned a lot from this encounter and apologize if a wayward attack hurt you. I will reflect on this encounter and improve because of it." Of course, trying to win your matches is important but of more significance is the manner in which one wins or loses. Regardless of the result, the competitor is expected to demonstrate self-control and respect to the opponent, the referees and the venue. Victory poses are considered to be *shitsu-rei* (loss of *rei* = rude). Leaving rubbish in your seat is *shitsurei*. Not bowing properly is *shitsurei*. Basically, being an ignorant, arrogant, obnoxious ass in any way is *shitsurei*. This goes for spectators as well as competitors.

in the study of humanity" by "putting an entire lifetime of exertion into each shot." ("One shot, one life" = *issha zetsumei*). To him, archery was to "see true nature in the shot" (*shari kensho*).

    In 1927, amidst opposition from some students who thought he was losing his marbles, he formed the Daishadokyo (Great Doctrine of the "Way of Shooting"). It was essentially a cult religion centered on the bow. Awa's ideology hinged on the concept of "building personality" and becoming unified with the cosmos. "The bow and arrow are not for piercing the evil of others but are a direct means of piercing the evil within oneself. The self then becomes one with the universe." His ideas were fringe, but Herrigel's enthusiasm for mysticism and his subsequent writings introduced Awa's esoteric take on archery to the rest of the world. It was then imported back into Japan in a kind of reverse backflow of Japanese culture.

> One day I asked the Master, "How can the shot be loosed if 'I' do not do it?"
> "It shoots" he replied....
> "And who or what is this 'IT'?"
> "Once you have understood that you will have no further need of me."

    This confusing dialogue provided the impetus for Herrigel's own epiphany. One day he shot an arrow and Awa apparently said "That's IT!" Herrigel ruminated for many years on this moment and came to take the outburst as acknowledgement of the "ultimate Zen shot," made with no-mind and

no-intent. "IT" happens. Personally, I think it should have been interpreted more along the lines of "Hey Eugen, that wasn't a bad shot. You're finally getting your technique down. Keep at it 'cos you've got a long way to go yet." Nevertheless, it was the central theme for the supremely optimistic Herrigel's now famous book and it solidified Awa's position in Kyudo folklore forever. Herrigel's volume was translated into Japanese in the postwar period, and connecting Zen with Kyudo, is now an influential book among Japanese Kyudo enthusiasts. Awa Kenzo's Daishadokyo is still the prevalent style but is no longer a religious movement. In any case, Awa Kenzo was, and still is, a controversial figure but he was undisputedly one of the most important martial artists of modern times.

Donn F. Draeger (1922–82)

The Japanese were immensely proud to host the Tokyo Olympics in 1964. It was time to show the world that Japan had risen from the ashes and was ready to host the world's premium sports extravaganza. What's more, Judo debuted as an Olympic event and was a guaranteed source of medals for the host nation. Indeed, the Japanese Judoka did claim several golds, but the most prestigious category—the open weight division—was the one they wanted to win the most.

The final was between Japanese superhero Kaminaga Akio and the giant Dutchman Anton Geesink. The Dutchman broke Japanese hearts with a resounding win in the newly built Budokan arena. This was an upset of monumental proportions! His countrymen were delirious with joy and prepared to rush onto the floor to congratulate their man. Geesink, however, with a face of grave solemnity extended his massive hand, signaling his supporters to stay

put. An invasion of the *tatami* after his victory would be nothing short of sacrilege and an unforgivable breach of Budo etiquette.

This action has become immortalized in the Budo world and was some consolation for the Japanese in coming to grips with the fact that Kaminaga had lost. At least the foreign victor had shown respect for the traditions of Budo.

Few people know, however, that a man who was instrumental in teaching Geesink such reverence for Budo traditions was an American by the name of Donn F. Draeger. He took care of Geesink at the Kodokan and not only taught him Judo techniques but also the all-important spirit of respect behind the art.

Draeger was born in Milwaukee and began studying Judo and Kendo as a child. After graduating from Georgetown University, he joined the US Marine Corps in 1943 and saw action at the Battle of Iwojima. He retired from the Marines in 1956 with the rank of captain and spent the rest of his life dedicated to researching combative culture, a field of academic inquiry called hoplology.

He was highly ranked in several modern Budo disciplines, including Judo, Iaido, Jodo, Kendo and Aikido. He was also the first foreign student admitted into the classical school of Tenshinshoden Katori Shinto-ryu.

His publications are numerous and are must reads for anybody wanting to understand the history and culture of martial arts, not just in Japan but throughout Asia. He was based in Japan from the late 1950s and traveled extensively through Asia on research missions. In 1979, he visited the Aceh people in Sumatra and fell gravely ill through some kind of poisoning.

Donn Draeger practicing *kenjutsu* with his mentor, Otake Risuke.

Personal friends of mine who were travelling with him believe that the poisoning was deliberate and was the cause of his subsequent decline in health. He died in 1982 of liver cancer.

Draeger is widely considered by many to be the first real non-Japanese pioneer of Budo. Those who knew him respected him, not only for his aptitude in all of the Budo arts he specialized in but also because of his humble demeanor.

As a case in point, the following is quoted from a letter that he wrote to his teacher in the Tenshin Shoden Katori Shinto-ryu, Otake Risuke. Otake wanted to give Draeger his sword, a great honor in anybody's books, and the significance of this was not lost on Draeger, who outlined the conditions which had to be met before he could accept the gift:

> "I would thus like to ask your permission to accept the sword under certain conditions. I have no heir to care for this sword with gratitude and honor upon my passing. As a result, I would like to ask a lawyer to prepare what I write below as part of my legal will and testament. Hencewith, this sword must be returned as soon as possible to its rightful owner in Japan, Otake-sensei or his family, within 60 days of my death. Should you agree to these conditions, I solemnly pledge that it would be my honor to humbly accept the sword to keep in my care as my most prized treasure until the day it is returned to you and your family. With my greatest respect, Donn Draeger."

To this day, I hear old Japanese Budo masters reminiscing fondly about that "big American Draeger-sensei" and what an incredible man he was.

BUDO TRAINING IN JAPANESE SCHOOLS

Martial arts were taught in domain schools for children of Samurai families during the Tokugawa period. It wasn't until 1911 that it became an established subject in the modern education system. Objectives for teaching Budo have changed with the times. It was employed as an important ingredient of militarism during war years but is now taught in schools to educate Japanese children about traditional values and respect.

Children demonstrate Aikido. There are no competitions in Aikido but demonstrations are quite a big deal.

Schoolboys doing sword exercises in the early 1940s. Given the role Budo played in the militarist agenda, a blanket ban on participation was enforced following Japan's World War II defeat.

Budo During World War II

In 1928, the Minister of Education decreed that "All imported ideas were to be thoroughly 'Japanized,' abnormal thought was to be purged and educators must firmly support the National Polity and understand its meaning." During the 1930s and 1940s, Budo was commandeered by the government as a means to ready youth to make the ultimate sacrifice. The National Middle School Curriculum was modified after the Manchurian incident in 1931 and Kendo and Judo were made compulsory subjects for boys to "nurture a resolute, determined patriotic spirit, and train both the mind and the body." Other martial arts were gradually included, and girls were made to learn Naginata or Kyudo from 1936. The objective was not one of personal growth as much as preparing younger generations for the exigencies of war.

In 1941, the relationship between Budo and militarism intensified. Practical combat training became the primary objective and plans were put in place to teach "Combat Budo" to elementary school pupils. Rules of engagement in Budo disciplines such as Kendo were changed to make them more realistic. In 1942, the government even commandeered the Butokukai, Kodokan and other martial art organizations to propagate state ideology through Budo more effectively.

Jingoistic rhetoric instilled cultural pride and an unwaivering belief in Samurai ideals of self-sacrifice. For example, guidelines for Budo lessons in middle schools stipulated that "Bodies will be strengthened and spirits forged to raise unyielding reserves of energy to augment the nation's capacity for defense and loyal service." The utilization of Budo during this period of Japan's history is not often talked about. It is not denied but is one of those inconvenient truths simply designated as a "dark age" and best left well alone.

The Postwar Budo Ban

When the war ended in defeat for Japan, authorities stopped teaching Budo in schools and the community as

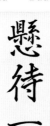

BUDO CALLIGRAPHY:
Kentai-itchi "Attack and Defense As One"

Kentai-itchi is the unification of attack and defense. The best form of defense is offence. That's why taking the initiative is important.

"combat training" and started promoting it again as a means for nurturing healthy bodies and minds. General Headquarters, led by General Douglas McArthur, was far from convinced of the veracity of intent. They saw the martial arts as dangerous tools for brainwashing and instilling nationalistic fervor. The Butokukai was disbanded and a comprehensive Budo ban was implemented that lasted to the 1950s.

> Traditional activities like Kendo, which foster the fighting spirit, must be abolished. Physical education must no longer be linked to "spiritual education." You must put more emphasis upon purely physical exercise; games that are not military training, and recreational activities.—SCAP directive

The reinstatement of Budo in the community and then the school curriculum was a piecemeal process. Judo was the first to be resurrected in 1950, and that was thanks to Kano Jigoro's early legacy of internationalizing it. There was a lot more sympathy for Judo and other Budo arts than Kendo, which was associated with the *katana* and wartime atrocities. The underlying condition for reinstatement was that Budo could no longer be taught as moral education but simply as "peaceful democratic sports."

Each Budo discipline created its own independent national body. Competition rules and techniques

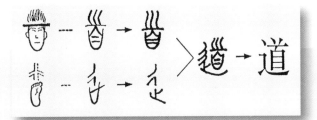

KEY BUDO CONCEPTS: *Michi* 道 "The Way"

Michi (aka *do*) is the word you will hear most in Budo circles. *Michi* is the *do* in Budo. The ideogram for *michi* (道 = Way) is made up of two radicals: *kubi* (首) and *shin'nyu* (辶). *Kubi* means "neck" and the *shin'nyu* radical is a kind of path. The path starts at the top of 辶 and rambles down into eternity. *Kubi* also has the nuance of "putting one's neck on the line." Together they can be interpreted as walking while turning one's head to look at the surroundings. In the context of Budo, the character for *michi*/*do* represents the application of Budo lessons in life. It is the path traveled throughout one's lifetime. It can also simply mean "street." Just 道 it!

The Japanese team marching in front of the home crowd during the 1964 opening ceremony of the Olympic Games.

were reassessed and emphasis on the austere side of training was softened as Budo was now supposed to be fun and educational. The physical education "Curriculum Guidelines" for junior and senior high schools were amended to allow Budo classes but the word "Budo" was banned. Instead, *kakugi* (combat sports) became the official designation and remained so until 1989. The Budo arts, mainly Kendo, Judo, Sumo and Naginata were taught as optional subjects in PE classes at most junior and senior high schools in Japan, but extra-curricular school clubs also flourished.

The 1964 Olympics

The Tokyo Olympic Games of 1964 were a momentous turning point in the postwar resurrection of Budo. Kendo, Kyudo and Sumo were featured as demonstration sports at the newly constructed Nippon Budokan and

Judo debuted as an official event. Judo's inclusion in the Olympics signified the start of reacceptance of Budo in the mainstream. Having been showcased at the greatest sporting event in the world, it was from around this time that Budo started gaining a dedicated following outside Japan too.

Budo competitions increased exponentially in all disciplines but Kendo and Judo were by far the most prevalent in terms of numbers in Japan. Parents enrolled their children in *dojo* with expectations that they would be taught discipline and etiquette. Children, on the other hand, stuck at it because they enjoyed competing.

A negative upshot of Judo's Olympic induction is criticism that it eroded its educational integrity as a form of Budo, transforming it instead into a "sport" in which the only concern is collecting as many medals as possible. In other

words, ideals of becoming a better person for the benefit of "self and others" as advocated by the founder of Judo became more about benefit of the self and a contempt for others. "Winning's not everything, it's the only thing." "It's not the process but the result that matters and the result justifies the means."

Such attitudes are seen as an abomination of the true Budo spirit. Some see it as having been brought on by a contamination of "Western sporting attitudes." At least that is the perception, which is paradoxical in a way because the Japanese media and general public are categorically unforgiving if their Judo heroes don't win gold! In any case, all Budo federations stress that the goal is not just about winning but becoming a better person. Still, gold medals are nice too.

Budo's Role in Schools Today

Budo is on a roll in Japanese schools today. In spite of the fact that the number of students in extracurricular Budo clubs is actually in decline, all Japanese kids now have at least tried Budo through compulsory education. In 1988, the government announced that its future education policy would aim at "Nurturing people with rich minds who are able to adapt to the changes in society as

Kendo was viewed with more suspicion than other Budo after the war. Kendo's revival was a drawn-out process that first saw the invention of a benign hybrid sport called Shinai Kyogi.

the twenty-first century approaches." Crucial to this lofty ambition was "Deepening international understanding and cultivating an attitude of respect towards Japanese culture and tradition." What better represented this ideal than Budo?

The following year, Budo was acknowledged as "Budo," not *kakugi*, for the first time in the postwar era. It was to play a role in children's education with expectations that exceeded other PE activities and sports. Budo was back and the stigma of militarism was officially buried. Budo = Japaneseness = International mindedness = Hale and hearty Japan and world peace—this became the official mandate. Given the previous four

decades of caution demonstrated by the government regarding Budo's role in character development in schools, this announcement was quite a coming out.

Momentum continued to build. In 2006, the government modified the "Basic Act on Education" for the first time since 1947. The new direction was to "Cultivate the zest for life," with "Enhancement of cultural/traditional education." Budo was made a compulsory subject for first and second year pupils in all junior high schools from 2012. The majority of schools teach Judo (around 70 percent), followed by Kendo (25 percent), and the remaining seven Budo in the Japanese Budo Association make up the rest.

BUDO CALLIGRAPHY: *Hinkaku* "Dignity or Class"

品格

This is quality in action and speech that emanates from the Budo practitioner who has trained for many years. Kano Jigoro espoused five factors that *hinkaku* is comprised of: etiquette (posture, appearance, correct deportment); lifestyle (living a dependable and frugal way of life); sociability (interacting with others with appropriate language); work ethic (using one's talents to the best effect); ideals (always maintaining high principles).

The Nippon Budokan

The Nippon Budokan is a building and also a foundation. The Budokan oversees the promotion of Budo in Japan. Its stated goals when created were:

"Encouraging the spread of the traditional martial arts of our country to the general public, especially among children, to nurture people of sturdy character, thereby contributing to the well-being of the Japanese people, and to peace and welfare throughout the world."

The monolithic Nippon Budokan martial arts hall was constructed in the vicinity of the Imperial Palace just in time for the Tokyo Olympic Games in 1964. It was to be the venue for Judo's debut in the Olympics and became a symbol of the postwar Budo renaissance. To this day, the Nippon Budokan Foundation is recognized as the governmentally endorsed caretaker of Budo culture. It is easily recognizable on the Tokyo skyline by the massive golden onion-shaped dome on its roof.

Ironically, the Nippon Budokan martial arts hall is used more often for high profile rock concerts than for Budo events. Even the Beatles played there in 1966, although security was high because right wing xenophobes were not exactly thrilled by the Fab Four's sacrilegious invasion.

Budoka can be seen climbing the Kudanshita slope to the Budokan for training or maybe a competition, but on alternate nights you will have to navigate your way through suspicious-looking

scalpers flogging tickets illegally to hordes of hankering band groupies. The syncretistic relationship between the Rocka and the Budoka is begrudgingly acknowledged as a necessary evil. Even the Budokan is not exempt from colossal tax bills that come with 10,830 sq m (116,530 sq ft) of land smack bang in the center of Tokyo.

One of the wonderful aspects of Budo is that people of all ages can practice together. There is no minimum age for starting and no retirement age.

BUDO IN JAPAN TODAY

For the sake of simplicity, I sometimes refer to Budo as "spiritual sports," but is this description entirely correct? The question of whether Budo is a sport or not is a hotly debated topic in Japan. Many traditionalists lament the apparent trade-off between Budo virtues of respect, modesty and courtesy for the desire to acquire medals and glory in the ring. Whether competing in a match or just training, practitioners are expected to exemplify the "spirit" of Budo. That is, winning with modesty, accepting defeat gracefully and always exhibiting self-control. In the following section, I will quote the six articles from the "Budo Charter" formulated by the Japanese Budo Association in 1987 to explain the Budo ideal as it stands today.

Why Budo?
Article 1: Objective of Budo
Through physical and mental training in the Japanese martial ways, Budo exponents seek to build their character, enhance their sense of judgement and become disciplined individuals capable of making contributions to society at large.

The "Budo attitude" is half-jokingly referred to as being somewhat sado-masochistic. There is a strict hierarchy in the *dojo*, with the *sensei* often bellowing at his charges like a merciless drill sergeant and throngs of students with grimacing faces sweating like there is no tomorrow. All Budoka at some stage have questioned, "What the hell am I doing here?" "Why do I have to endure such extremes of temperature, painful blisters, aching muscles, this wretched stench of blood, sweat and tears, and apprehension for what's coming next?" Welcome to the world of Budo.

The whole point of training is to seek and destroy your own physical and psychological limitations and get over feeling sorry for yourself. We humans are inherently soft. We will take the easiest route for everything if presented with one. But there comes a time in life where you have to challenge yourself. At any given moment, you may be forced to stray out of your comfort zone whether you like it or not.

Shugyo in the martial arts is all about extending the boundaries of your comfort zone and going to places you have never been before. It's like exploring the Wild West of your mind and body, riding on your trusty but sometimes unpredictable steed called "Budo." The ideal *sensei* will help you chip away at your self-imposed inhibitions at a reasonable pace, although it may not always seem reasonable at the time. Nothing is more satisfying, gratifying and empowering than pushing through a training session that leaves you with just enough energy to crawl home and into your futon to assume the fetal position.

You may have a feeling of dread leading up to the next session and will be tempted to make an excuse, any excuse, not to go. Then you will feel guilty and end up forcing yourself to the *dojo*. You will crawl home pooped again but happy that you went.

Before long it actually gets easier. You become more confident in your abilities, and your mind and body start to crave the workout. You will enjoy pushing yourself beyond your limits. You will revel in the dichotomy of pre-training trepidation and post-training elation. That's heaven and hell all in one day.

Budo is hard work but those who excel at it know how to knuckle down and make the best out of any situation. A group of Kendo kids enjoying some downtime between matches.

Kan-geiko the Karate way. At least you don't have to wash your *dogi*. *Kiai* tends to be unusually high pitched.

And you will form incredibly strong bonds with the people you train with. You won't get there without making an effort and persevering but it will be worth it when you do.

Can you hack it? Of course you can. But make no mistake, it's not supposed to be easy. Like they say, if it doesn't kill you, it's gotta be good for you. You will become a stronger and more dependable person, brimming with self-belief. That's the objective. That's why it's worth it.

Training or Keiko?
Article 2: Keiko

When training in Budo, practitioners must always act with respect and courtesy, adhere to the prescribed fundamentals of the art and resist the temptation to pursue mere technical skill rather than strive towards the perfect unity of mind, body and technique.

We don't "play" Budo and the word "training" is actually frowned on in Budo circles in Japan. The inference is that Budo is much more than a simple physical exercise which one enjoys like any other sport. Thus, we don't play Budo, we *keiko* it. Not to be confused with the very common woman's name, the *kanji* for *keiko* is *kei* (稽), meaning "contemplate," and *ko* (古), which

means "antiquity." In other words, engaging in *keiko* is to contemplate past teachings. Early reference to the word can be found in the ancient text *Kojiki*, in which *keiko* is combined with *shokon*, which literally means to "illuminate the present." Accordingly, the mindset of Budo is to "contemplate the ways and wisdom of the ancients in order to make sense of one's predicament in the present day."

Perhaps the closest term in English to *keiko* would be study. Saying that "I study Kendo," or "I study Karatedo" is perfectly acceptable. Just don't "play" it, 'cos it ain't no game! *Keiko* is also used in reference to artistic pursuits, such as the tea ceremony, flower arranging and even playing the piano, but it is never used with mainstream sports. If you said "I'm going to baseball *keiko*," the likely response would be "Yeah? Where does she live?"

Compared to other sports, Budo often seems quite draconian but there is method behind the madness. It's all about tempering mind and body to operate well in the most inhospitable of conditions. If you can do this, then it's all the easier in optimal conditions. To this end, one tradition that many of the Budo disciplines engage in is *kan-geiko*—early morning training at the coldest time of the year. One of my *sensei* used to take

it an extra mile by soaking his *gi* in water each night and hanging it on the clothesline to freeze.

Kan-geiko usually lasts for a couple of weeks, sometimes more, during the winter months of January and February. Often with snow on the ground, the biggest struggle is overcoming the intense displeasure of hearing your alarm go off and having to leave the safety and warmth of your bed. Scoffing back a banana and a hot coffee, you then make your way down to the *dojo* at around 5:00 am trying desperately to flick the stubborn switch inside your head over to "harden up" mode.

Kan-geiko is notoriously rigorous because it's too damned cold to stand around. You will be training and sparring at full velocity for around 90 minutes. The floorboards will feel as cold as ice and will become quite slippery through all the condensation falling from the white clouds of heavy breathing. But that's okay because your feet and toes will be completely numb with the cold anyway. *Kan-geiko* is all about strengthening the body and building stamina in a refrigerator.

Then, there's summer. *Shochu-geiko* involves training at the hottest time of the day in the hottest months of the year. Different to *kan-geiko* where building stamina is the name of the game, training in the heat is more about refining technique. Of course, you still need stamina and it is very difficult to maintain focus in the dog days of summer, but that is the point. Rather than moving around attacking at full pace, *shochu-geiko* is a little more subdued as different senses are honed. Once you have survived Budo in a sauna, training during the fall and spring months is an entirely pleasant experience.

百
錬
体
得

BUDO CALLIGRAPHY:
Hyakuren-taitoku "Practice 100 Times and Make it Yours"

The standard way of learning martial arts is through constant repetition. Think of the classic line in the *Karate Kids* movie—"Wax on, wax off...." Over and over until it becomes second nature.

Budo Versus Sport
Article 3: Shiai (Competition)

Whether competing in a match or doing set forms (*kata*), exponents must externalize the spirit underlying Budo. They must do their best at all times, winning with modesty, accepting defeat gracefully and constantly exhibiting self-control.

Parents in the 1960s and 1970s urged their children to take up Budo recognizing it as a valid means for promoting discipline and learning manners. Community and police *dojo* found it impossible to accommodate the large number of hopefuls queued up to register their young ones in beginner courses. For most children, however, motivation to continue was in competition rather than an appreciation of the discipline forced upon them by zealous instructors. Successful tournament results can help a kid gain entry into a prestigious school or university on a sports scholarships. It can even lead to employment. Winning is, therefore, important, and a commonly debated theme is whether or not Budo should be defined as a "sport."

What is a sport? Of course, it depends on the sport, but if we go by Allan Guttman's definition it entails "secularism—equality of opportunity to compete and in the conditions of competition, specialization of roles, rationalization, bureaucratic organization, quantification, the quest for records." Budo certainly fits the bill. Then there are "purposive sports" in which goals, home runs, tries and touchdowns are counted as points regardless of the means by which they are scored. In "aesthetic sports" such as ice skating and gymnastics, artistic form and performance attitude is an important factor in judging victory or defeat. Budo has elements of both but leans more towards "aesthetic sports."

Semantics? The arguments surrounding the difference between Budo and sports has always been passionately debated. It points to the crux of Japan's sense of "uniqueness" vis-à-vis the rest of the word. It's a point of pride, with the prevalent argument being that Budo should never be reduced to matters of "victory or defeat." It's not the result but the process that really has meaning, or so the standard rhetoric goes. After all, we don't "play" Budo, we "study" it, so this means that it's more than "just a sport."

But the reality is that even in domestic competitions in Japan, the rivalry and will to win at all costs is intense.

Older martial art enthusiasts now weep over the perceived decay of Budo through the egotistical pursuit of trophies and glory. And this is usually blamed on globalization.

I prefer to look at the issue from a different perspective. "What are the characteristics of Budo *as* a sport? Each sport has its own values, as does each Budo. Some are competition oriented, some are not, and some look for a balance somewhere in between. Each Budo has many faces. These change over time as the practitioner matures. All said and done, the value of Budo is in the eye of the beholder. There is no such thing as one size fits all. Nevertheless, winning with modesty, accepting defeat gracefully and constantly exhibiting self-control is *not* negotiable.

The Meaning of "Dojo"
Article 4: Dojo (Training Hall)

The *dojo* is a special place for training the mind and body. In the *dojo*, Budo practitioners must maintain discipline and show proper courtesy and respect. The *dojo* should be a quiet, clean, safe and solemn environment.

Dojo literally means "Place of the Way." It is a translation of the Sanskrit word *bodhi-manda*, which refers to the

Above Oh yeah! Who da man! And, oh woe is me. Not exactly the right Budo attitude.

Left Kyokushinkai Karate competitors getting ready to rumble.

"Diamond seat" where Gautama attained nirvana sitting under the Bodhi tree. Thus, *dojo* originally meant "a place where Buddhism is studied." Budo is not Buddhism, but because of the deep spiritual connotations and ascetic training in search of a higher consciousness, the same term was adopted to mean "a place for studying the martial arts."

The quaint wooden-floored *dojo* that we are familiar with now didn't exist in Japan until around the late 1700s. Before this, training was mostly conducted outside on the dirt. Over time, Samurai took their training inside, in the hallways or on earthen floors, and then ultimately in specially designed rooms.

Not all Budo is conducted in specialist *dojo*. Often clubs will hire venues such as gymnasiums or school halls. Whatever the case, however, when Budo practice is under way, that space becomes a *dojo* and special rules apply. According to the "Budo Charter," the Budo practitioner must always be respectful and the *dojo* must be kept "a quiet, clean, safe and solemn environment."

This means taking your shoes off and placing them neatly in the shoe boxes at the entrance and removing your hat and headphones before going in. Always bow deeply to the *shomen* when entering and exiting. Immediately seek out the *sensei* and greet him or her. Help keep the *dojo* clean by mopping the floor and taking any rubbish away with

you. Under no circumstance should you fool around and act inappropriately, just as you wouldn't in a church, mosque, temple or synagogue. When you are not training, sit quietly out of the way, preferably kneeling in *seiza*. If your knees can't take it, you can sit cross-legged, but never have your legs splayed out like you're lounging on a couch at home.

Sometimes you find *dojo* students in Japan breaking all of these basic rules with impunity. Don't copy them. You'll be praised by the *sensei* for doing things properly. "Look! The *gaijin*'s doing it right. Why can't you lot?"

The Meaning of Sensei
Article 5: Teaching
Teachers of Budo should always encourage others to also strive to better themselves and diligently train their minds and bodies while continuing to further their understanding of the technical principles of Budo. Teachers should not allow focus to be put on

winning or losing in competition or on technical ability alone. Above all, teachers have a responsibility to set an example as role models.

The literal meaning of *sensei* is "person born before another." In general usage in Japan, it is added after a person's name and means teacher: Takahashi-sensei, Watanabe-sensei. It's used in all sorts of occupations. A kindergarten teacher will be referred to as *sensei*, as will university professors, doctors, politicians, lawyers, priests, artists, musicians and Budo instructors.

Basically, anybody with a position of authority who is respected in the community will be called *sensei*. It is a handy word when you forget the name of somebody important. You can get away with just calling him or her *sensei*.

All Budo instructors are called *sensei* as a generic term but other titles are also used depending on the discipline. For example, the master of a Sumo stable will be called *Oyakata*. Kano Jigoro is referred to as *Shihan* by Judo practitioners. *Shihan* actually means "chief instructor" and has nothing to do with grade. Aikido devotees call Ueshiba Morihei *Kaiso* (founder) as do Shorinji Kempo trainees with regard to So Doshin. *Doshu* is another word heard in Aikido for the leader of the Aikikai, as is *O-sensei* (venerable teacher), which is reserved for Ueshiba Morihei. *Shisho* is for a martial arts instructor who heads a *dojo* and *Shidoin* refers to the teaching staff. In all cases, *sensei* is attached to the surname. Nobody calls themselves "XXX-sensei." Beware of people who blurt out a string of titles like Sensei Shihan Hanshi Ben Dover Sama PhD 13th Dan

阿呼呼吸

BUDO CALLIGRAPHY:
A-un-no-kokyu "Synchronizing One's Breathing with the Opponent's"

Buddhist temples often have fierce-looking guardian statues at the gates, one with his mouth open (a = breathing in), and the other with his mouth closed (un = compression). In Budo, it indicates an inherently harmonious relationship between the two protagonists.

Soke of Cowboy-ryu. Such an esteemed Budoka probably sells black belts for $50 plus a free set of steak knives.

The role and accountability of a genuine Budo *sensei* is immense. As stated in the "Budo Charter," teachers of Budo should always encourage others while also striving to better themselves. They must diligently train their minds and bodies and continue to further their own understanding of the technical and metaphysical principles of Budo. Instructors should not allow focus to be put solely on winning competitions, nor on technical ability alone. Above all, teachers have a responsibility to set an example as role models—to walk the talk.

Unfortunately, many who teach Budo fall short on these criteria. It's said in Japan, "Better to wait three years and find the right teacher, than start three years sooner with a doofus." Studying martial arts under a *sensei* of dubious moral fiber or questionable teaching methods will lead to a distorted view of Budo. This makes it dangerous at worst, meaningless at best.

Budo's International Outlook
Article 6: Promoting Budo
Persons promoting Budo must maintain an open-minded and international perspective as they uphold traditional values. They should make efforts to contribute to research and teaching and do their utmost to advance Budo in every way.

The quest for internationalization by Budo federations has been an ongoing issue for decades. All Budo organizations in the Japanese Budo Association have international federations except for Jukendo, but they are looking into this now. Budo first left the shores of Japan with Japanese immigrants around the turn of the twentieth century. Countries with long-established communities of Nikkei, that is people with Japanese ancestry, usually have a strong Budo presence. Budo migrated to Europe and the rest of the world mainly from the 1970s.

The international spread of Budo is seen in both a positive and negative light. On the one hand, promoting Budo overseas contributes to Japan's identity as a "soft power." Providing the world with a framework for personal growth, mutual understanding and respect is Japan's contribution to world peace. On the other hand, and somewhat paradoxically, the more Budo is successfully promoted outside, the more Japan fears that it may lose its position of leadership. Authorities in Japan have demonstrated an obses-

sion with preserving Budo's technical and spiritual veracity and insist on conveying it "correctly," that is, promoting it the way it would be in Japan. This reeks of cultural imperialism. It is a gross misconception that non-Japanese study Budo because they want to be like Japanese people.

As one of my Japanese Kendo colleagues admitted, the global spread of Budo is important because it provides Japanese with an incentive to reflect on the state of Budo in Japan. The international migration of Budo is not only inevitable but is a crucial aspect of its evolution. Cultural friction can function as a catalytic agent to revitalize all practitioners, regardless of nationality.

An old Naginata teacher, Mitamura Takeko, once said to me, "Wow, Alex. You really are trying very hard. You've learned the language and try to abide by all the Japanese rules. Just remember that there are bad things about Japan and good things about New Zealand. You don't have to try to become Japanese you know." That was one of the most liberating, open-minded, internationally astute instructions I ever received in a *dojo*. It's things like this that help you recognize a real *sensei*.

Many non-Japanese Budoka come to Japan on short trips to visit the headquarters or *sensei* of their martial art. Most Japanese people are totally unaware of how immensely popular Budo is overseas.

CHAPTER 5

LIFE IN A JAPANESE DOJO

Studying martial arts in a *dojo* under instructors of dubious moral fiber or questionable teaching methods will lead to a distorted view of Budo. Many a keen martial artist has become disillusioned and eventually given up altogether because the *dojo* took them down the garden path instead of the Budo path. Being a foreigner in a Japanese *dojo* has its own challenges on top of knowing what is legitimate or wrong. Fitting in may come with some unreasonable expectations to suddenly act and behave exactly how a Japanese does. I, for one, don't do Budo because it's Japanese. I do it because it is meaningful to me and I enjoy it. But if something doesn't seem right, is it you that's the problem or the *dojo* itself? How can you identify the "false gods" and problematic clubs? How do you discern the parameters for acceptable and unacceptable behavior? The *dojo* is a complex place. In many ways, it is a microcosm of Japanese society, and what you learn there will be applicable in many aspects of your daily life in Japan. The rules may seem confusing at first and things won't make any immediate sense. This section will give you the info needed to navigate the murky shadows when embarking on a journey of Budo exploration.

FINDING YOUR PATH

What should you expect when you first arrive in Japan to study Budo? The Samurai text *Hagakure* advises: "There is a lesson to be learned from a downpour of rain. If you get caught in a cloudburst, you will still get drenched even though you hurry to take cover under overhanging roofs. If you are prepared to get wet from the start, the result is the same but it is no hardship. This attitude can be applied to all things." Indeed, being ready and willing for seemingly irrational occurrences will make your time in Japan more enjoyable and better for your blood pressure. Studying Budo is a surefire way to keep your head in the game, and provides a map to hidden doors and a peaceful Zen outlook on all manner of things.

Which Budo Is Best for You?

"What Budo is best for me?" I often get asked this by people interested in taking the plunge. My standard reply is, "How long is a piece of string?" There are too many factors involved to answer this question succinctly. For example, much depends on where you are based in Japan. If you are in Tokyo or one of the main centers, then the world is your oyster and you will have access to pretty much anything you want to try your hand at. If you are on a Study Abroad program, then you will have several club options at your host institution. If you are working, then your job schedule will determine your mobility and timetable. Ask yourself why you are interested in Budo. What are your goals and motivations? Are your expectations realistic? The following considerations may provide some clues:

1. Are you an anime freak who wants to do a martial art because it looks "cool"?
2. Do you enjoy the thrill of competition?
3. Do you want to learn how to fight (in self-defense) and stay fit?
4. Are you interested in spirituality or traditional Japanese culture?
5. How long will you be in Japan?

If (1) is the first thing that comes to mind, you won't last long. Time for a reality check. Budo is hard work and most of the time when you are slugging away in the *dojo* the only "cool" thing you'll be wanting is a big lake to jump in. (2) All of the Budo disciplines, apart from Aikido and Kobudo, have competitions you can enter. For Aikido and Kobudo, demonstrations (*enbu*)

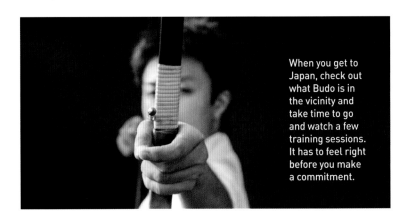

When you get to Japan, check out what Budo is in the vicinity and take time to go and watch a few training sessions. It has to feel right before you make a commitment.

provide an exhilarating experience where you "compete with yourself" and demonstrate the fruits of your labor in the *dojo*. If you love competing in the conventional sense, amateur Sumo, Judo and Karate would be the easiest options. Kendo, Naginata, Jukendo and Kyudo are also quite competitive but they take a lot longer to become proficient at because they involve the use of weapons. (3) All Budo (apart from Kyudo) will give you a decent cardio workout and keep you fit, but if your goal is to learn some useful self-defense moves, Judo, Karate and Shorinji Kempo might be the ticket. (4) Closer to the spiritual end of the spectrum would be Aikido, Kyudo and perhaps Shorinji Kempo with its teachings of Kongo Zen. (5) Other considerations include how long you plan to be in Japan. Weapon disciplines

take longer to get a handle on and may require expensive purchases of equipment. So if you're only going to be around for a few months it might be easier to try something that only requires a *dogi* (training top). Also, Judo, Karate and Aikido are ubiquitous Budo all around the world, whereas the others, especially the Kobudo schools, are unlikely to be found in your backyard when you return home and you may have to go cold turkey. If you get hooked, you might end up having to stay in Japan a lot longer than you bargained for (like me).

There is no simple answer to what you should do. Ultimately, it boils down to what "turns you on" the most and just trying it. The following is a very loose synopsis of the characteristics of each Budo. Keep in mind that every *dojo* is different.

Emphasis on Tradition	Tradition and Competition	Emphasis on Competition
Kyudo	Kendo	Judo
Aikido	Naginata	Karate
Kobudo	Jukendo	Sumo
	Shorinji Kempo	

Left So many patches for so many *dojo*. Compared to other sports, however, Budo is typically low key and people tend not to advertise the fact that they do it in Japan.

Ye of Previous Experience

If only I had 100 yen for everyone I've met who came to Japan to continue their Budo habit, only to fizzle out like a damp squib. They come over to live their dream but then lose sight of what that dream was. The reasons are endless but usually include expectations that aren't met: "The style/methodology is different to what I learned back in the US." And a misguided sense of entitlement: "I'm a black belt but they treat me like a beginner in Japan." Procrastination is another big reason: "I just need to get myself settled first, get a job and then I'll get into it." Often underlying all of this is a degree of subconscious apprehension, an element of fear born of frustration at not being able to speak Japanese and not knowing what is happening around you. Another reason for the fuse never igniting is a false sense of security that, even if you train less than you did back home, the level in Japan is higher and you can just learn by osmosis. Wrong! If anything, you need to work harder in Japan to improve precisely because of the language issues and different training and teaching methods. My advice to those who are already experienced in Budo is:

- Get an introduction through your *sensei* or contacts in your home *dojo* if at all possible. The feeling of obligation and not wanting to disappoint can be a good motivator to get you going when you arrive in Japan.
- Don't put it off. Get into the fray

Above Every Budo is different. Some are more competition oriented while others are more spiritual in nature.
Right Higoanna-sensei on the left is a world-renowned Karate teacher in Okinawa. His teaching focuses on the cultural traditions of Karate.

as soon as you can. Life in Japan falls into a routine very quickly and if Budo is not part of that routine right from the start, it will be harder to include later on (especially when you get a girl/boyfriend).

- Most important of all, come with the intention of starting from scratch. Enjoy going back to being a "beginner," even if you're not. It will be different in Japan so realize this from the outset and purge yourself of any

preconceptions. You are not entitled because you already know a bit or have a black belt. *Everybody* has a black belt in a Japanese *dojo*. Humility is the name of the game here, so go back to basics and revel in the new journey as you learn the lay of the land.
- Study Japanese seriously. Take a course!
- Get hard.
- If you quit, please send me 100 yen.

BUDO CALLIGRAPHY: *Nyumon* "Entering the Tutelage of a Master or School"

Literally meaning "enter the gate," this word is used when people join a *dojo* or a traditional school of artistry. Incidentally, being kicked out of a *dojo* is referred to as *hamon*, literally, "deprived of the gate."

KEY BUDO CONCEPTS: *Zanshin*
残心 "Lingering Heart"

The Budo arts abound with old sayings and tenets of wisdom that can be a framework for life. One such concept is that of *zanshin* or "lingering heart." In movies, the bad guy always seems to get up for one last gasp attempt to kill the hero when you least expect it. As the old Samurai adage goes, "When you think victory is at hand, tighten your helmet straps."

In modern Budo, making a successful attack is only half the equation. Like the Samurai warrior, a Budoka must never let his physical or psychological guard down. He must remain vigilant, calm and collected at all times and somehow manage to contain the intense emotions and adrenalin surging through his veins. This is not just a matter of survival but is also a sign of respect for one's opponent. Indeed, it is the emphasis on *zanshin* that distinguishes Budo from all other sports. Triumphant players dash around the pitch congratulating each other with delirious enthusiasm when a goal is scored in soccer or after hitting a home run in baseball. In Budo, scoring a point is theoretically taking a life. It is highly inappropriate to show pleasure, and throwing one's arms in the air with joy is clearly an act lacking *zanshin*. Learning to stay focused, attentive and respectful regardless of the situation is the crux of all martial arts study. It is concepts like *zanshin* which can be applied to one's activities and conduct outside the *dojo* that make Budo a lifelong spiritual journey. *Zanshin* represents the very essence of the spirit of Budo.

Choosing the Right Teacher

Joining a *dojo* with the right teacher(s) is probably the most important thing of all. Sometimes you don't have a choice because of your location. Sometimes teachers choose you and you somehow have little say in the matter. You must be able to respect the person who teaches you Budo. Remember, "trust is a must."

Just because he or she has a high rank, or boasts an illustrious competitive career, doesn't mean that they are necessarily the right person for you to learn from. Everybody has different values and outlooks. It is said that we don't get along with 30 percent of the people we meet in life. Believe it or not, Budo teachers are people, too. You'll become demotivated quicker than a chicken tied to a helium balloon in a Samurai bar if you don't gel with the person calling the shots.

When you watch training for the first time, don't be freaked out by the intensity or Spartan style of the *sensei* barking orders like a possessed megalomaniac. Such scenes might shock the sensibilities of the uninitiated foreigner but strict discipline and harsh instruction come with the territory. Second point, if you're expecting to find some kindly old soul who speaks like Yoda to blow your mind with cosmic awesomeness, then it's time for that reality check again.

Another thing to consider is the caliber of students in the *dojo*. Are they polite and accommodating or do they act like arrogant thugs with no decorum? Again, this is something that might be hard to tell if you're not used to the ferocity of a Japanese *dojo* setting, but a good indication is whether or not they greet you in any way, no matter how fleetingly. You'll find that the culture of every *dojo* is very different. Some are friendlier to foreigners than others. Find a *dojo* that puts emphasis on etiquette and good manners. That's a good sign that the teacher runs a tight ship and the respect is there. So, how do you know if it's right or not? It's all in the gut. If it doesn't feel right, keep looking until it does.

One more thing to keep in mind is your own deportment. It's fair to say that, to varying degrees, Japanese Budoka harbor preconceptions about foreigners joining their group. It's not always negative but "lumbering" and "loud" probably come to mind more often than not. Go to the *dojo* and meet your prospective *sensei* as if you were heading to a job interview. Most *sensei* are fairly conservative. That means that you should not dress in a T-shirt and shorts/miniskirt. Remove nose piercings and other bits of metal from your face. And for the love of Amaterasu, cover up the ink! Tattoos are taboo in Japan because of the perceived association with organized crime. Like anywhere else in the world, first impressions are everything. If you like what you see, follow up with a handwritten letter to the *sensei* explaining your desire to learn from him/her. Dress neatly and be respectful. This sense of propriety may seem old fashioned but will definitely be appreciated.

Karate has been a comparatively minor Budo in mainland Japan until now. More children have taken it up recently with the decision to include it in the 2020 Tokyo Olympics.

School Kurabu

You might be working or studying at a Japanese school and want to join a club activity. This is usually not a problem but it helps to have an idea how clubs work in Japan. Pupils start extracurricular club activities from junior high school. Called *bukatsu* or *kurabu*, they are notorious for the amount

Above Called *yakyu*, baseball is by far the most popular sport in Japan.

Right Japanese children are subjected to a rigorous regime of study from early on. Many will also go to cram schools in order to pass competitive entrance exams.

Below One of the most anticipated days on the Japanese school calendar is the sports festival.

University clubs have a decidedly social aspect to them. College students are old enough to drink alcohol, and drink they do. Particularly perilous are the *izakaya* "happy hour" sessions that target students with all-you-can drink deals (*nomihodai*), often as cheap as 1,000 yen for 90 minutes of crazed binge drinking! Getting carted off in an ambulance with alcohol poisoning caused by unrelenting *senpai* (senior) pressure was once a badge of honor. Fortunately, the *aruhara* (alcoholic harassment) that once typified university sports clubs in my student days has been toned down considerably in recent years. The media is quick to jump on deplorable, decadent and sometimes illegal shenanigans of drunken student athletes. With the current declining student numbers in Japan, universities are paranoid about having their reputations tarnished by scandalous club behavior getting plastered all over the news. Universities have clamped down on alcohol abuse with the threat of disbanding offending clubs, expelling students and firing staff involved if it all goes pear shaped.

At all levels of schooling, teachers or professors are assigned as advisors to the clubs, even though they may not, or never have, actually practiced the sport. Students themselves are usually responsible for the running of club activities, with the seniors taking a leadership role.

of time and dedication expected in their undertaking. It is not uncommon for school clubs to require attendance seven days a week for at least a couple of hours each day. Japanese kids join only one club for their entire time at school. There is no real concept of seasonal sport and belonging to two clubs simultaneously is never done in Japan.

Compared to junior high, senior high school clubs are even more arduous. They are akin to military training in terms of ferocity of content and strict hierarchical relationships. There may be a teacher at the school with experience in the sport. Typically, he or she will be a PE teacher who graduated from a sports university or excelled in their college club. These teachers are usually feared by the students as they instruct with an unmerciful degree of intensity that leaves heads spinning. Overseeing clubs is a volunteer activity for teachers and they devote much time to it, above and beyond the call of duty. Not all kids join a club although it is generally encouraged by teachers and parents. Some prefer to hang out in culturally oriented clubs like calligraphy, music or English, but the same dedication is expected for the entire three years of high school.

University sports clubs usually come in two styles: the hard core "Taiiku-kai" (athletic association) clubs, which are tremendously competitive and often have scholarship "ringers" brought in solely on the basis of their high school record in that sport. Then there are the more relaxed "circles." These consist of students who love the sport but not to the extent that they are prepared to dedicate every waking moment of their newfound freedom to being a cog in a jock-heavy athletic club. The teaching role in these clubs is usually assumed by alumni or seniors, except in sports oriented universities where the instructors are typically also professors.

Bun or Bu?

Some schools are famous for sports while others are better known for academic achievement. Some are renowned for both. If a kid is particularly talented at a sport, he or she might end up focusing on that rather than on their academic studies. This is possible because career paths are available for successful teenage athletes. They may go to university on a scholarship or even find employment straight out of high school. High-

Above and below Budo is hard work but the down time is very relaxed. Judo lads tucking into lunch during a tournament.

Left College Sumo students give some kids a taste of their art.

profile athletes bring companies the kind of advertising that money just can't buy. Depending on the school, there will come a time when a student has to make a big decision—whether to excel in sport and go all the way or study hard and go the academic route. *Kurabu* activities are often too physically demanding to effectively do both.

The problem with this system is that education can become seriously unbalanced. I deal with many students on sport scholarships at university who only know about sports. They don't know how to study but are somehow fed through the system until they graduate, after which they might be employed by a company with an in-house team for that sport. They may become a professional athlete or, if they study hard, a PE teacher. In the case of Budo, the crème de la crème of school club athletes can never hope to enjoy the life of a celebrity the way a baseball or soccer professional can. Success in the Budo competitive arena might open doors for a career in the police, as a PE teacher, or in companies with Budo teams (usually Kendo or Judo).

Schools that perform well in regional and national competitions for any sport bring considerable prestige to the institution and instructors. This is another reason why they are so zealous in their coaching. The no pain no gain, cruel to

be kind mentality of school sports coaches is pervasive in Japan. If their apprentices fail competitively, at least they will be equipped with the mental toughness, discipline and *gaman* (self-control) qualities that are highly cherished in Japanese society. That's the thinking anyway.

Toeing the Line

Under classmen (*kohai*) will have a very tough time of it. They are expected to do the cleaning and menial tasks and obey the selfish dictates of their seniors (*senpai*). Even if the senior is significantly less skilled than the *kohai*, the *senpai* is still king. In this way *bukatsu* are seen as effective ways to socialize Japanese youths and prepare them for the adult world. Students learn manners, how to speak appropriately to "superiors," self-restraint and guts through the rigorous *bukatsu* lifestyle.

As an outward sign of their dedication, boys will regularly shave their heads in a style known as *bozu*, an informal term for Buddhist priests. This is a sign of sincerity, not neo-Nazism, so don't be surprised if you see a bunch of skinheads in the *dojo*. Girls will also have short hair, but not shaved! Perhaps a common exception to the rule here

are soccer lads. They are more likely to sport long, semi-bleached hair, grooming themselves in the mirror like rock stars. A relative newcomer in terms of popularity, soccer players don't uphold the hard-core traditions seen in sports like baseball and Budo. Although school soccer teams train with the same rigor, more emphasis is placed on independence and individual flair.

Quitting a club at any stage is a big no no and those remaining will feel betrayed. Students in the last year of school, however, will retire around six months before graduation to concentrate on studying for their entrance exams for university.

For college students, participating in club activities is a factor in finding employment after graduation. From an employer's perspective, a student who has survived club life has obviously learned to "toe the line" even in the most unreasonable of circumstances.

Students of the Naginata Club at the International Budo University take a breather from training. Budo isn't always done inside a *dojo*.

He or she will not shy away from working overtime and will be easy to train on the job.

Belonging to a club at any stage of school life in Japan is hard, but many look back on it with nostalgia and are proud to maintain their affiliation as OBs (old boys) or OGs. It is a rite of passage for many, and the bonds forged through blood, sweat, and tears last forever.

Joining a School Budo Club

All Japanese junior high school students now get a taste of Budo as a compulsory part of their education. Nevertheless, Budo is not nearly as prevalent as it used to be as a club activity. Baseball, soccer and volleyball are much more fashionable. Of the various Budo, Kendo and Judo are by far the most common with only a smattering of the others.

Pre-junior high kids may learn a Budo at a community *dojo* but school clubs become the priority from junior high. A unique feature of Budo clubs at all levels of schooling is that girls and boys train together. They compete separately but training sessions are combined, which is not the case with other sports.

The motivation to continue mainly derives from the thrill of competition and a sense of belonging. Even though most teachers preach the "party line" in promoting the holistic benefits of Budo, they are not averse to teaching strategies to win matches by any means possible. Budo at schools, like other sports, is predicated on competition first and foremost. You will generally find that schools with strong Budo clubs have a specialist hard-ass Budo teacher in charge rather than a random member of staff who was press-ganged into looking after the group. Experienced teachers have been through the system so their truculent Budo methods are perpetuated.

School Budo clubs are meant to be tough. So should you join one? If you are at a junior high school, you will probably be there as an English teacher rather than as a student. If you have an interest in joining a school club (prob-ably limited to Judo, Kendo, Sumo, possibly Naginata and Karate), you will be treated like a s*ensei* even though you might be an absolute beginner. The other teachers and kids will love to have you in their midst. It can be a fabulous way to connect and you will be looked after. It would be a perfect introduction to learn the ropes in an environment that is not too daunting. The same applies if you are teaching English at a high school.

Your position within a high school club as an actual student will be very different and you will be expected to become a part of the machine like all the others. This means training every single day, if necessary. Say goodbye to weekends and holidays. The club members will become your best friends. As a foreigner who "knows no better," they will turn a blind eye to the occasional non-conformist behavior and truancy. If you really want to have a meaningful experience, however, you need to knuck-le down and subject yourself to the same trials and tribulations as your peers. Copy what they do and fit into the hierarchy by following their lead. Your Japanese language will go through the roof after six months and you will learn to operate within the complex fabric of Japanese society, of which the *dojo* is a perfect microcosm. The friendships you forge will be lasting but are requisite on making a serious commitment. If you do that, you will be rewarded. If not, you will be ignored as a curiosity. It's pretty much all or nothing.

University clubs are a different animal altogether. Mostly run by the students themselves, they have a strict hierarchy and firmly entrenched ways of doing things. National universities are generally more liberal in their approach compared to private ones, but the hierarchy is still absolute.

The new student intake for school clubs starts in April each year. Freshmen are recruited as novices, not necessar-ily in the Budo but in the context of the club's system. Those with experience in Budo from their high school days and earlier will seek the club out themselves (or avoid it like the plague). If there on a sport scholarship, the student has no choice but to muck in before anyone else. Regardless of skill or experience, howev-er, they all start together on level pegging as first year students. Once sweet-talked into the club with atypical conviviality by seniors, they dwell at the bottom of the totem pole for the rest of the year. They are tiny little fish in a little pond. The oversized sharks circling menacingly at the top are the fourth year students. The club itself is a bit like *Hotel Califor-nia*. Once you've checked in....

Joining a College Club

Each age group in a college club has specific responsibilities and expectations placed on them, which can be difficult to manage for a foreign student on a one-year Study Abroad program. This is especially true if you arrive halfway through the Japanese school year in the Fall Semester (September–). The stu-dents won't know where to place you in the scheme of things, especially if you already have some experience.

Japanese students in college Budo clubs are not very flexible and have little knowledge or patience for things outside

A children's Kendo team warming up outside before a tournament.

their own world. Although you will generally be welcomed, you will possibly be seen as a small spanner in the works. College athletic association Budo is totally competition-oriented and students are more focused on improving their own performance than helping a beginner who doesn't speak much Japanese.

Occasionally, you may even be ignored by more surly members of the club, and they might even refuse point blank to train with you. This is a total breach of Budo etiquette but is a sad fact of life at some clubs. Suck it up and feel sorry for them. They are the frogs in the well who know nothing of the great ocean outside.

To get anything out of belonging to a college Budo club requires nothing short of total dedication. Even if you are experienced, start by fitting in with the first years and do what they do. You will have to take part in the usually good-natured hazing rituals and help with the endless list of menial chores. If the club trains every day, then so must you. You'll clean the *dojo* floor, sacrifice your weekends to support the team at tournaments, be called to impromptu drinking parties, etc. Become a part of the club's culture, no matter how silly some of it seems, otherwise you will never be included in anything.

If you're not prepared to make such a big commitment, an alternative is to join a less formal "circle." These groups are made up of students who are not keen on the culture and rules of athletic association clubs. They are there primarily for social reasons and are much more accommodating and willing to take on beginners. Students will typically be more internationally minded as well. They do participate in competitions. The training is still challenging, but is usually more manageable at two or three times a week.

If you are a diehard Budo practitioner with a track record and are focused and motivated enough to go the distance, join an athletic association club. If you want to dabble, join a circle. In either case, fit in with the first years unless otherwise directed. If you are a teacher at the university, you will be treated politely and helped along at your own speed in either group. You won't be expected to fit into the student hierarchy, but this actually makes it harder to learn and you will need to be strict on yourself to make any progress.

The Community Dojo

Every prefecture in Japan has a big bad Budokan, a large center dedicated to the martial arts. These are usually situated close to the largest city in the prefecture and are publicly funded. That means they are very cheap to utilize. They have facilities for all Budo arts classes at various levels. Space can be rented by local clubs for training and competitions.

A problem for novices is that "beginner classes" for some modern Budo disciplines often actually mean "children's classes." If you are in your late teens or older, it could well be difficult to find

Children get to grips with some Judo basics. The instructors are purely volunteers in most community *dojo* in Japan.

a class to comfortably slot into. Adult free-for-alls are ordinarily held after children's classes, but these sessions are generally not structured in a way for older beginners to get the instruction they need. That is not to say you won't be taught, but the members there may be more focused on polishing their own techniques and blasting away the day's stress. It all depends on the *dojo*.

Having said that, the local Budokan is a good place to start looking. Being a public space, training sessions will be "civilized" and the atmosphere very affable.

Other common venues for community Budo activities are school halls in the evening. Local clubs will hire the halls after school hours. Although the club will be unrelated to the school itself, it will have the usual children's classes followed by free for all sessions for adults.

Then, there are the *senyo dojo*—private Budo salons as opposed to public facilities—which are becoming less common in Japan these days. The main reason for their scarcity is the dwindling number of children taking up Budo. Kids provide the bread and butter for private operations. Also, being such a crowded country, private *dojo* located in residential areas have to be conscious of noise and neighbors. Tolerance in the community for screaming, battling Budo nuts is not what it used to be.

Other places that you can find instruction are at police *dojo* (mainly for Kendo and Judo), but again these are usually targeted at children. Company clubs are another option if you know somebody who works there. Wherever you go, expect to pay a nominal monthly fee.

Far left Once you've exceeded your pain threshold, that's the time to tap out.

Left There will always be an element of discomfort in Budo. You'll get used to it.

Dojo Violence and Abuse

My induction into the world of Budo was as an exchange student at a high school in 1987. The school Kendo *dojo* had a low ceiling and foreboding bars on the windows. Inside was a swarm of hyperactive trainees trying to smash each other with bamboo sticks. To my untrained eye, it all seemed senseless, painful violence.

My attention was drawn to a scene in the far corner. There was a big, fierce dude with a bigger stick than anyone else. I could've sworn it was Darth Vader. He was being attacked furiously by a lesser mortal, but to no avail. Vader casually warded off the would-be challenger as if he was swatting a pesky fly. The suicidal Jedi in training screamed defiantly, trying not to fall flat on his face as the big guy calmly deflected all the blows.

After a while, his relentless effort paid off as he was permitted to land a few cracking blows on Vader's head. The sweet taste of victory was short-lived. Vader upped the ante and retaliated with vicious thrusts, whacks and foot sweeps, reducing the attacker to a sweaty heap of tangled limbs and armor on the floor. Still, just when it looked as if all was over, the poor little Jedi found his second wind, summoned the "Force," and the long, painful process started all over again, and again. Corporal punishment had just been outlawed in New Zealand, and as I witnessed the carnage, thoughts that someone should call the police did cross my mind.

I'll never forget that experience. It shocked the hell out of me but strangely drew me in at the same time. I was intrigued by the intensity of it all and the never say die attitude.

Subsequent decades of experience have shown me that there is a gray zone separating violence and education in Budo. After all, the techniques of any Budo discipline derive from combat. You are not kicking a ball into the back of a net, you are attempting to kick somebody in the head.

ERR... DID SOMEBODY CHANGE THE RULES AND NOT TELL ME?

The techniques of Budo were originally designed to kill or maim.

The training has to be hard, but where is the line dividing what is acceptable and what is not? This is difficult to answer because it is so often subjective. There is no option of giving up midway in training as that is considered cowardly and weak. Overcoming your fear of being pushed beyond your limits is precisely what builds strength of character. Few people are able to press themselves beyond a certain point, which is why a teacher is necessary to throw some fuel on the fire to keep you honest and fired up.

This is precisely why "trust is a must" when you seek tuition at a *dojo*.

A good teacher will drive the students but knows when enough is enough. It is a huge responsibility, and knowing just how much is "enough" is learned only through personal experience in the same hard ass treadmill. The intention has to be to "teach," not to "hurt."

More than the *sensei*, however, it is the senior students or *senpai* who can often be the unwitting abusers of this trust. They are usually very young themselves and have no real idea of the implications of their "power" or their own strength.

There have been more than a few tragic incidents in school Budo clubs over the years. Sometimes it is the result of outright bullying, while other times it comes from pushing the student too hard to experience the "never say die" attitude.

In recent years, violence and bullying is a much publicized problem in school clubs, not just Budo. The last decade or so has seen a distinct move away from over the top training. The tradition of "hammering out the iron" has been watered down to the extent that some Budo practitioners believe it has gone the other way and become too soft.

You need a kick up the backside sometimes to really understand the essence of Budo. You need to peer into the abyss and for somebody to knock you over the edge every once in a while. Sometimes you need to "die" in the figurative sense to tap into the deep internal well of life.

If there is obvious unbridled violence being committed by the *sensei* or the *senpai*, where people are getting injured or traumatized, then this is not acceptable.

Appearances may be deceptive due to the combative nature of Budo, but if you feel what is happening in the *dojo* exceeds the boundaries of simple hard training, then take a step back and reassess. But remember that Budo is not tiddlywinks either.

BUDO CALLIGRAPHY:
Seme "Applying Pressure"

Sometimes translated as "attack," *seme* is the process leading up to the unleashing of a technique. Applying physical and/or psychological pressure to unsettle your opponent.

HOW A DOJO OPERATES

The *dojo* is a sacred place where Budoka train their bodies and minds. Irrespective of the Budo discipline, each *dojo* will have its own idiosyncrasies, rituals and ways of doing things. Everyone in the *dojo* knows their place and how to behave and you need to learn how to fit in quickly.

The Dojo Hierarchy

Just about every aspect of Japanese society and culture is based on a hierarchy dictated by seniority in age, experience, occupation and gender. The terms *senpai* (senior) and *kohai* (junior) are used to distinguish seniority in schools, companies, organizations and the *dojo*. There is always a power dynamic present in which the *kohai* is expected to be obedient, speak politely and act deferentially. Nowhere is this more pronounced than in the *dojo*. At the top is the *senpai* and everyone else slots into place underneath according to a pecking order that may be difficult for Westerners to interpret.

The hierarchy in school clubs is simple. Seniority is determined by age group but not necessarily age. For example, a student who fails the university entrance exam one year will spend the next year studying to try again. These students are called *ronin*—masterless Samurai. When they are successful, they might end up in the same year group as somebody who was previously their *kohai* in high school. This can complicate things somewhat but their current school cohort takes precedence.

In a community club, however, the order is not always so clear cut. Usually it will be based on Dan rank. If a number of people have the same rank, positions will be further divided by who took the grade earlier. If the grades were taken at the same time, then age will be the deciding factor. This pecking order has nothing whatsoever to do with skill. Even a World Champion will sit at the bottom of the line if he is younger or has a lower grade, and will politely listen to advice and orders from his weaker *senpai*, even if it's meaningless and off the mark.

The *dojo* is not a democracy. It is the job of the *senpai* to teach and help their *kohai*. If they do it badly they will be reprimanded by the *sensei*. Often it is *senpai*, not the *sensei*, who acts as the enforcer of discipline in the *dojo*. *Senpai* will foot most of the bill for their *kohai* if they go out for a meal and typically show kindness as a counterbalance to acidity in training. This might seem restrictive but it works well when the system is not corrupted by bad-natured blockheads. It's bearable if all they do is pontificate, but "senpai-itis" can get abusive and that's when problems can arise. In the West, we'd tell an abusive teammate to sod off, but this is not appropriate in a *senpai–kohai* relationship; *kohai* have to hold their tongues. As the figurehead of the *dojo*, the *sensei* will usually step in if things get out of hand.

Dojo Etiquette

Being a sacred place, proper etiquette in the *dojo* is mandatory. Always try to arrive early. When you enter the *dojo*, take off your hat and place you shoes neatly in the shelf or at the bottom of the step with the toes pointing away from the *dojo*. Bow towards the *shomen* or *kamidana* (front, and most hallowed location in the *dojo*) while lowering your eyes and say *shitsurei shimasu* ("I am about to be rude"). This serves as a greeting, not a preemptive warning for an unfortunate escape of gas. Bowing to the *shomen* is also a sign of respect to the *dojo* environment, the people you train with and the traditions of your Budo. Go and greet the *sensei* and *senpai* . It's good form to kneel on the floor and do a seated bow to the *sensei*. Always say hello with a standing bow when greeting the others.

Remove all jewelry and accessories and get changed as quickly as you can without talking loudly. As soon as you are in your gear, find a corner to prepare by yourself before the group warm-up starts. You might also want to do a bit of cleaning, but this depends on the *dojo*.

Have all your equipment ready beforehand and jump at the order to line up. If you are new to the *dojo*, some people will try to be polite and put you in a higher position in the line. Refuse politely by lowering your head and shuffle toward the lowest spot. The *sensei* will then show you where you should sit and the matter will be settled. When in doubt, go low!

A group of Shorinji Kempo practitioners enjoying lunch during a seminar. Attending tournaments, seminars and demonstrations is an important part of *dojo* life.

KEY BUDO CONCEPTS: *Kamidana* 神棚 "God Shelf"

Almost all private *dojo* have a *kamidana* (literally "God Shelf") or Shinto altar. There might be a small Shinto shrine placed in the most prominent part of the *dojo*, which is called the *shomen*. Or there might be a Buddhist altar, a calligraphy scroll or a flag instead. If the training in conducted in a public facility like a gymnasium, there shouldn't be a *kamidana*, as organs of the state are not legally allowed to sponsor religion. The law is flouted a lot, however, especially in public schools, but was written into the postwar constitution of Japan as a safeguard following the rise of militarism through state-controlled Shinto. Back in 1936, the government connected the study of Budo to state consciousness through a decree that *kamidana* were to be installed in all *dojo*. Items of veneration such as scrolls and the like sometimes featured in *dojo* in the Tokugawa period but there

were few examples of Shinto altars being present until government sponsorship of Shinto from the Meiji era that positioned the emperor as a living god.

The *kamidana* decree effectively forced a direct relationship between Budo and reverence of the imperial way (*kodo*). Whenever a training session commenced or finished, all students bowed to the *kamidana* as a sign of reverence to Shinto deities, the emperor and the state itself. The ultimatum was later criticized as having been designed to indoctrinate nationalistic ideals.

Nowadays, whether a *kamidana* is present or not is entirely contingent on the *dojo* and the political and/or religious leanings of the people running it; but in most cases the *kamidana*, or objects placed in the *shomen* area of the *dojo* symbolize the sanctity of the space. Bows to the *shomen* will always be conducted at the beginning and end of a training session. It doesn't necessarily need to be interpreted as a religious act per se. Nevertheless, it is a ritual that is done according to the *dojo*'s protocols, so not participating will raise a few eyebrows and be seen as disrespectful. Think of it as similar to standing for the national anthem before an international sports match, even though you might not be a citizen of that country.

Each *dojo* has its own rituals for the start of training. A fairly standard set of protocols will have you all kneeling down in *seiza*, meditating for about a minute, followed by bows to the *shomen*, to the *sensei* and *senpai* sitting in front, and then one more for good measure. This order is reversed at the end of training. If you are just there to watch, kneel on the floor for the starting and ending ceremony. Never remain seated in a chair.

A *senpai* offers advice on the correct stance for maximum punching power during a Karate class.

Training Etiquette

When training commences, it is rude to put less than 100 percent effort into your drills. You will get hot and thirsty during the training but don't fall out and get yourself a drink while everybody else is still active. There will typically be a break halfway through when you can rehydrate, but consume the liquid as inconspicuously as you can; don't walk around with a bottle in your hand and glugging it back.

Sit in *seiza* in the *dojo*. This will kill your legs and be uncomfortable, but try to keep it up for as long as you can. When you are at the end of your tether, do a seated bow to the *shomen* and sit cross-legged. Never sit with your legs splayed out like you would in front of the TV at home. Don't eat, smoke, swear or engage in any form of tomfoolery. You might see others breaking the rules of propriety, but don't do it yourself.

When the bosses are talking, stop and listen. Reply to any advice with a loud clear *Hai*! to show that you understand. (Only Karateka say *Oss*!) Never respond with something along the lines of "Yeah, but what if…." Just shut the hell up and take the guidance. If you have a question, it's best to wait until the end of training and ask the *sensei* privately. Training is not the time to ask nitpicky questions or show how much you think

IAIDO: TIME-HONOURED ART OF SPIRITUAL DEVELOPMENT.

Karate is not just about kicks and punches. Locks, holds and pressure points are all part of the technical syllabus.

you know. You're there to absorb information, not quibble about it or show off. As a rule, unless you are a *senpai* and have been asked to help other members, you should *never* take it upon yourself to teach. Sometimes you might see people doing something wrong but it is not your place to correct them.

Always bow to each partner before and after drills. It doesn't matter how exhausted you are, bow properly with clear intent. You don't need to say please or thank you each time but look into their eyes and convey your gratitude with sincerity.

When training has finished and you have bowed out, don't rush off and guzzle two liters of water. Instead, go straight to the *sensei*, kneel down and say thank you once again. This is when you can ask for some tips or clarify what you were taught during training. The *dojo* will be cleaned after the session, so try to be the first to go a find a broom or mop. When the *dojo* has been tidied up, go into the changing room and get changed as quickly as you can. Fold your gear up neatly, don't just roll it up and chuck it in your bag. Be sure to say goodbye to the *sensei* and bow deeply to the *shomen* as you leave.

It seems like a lot to remember but basically you should be on your best behavior at all times, keep your mouth shut, train hard and learn. When in doubt, follow what others are doing. Every *dojo* is different.

Religion, Ritual and Meditation

There was a famous court case in the US concerning bowing in Judo. In 1997, some US-based Judoka claimed that being "forced to bow" to inanimate objects before a competition, such as flags or pictures of Kano Jigoro, is religious and is therefore in violation of the Civil Rights Act of 1964. They maintained that such a rule should not be mandatory in a public facility where tournaments are held. They opposed the Judo Federation's stance that if they don't bow, they can't compete.

Apparently, the plaintiff was a Japanese Buddhist and didn't want her children being forced to participate in "Shinto

Meditation before and after training is an important time to control your breathing and get your mind where it needs to be.

rituals." In 2002, after several hearings and submissions, the judge rejected their assertion that mandatory bowing is a violation of their rights and the case ended there.

Indeed, there are many religious aspects in ceremonies conducted in the *dojo*. Kyudo has a number of Shinto-based rituals. The Shinto-derived Omoto-kyo religion had a profound effect on the philosophy of Aikido. Shorinji Kempo includes teachings of Kongo Zen, and most other Budo start and finish training with short periods of meditation with the hands held in the Cosmic Mudra pose. *Kamidana* are small shrines found in many *dojo*, adorned with branches of the sacred *sakaki* tree, and they are bowed to "religiously." The list of examples goes on, but does that mean that someone with their own religious beliefs should not participate in *dojo* rituals if they don't want to? The common seated bow, for example, very much resembles how a Muslim would prostrate in the direction of Mecca. In all the Abrahamic religions of Judaism, Christianity and Islam, idolatry—the worship of inanimate

objects—is forbidden. Bowing to a *kamidana* or decorative scroll in the *shomen* could easily be interpreted as an act of idolatry. What to do?

Religious rituals permeate just about every aspect of daily life in Japan, but many Japanese refer to themselves as *mushukyo* (non-religious). This actually means that they may not associate with a specific religious organization, but still take part in numerous acts of worship. Important ceremonies in life are a real mishmash of Taoism, Confucianism, Shintoism, Buddhism and even Christianity. All sorts of ceremonies are conducted in a *dojo* but most Japanese Budoka don't think of them as religious in the typical Western monotheistic sense of the word.

Each individual has to decide whether or not participating in religious-based rituals violates their own faith and beliefs. It is not for me to say that it doesn't. Nevertheless, point blank refusal to participate will generally be looked upon with scorn by Japanese Budoka. "When in Rome…. Otherwise, go home." If it really is a problem, I suggest you consult with the *sensei* beforehand and explain your predicament.

Ultimately, though, many of these rituals are interpreted differently by each individual. In other words, the rituals mean what you want them to. The *kamidana*, for example, doesn't necessarily need to be symbolic of Shinto if you don't want it to be. It can be thought of as representing the environment, or even "peace on earth" if you want it to mean that. Bowing to it doesn't have to be taken as a religious act. It is perfectly acceptable (if not the norm) to bow as a formality simply to show respect. And meditating doesn't mean you are suddenly a Zen Buddhist. If anything, it is a quiet time to settle your nerves, control your breathing and get your mind and body in sync. It's really up to you how you interpret these things.

Warm-ups and Cool-downs

I once asked a *sensei* why he never seems to stretch before training. He replied, "Because it's a waste of time

KEY BUDO CONCEPTS: *Mushin* 無心 "No-mind"

This is the elusive mental state which Budoka aspire to attain. It is the "mind without mind," but doesn't mean mindless! It is a mind that is not fixed on any one thing (winning, striking, escaping) or bound by emotion. It is the mind that can react intuitively to any situation without intent. To achieve this, the Budoka's mind must be liberated from fear, surprise, doubt, hesitation and ego. It supersedes the desire to win through ploys or strategies. It sounds like cosmic hocus-pocus but is an integral teaching in Zen from whence it was introduced into the martial arts canon. *Mushin* amounts to an absolute liberation in movement and method—free of desire and oblivious to the result, live or die.

In the martial arts, the mind is trained to flow. Death is the probable result if it stops and becomes attached to the existence of the enemy. Understanding and experiencing this mindset is an important objective in Budo and is why *kata* is practiced *ad infinitum* until the techniques, breathing and movements all become second nature. In other words, they become a part of the martial artist's being. This leads to deeper awareness in all aspects of the warrior's life.

The monk Takuan Soho explained, "When the swordsman stands against his opponent, he is not to think of the opponent, nor of himself, nor of his enemy's sword movements. He just stands there with his sword which, forgetful of all technique, is ready only to follow the dictates of his subconscious."

This concept can be equated with "flow" or getting into the "zone." According to the psychologist Mihály Csikszentmihályi, flow is a single-minded immersion in an act, be it work, sports, music or video games, and involves an intense and unobstructed concentration on the present. It is characterized by "merging action and awareness," "loss of reflective self-consciousness," "a sense of personal control or agency over the situation or activity," "a distortion of temporal experience," "experience of the activity as intrinsically rewarding." If you've experienced "being in the zone" in something you enjoy doing, then this is something akin to *mushin*. To feel it in Budo training takes a long time, and as much as I want it to be it is never constant. Maybe that will come with time. When it does happen, it is inspiring and cathartic—like "moving Zen."

when I could be fighting. That's why I warm up *before* coming to the *dojo*." Warm-ups and cooling down exercises in a standard Japanese *dojo* are decidedly inferior to what you may be accustomed to in other sports. Budoka are quite stubborn and are wary of changes to traditional methodologies. Common sense based on the latest sports science info (which is always changing) is often disregarded

as irrelevant or just not known about. This is partially because there is no retirement in Budo. Those in teaching positions are long-time practitioners who tend to perpetuate the outdated methods that they learned decades ago. Almost all *dojo* do warm-ups but these are not particularly thorough and seem more like going through the motions. Proper cool-downs are even rarer, and few *dojo* have ice for post training icing of joints and muscles. If there is ice, it's destined for cold drinks, not fatigued bodies.

My point is that ultimately your body is your own responsibility. The jury is out on the physiological efficacy of static stretching just before explosive exercise, but you should never go into something cold. From personal experience, I suggest arriving at the *dojo* early and get the blood and muscles pumping before the formal warm-up. If you can, stay a little longer after training to cool down as well. You might be the only one doing it, but your body will thank you for it.

Hygiene

They say that "Old Budoka never die, they just smell that way." Given that most Budo involves lots of contact, it is important that you turn up to the *dojo* with clean gear, cut nails and not smelling of garlic-filled *gyoza*! You will sweat a lot, and as gross as it sounds, there will be fluid transferred in the tangle. If you are feeling ill or have a nasty virus, don't train! It will spread through a Budo club like wildfire.

Be sure to wash your gear each time after training to remove the blood and sweat. Don't leave it in your bag or else it will start reeking of ammonia. The summer weather is so humid in Japan that it only takes one day for a sweat-drenched *gi* or other equipment to begin cultivating a small forest of revolting fungi. Always dry your gear out, and maybe even use a disinfectant spray like Febreze for good measure. Remember, this is not only for your own comfort but for those whom you train with. Cleanliness is Budoness.

Injuries

Minor niggles in Budo are not uncommon. The problem is that Budoka in Japan continue training even when they are injured. It's seen as a sign of weakness to stop so they just keep pushing through the pain barrier to finish the session. There is pressure to not take time off training, so injuries will get taped up and unrehabilitated in the rush to get back.

Of course, from a Western athletic perspective this kind of mentality is ludicrous and likely to make a bad situation worse in the long run. On the other hand, I have encountered foreigners who linger unashamedly on the opposite end of the scale. A little bruise will keep them away for a week. I once tried to get an afternoon off training because the soles of my feet were covered in blisters. My *sensei* laughed, pulled out a lighter and needle and drained the blisters with ruthless efficiency. "Now get your butt back out there you gutless creampuff!"

If you get injured (torn muscle, sprain, broken nose, etc.), stop! Quietly make your way to the side of the *dojo* without making a fuss and assess the situation. Excuse yourself and then do what is necessary. If it means taking time off training to rehab, do it. Just be sure to turn up to the *dojo* to observe trainings, showing that your heart is still on the floor. Don't make a big song and dance about your war wounds. People will laugh at you behind your back. Are

Top Never forgo your warm-up. Get the blood pumping first and avoid those silly injuries. It's your responsibility.
Above Karate practitioners working on core strength during training.

you a hypochondriac in desperate need of toughening up? Only you know your own body but be honest with yourself. Bruises, blisters, and broken nails are never an excuse.

Hydration

Another important consideration when training in the wet muggy heat of Japan is hydration. Heatstroke is a common and sometimes fatal affliction in the summer months. The symptoms may not be obvious but you will start to slow down, feel dizzy and slur your words.

The problem in Japan is that sports buffs have been taught never to drink water during exercise! This foolish convention came about way back in 1904 when a Japanese university professor claimed "the only way to build physical dexterity is to minimize water intake." A

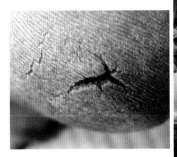

crazy notion, but it became "common sense," and generations of Japanese athletes have suffered needlessly in the heat as a result. Only recently has the situation begun to change. In 2008, Japan's Health, Labor and Welfare Ministry started a campaign to educate teachers and athletes of the necessity to keep their fluids up! My favorite poster said "We're thirsty. Sensei, let us drink water."

Outrageous as it is, this fallacy that water intake should be limited is still stubbornly adhered to by old school Budoka who see the need for rehydration as a sign of frailty, or drinking while training as just plain rude! It has finally become "relatively" acceptable to rehydrate but it has to be done without making it too obvious. Turn and face the *dojo* wall and squat down as you take a few sips. Make sure that it's at an appropriate time, like during a break.

You need to rehydrate around 70–80 percent of what you sweat. If you perspire anything like I do, this means a copious amount of water, or the famous ion replenishing drink "Pocari Sweat." I still haven't worked out what kind of animal a Pocari is, but it tastes pretty good when dying of thirst. (It was originally developed as a drink for rehydrating burn victims.) By the way, *dojo* students have an unhygienic habit of sharing water bottles and cups. It's best not to.

Weight Training and Fitness

People believe that Budo will keep them fit. I believe that you should keep fit for Budo. Although you will get a good workout in most forms of Budo, the movements tend to put more stress on one side of the body than the

Above left It doesn't even count as a flesh wound but cracked heels are a painful part of the cold, dry Japanese winter months.

Above Accidents do happen. That's why it's important to have insurance coverage.

other. Training only in Budo can lead to physical imbalances. It might not be immediately obvious but will eventually lead to niggling injuries when you get older. I am just starting to find this out now!

An effective way to remedy this is weight training. With the exception of Judo, weight training is largely discouraged in Budo circles. The standard criticisms are "You'll become muscle-bound." "You don't need big muscles in Budo; it'll slow you down." "Budo technique is not about power, so stop wasting your time." Or "If you've got time to go to the gym, you should be in the *dojo* instead."

These traditionalists are missing the point. Not all weight training is about bulking up! Given the hip-centric movements employed in most Budo, the lower back is prone to soreness. The legs are also common injury spots, along with shoulders, and everywhere actually. To strengthen these areas and prevent debilitating injuries, I subject

myself to a simple regime of dead lifts and squats, and a mixture of free weight upper body exercises with kettle bells followed by stretching. Dead lifts and squats are excellent for tempering your core and building overall strength. My body has become significantly more resilient as a result. More balanced, I am now lighter on my feet and more energetic.

You can find the necessary equipment in any school or commercial gym and it doesn't take long to go through the routines. Don't be surprised when your *sensei* tells you that you don't need to do weights. Say *Hai*! and just continue behind the scenes without making a big deal out of it. It's the extra work that will take you to a level above everybody else.

Language

Language is perhaps the biggest barrier for a budding *gai-sam*. Orders are barked in Japanese and the tone is often angry. It's hard to follow at first, but as you get used to the way things are done in your *dojo* you will start to see patterns and understand intuitively. When you're not sure, always reply with a short sharp *Hai*—"Sir, yes sir"—because more often than not what you are hearing is an ultimatum.

Equipment should always be neatly placed when not being used. This goes for shoes in the *dojo* entranceway. The brooms and mops in the background are for cleaning the floor before and after training.

The finer points of instruction will go over your head, and there are safety concerns if a member of the *dojo* is oblivious to what is going on. To counter this problem, the *gai-sam* with limited knowledge of Japanese will often be assigned a "minder" who speaks some English. There is almost always somebody in the *dojo* who is "more international" than the others and supposedly speaks good English. Even if s/he doesn't speak that well, they will be the ones tasked with looking out for you. Sometimes, younger members of the *dojo* are allotted this responsibility because they studied English at high school or university, so "must" be good at it.

Adding to the confusion are the different modes of Japanese spoken in the *dojo. Sensei* and *senpai* will often converse in informal Japanese, whereas junior members will be expected to use politer forms. A beginner in Japanese will not be able to make the distinction at first and will inevitably screw up.

Don't worry about it though. The Japanese are open minded about this when it comes to foreigners and are amazed if you can utter even a few words in Japanese. You will learn, but be sure to put as much time into learning Japanese each day as you do in the *dojo*.

Outside the Dojo

Part of belonging to a *dojo* involves doing lots of things outside training times as well. *Dojo* are very social entities and you will be invited to drinking

FIFTEEN FAMOUS JAPANESE CULTURAL IDIOSYNCRASIES

1. **Black Belt Sleepers** Japanese people are incredibly adept at sleeping anywhere, anytime, anyhow, even while standing in a train. And they know the exact moment when they have to wake up.
2. **Toilets** Apart from the bright red toilet slippers that *gaijin* often forget to take off after visiting the loo, Japanese toilets can be a minefield to operate, especially if you can't read the *kanji* to switch the bidet/butt washer off. Some have butt blow dryers and recordings of flushing sounds to camouflage embarrassing bodily explosions.
3. **Cosmetic Surgery for Teeth** Not to fix them but to get what are called *yaeba*, or snaggle teeth (sort of upper canine fangs) which are considered *kawaii* (cute).
4. **Christmas Eve KFC** No turkey for Christmas in Japan. Young Japanese couples traditionally spend Christmas Eve together enjoying a bucket of Colonel Sanders' finest. It never occurred to me before, but the Colonel actually looks like Santa! I wonder if this is why.
5. **Pachinko** Vertical pinball machines lined up in rows in noisy, smoky, crowded parlors full of zoned-out zombies trying to get rich. Flick a ball bearing in the right hole and win the spin. The machine then spits out hundreds of balls which are put in plastic containers. These are exchanged for tokens, which are then taken off the premises and cashed in. Serious gambling exploiting loopholes in the law and found absolutely everywhere in Japan. Probably the most popular pastime for Japanese over the age of twenty.
6. **Maid Cafes** Young ladies dressed up in French maid outfits. Their mission? To pamper you and sing for you and even bring you coffee. Full of middle-aged male clientele.
7. **Love Hotels** Secret love dens that couples hire for a couple of hours or a night training in the marital arts. Eyesores from the outside but inside it's a different story with theme rooms to cater for every fantasy.
8. **Kancho (Enemas)** For some reason when you least expect it, Japanese children (and a few puerile adults) insist on clasping their hands together, extending both forefingers, and stabbing you in the butt shouting *kancho*! It really hurts.
9. **Wet Fish Handshakes** The traditional greeting in Japan is the bow but the handshake is becoming more common. Most Japanese have never been taught to give a good firm shake while looking you in the eye. It results in you grabbing a limp hand. Added to this, people don't know when to let go. You may end up having an awkward marathon handshake lasting for five minutes!
10. **Opening Presents** Japanese love to give and receive presents but never open them in front of the giver. Very rude.
11. **Blood Type** Japanese like to ask about your blood type. Many people believe that blood type is directly associated with personality. That's why I never tell them mine for fear of being pigeonholed even more! I don't know it anyway.
12. **Age** Being a hierarchical society, Japanese are fixated on age and will often ask how old you are. Age is an indicator of where you should be in life. Fortunately, there is not as much pressure for women to marry by the age of 25 anymore. A 25-year-old spinster used to be cruelly referred to as "Christmas Cake"—something that nobody is interested in after December 25.
13. **You've Put on Weight** A common greeting in Japan, even if you saw the person as recently as yesterday. Losing weight is mentioned tentatively as it may be a sign of illness.
14. **Ear Wax** Japanese use little bamboo sticks called *mimi-kake* to scrape their earwax out onto the table. Strangely enough, Japanese earwax is white and powdery and you may think that they are setting up a line of cocaine. This actually happened to a Japanese friend of mine in New Zealand.
15. **Sniffing** Japanese do not like to blow their noses in public. A handkerchief is for wiping sweat off one's brow or smothering a cough, not for snot removal. Instead, they will sit there sniffing and sniffing and sniffing. It can be very irritating.

A neat little bar in Okinawa run by an expat Karateka.

parties and seminars throughout the year. Such gatherings are a fantastic setting to ask potentially silly questions that are too embarrassing to bring up in the *dojo*. It is a jovial time where members will open up and become sociable to degrees that they never would inside the *dojo*. It's also a time when *sensei* (and wannabe *sensei*) wax lyrical about the wonders of Japanese Budo and you can pick up lots of insights and advice. The hierarchy is still there and liberties should not be taken, but it is a lot more relaxed.

Depending on the club, drinking parties can be frequent or extremely frequent events. In fact, the code name for a post-training "debrief" over a brewski or three is "Second Dojo." This is never a problem if you enjoy alcohol. But what if you don't? Fortunately, expectations for drinking have become more tolerant in recent years. Two simple excuses will get you off the hook with no questions asked: *Dokutaa Sutoppu* (The doctor has advised that I should stop drinking for health reasons) and *Unten* (I'm driving.) DUI is a serious crime in Japan now. Don't say "I hate alcohol and don't drink," as such candidness will be thought of as unfriendly. If you are under aged (the drinking age is 20 in Japan), then it's not an issue.

While I'm on the subject of drinking, never pour your own. You'll be the poorer for it. Also, never drink from the bottle. Both are seen as antisocial. When bottles are brought to the table, take one and pour your *sensei/senpai* a beer with both

hands, keeping the label on the bottle facing upwards. This is the polite way of pouring. Never do it with one hand as this would be discourteous to a senior. When you are poured a drink, hold your glass up with both hands for the same reason, not with one hand. Then reciprocate.

This is one of the many ways in which the hierarchy is evident. The place where you sit at the table is also determined by your position in the *dojo*. As a foreigner, you might be asked to sit in front of the *sensei* as a special guest at first. As they become accustomed to having you around, you will be treated like everybody else.

Also, never touch your chopsticks or eat any of the food on the table until the *sensei* has taken the first bite. At the end of an informal gathering, you should go for your wallet and look like you want to pay but you will be told to put it away. In fact, the bill (or most of it) will usually get paid by the *sensei/senpai* before you even realize it. It's just the way it's done in Japan, which isn't bad unless you are the *senpai*. Be sure to say thank you when the bill has been

paid! It's amazing how many people don't.

In the case of formal parties, like end of year shindigs, all members will be expected to pay the same amount no matter how much they drank, which will be collected by one of the minions in charge of cash.

Other occasions where you will gather outside the *dojo* will be for *gasshuku* (training camps) or official events on weekends. This could be a local or regional tournament or seminar. Whatever the case, you should make an extra effort to participate and dress appropriately with a shirt and tie. You might not be competing but you will be expected to come down and support members of your *dojo* or maybe help with setting up the venue and cleaning up.

All Budo events are run by volunteers and you should be one, too. Your participation outside of usual training times will be noted and duly appreciated, even if you do prove to be a liability by getting in the way. Be prepared for the post event Second Dojo.

Gender Issues

There is a term that describes the traditional position of women in Japanese society—*danson-johi* ("Respect for the male, contempt for the female.") Women are not held in "contempt" per se but the mere existence of the term is an indication of the patriarchal nature and attitudes in Japanese society. The world of Budo is predictably patriarchal also. It varies according to the discipline, but in almost all cases (except perhaps Naginata and Kyudo), women are a minority.

Japanese women are accustomed to the blatantly misogynistic attitudes shown by some men and take it with a grain of salt. Nevertheless, instances of unconcealed sexism may come as a horrible shock to non-Japanese trying to navigate Japan. You may feel as though you are being looked down upon and even the object of sexual harassment.

I'M JUST SAYING, ISN'T IT A BIT ODD TO PRACTICE FOR ONE HOUR, AND THEN DRINK FOR THREE...?

A Budo Seminar for Foreigners

The International Seminar of Budo Culture is conducted for three days at the beginning of March every year at the Nippon Budokan's Kenshuu Center and the International Budo University in Katsuura, Chiba prefecture. This is about 90 minutes from Tokyo Station. The purpose is to provide foreign residents who study Budo with a deeper knowledge of the theory and techniques. There are lectures about the history, philosophy and culture of Budo, and also practical lessons in which the top *sensei* of each Budo discipline in Japan offer instruction. The seminar is sponsored by the Nippon Budokan, Japanese Budo Association and the MEXT Sports Agency in the hope that it will contribute to fostering international goodwill through Budo. The seminar costs the paltry sum of ¥5,400, which includes food and accommodation.

You will be able to train in your own specialist Budo with the top instructors dispatched from each federation. There is a Kobudo *ryuha* invited each year to introduce modern Budoka to one of the classical schools. The most popular aspect of the seminars are the two-hour sessions where you can try your hand at something you've never done before. If you've always wanted to give Sumo a go, for example, then you'll get to put on a *mawashi* and slip and slide around the *dohyo* to your heart's content. Such opportunities to try out all the different kinds of Budo in one place are rare in Japan and are the best way to see which ones work for you. It's a lot of fun. Check out the Nippon Budokan's website for details.

☞ **Nippon Budokan and Budo Seminar**

Sekuhara is a Japanese word deriving from the English "sexual harassment." That this word exists in Japan shows that such behavior is no longer socially acceptable by any means. Mention of the word *sekuhara* is enough to send shivers down the spine of the most shameless touchy-feely male chauvinist pig.

It is on the cards that you will encounter some offensive behavior. Sexist attitudes are an unfortunate aspect of Japan's social hierarchy. Conversely, although not sexism I have witnessed many instances where women *senpai* in college clubs have run their male *kohai* ragged with unreasonable demands and intimidating behavior. In any case, you will need to be a little thick skinned about misogyny but don't let it hold you back! Be aware that it is easy to read too much into looks and words, especially when trying to get on in an unfamiliar culture. But if there are obvious problems that are too much to bear, be sure to consult with a school counsellor or colleague whom you can trust.

Nationality Issues

When I first came to Japan in 1987, so rare were foreigners even in the big cities that there wasn't a day that went by without hearing the vapid expression *Gaijin da!* ("Yikes! It's a foreigner!") After nearly three decades in Japan, it suddenly dawned on me recently that I haven't heard this irritating phrase for some time now.

Two women Kendo teachers perform a customary *kata* demonstration before the start of a tournament.

Moreover, people no longer assume that because I'm Caucasian I must be American although they do try to speak to me in English. What if I was Russian or French?!

In any case, although it's no longer polite to brazenly point out alien presences anymore, foreigners not of Asian descent still stick out like sore thumbs. You will catch people gawking at you from afar, but the attitude toward foreigners is much more lackadaisical than it used to be.

The Japanese-speaking *gaijin* is no longer the zoo attraction s/he once was. This is because more young Japanese are experiencing life overseas on exchange programs, and more non-Japanese people are laying down their roots in Japan. Not to mention the growing number of kids born of mixed parentage in Japan—one in fifty. Despite the myth of homogeneity, Japan is now very much a multicultural society.

Nevertheless, you will be a bit of a novelty item in the *dojo*. Get used to it. At first, you will be an enigma as the members try to work out exactly where you fit into their ecosystem. You will feel quite self-conscious, and even though you just want to blend into the *dojo* crowd, it ain't going to happen right away.

The beauty of Budo is that once you prove yourself capable of surviving the rigors of training without shirking off, you will be treated as one of the team. With effort, you will become a genuine member of the club, albeit still a bumbling *gaijin*. The difference is, you will be "their *gaijin*" and they will be delighted to have you. You might even become a welcome source of entertainment because of your bumbling, which isn't always a bad thing.

The transition will be easier if there are other respected foreigners in the *dojo*. But, one *gaijin* ass who trampled on the hallowed *dojo* traditions ten years ago will still be remembered today, and you may find yourself having to atone for a previous alien miscreant's misdeeds. Roll with the punches and don't take things too personally.

Like every country in the world, there are bigots in Japan. Bigotry is born of ignorance. Budo, in particular, is very old-fashioned, exclusive and xenophobic even by Japanese standards. You will come across the odd grumpy Budoka who resents having you there. It might not be expressed in words, but you can tell by the scowls and grunts of disapproval whenever you don't act the way a Japanese would.

Then again, you might also find that the one who scowls the most is actually the person looking out for you behind the scenes, and is just embarrassed for you as you blunder your way through *dojo* life.

Whatever the case, just deal with it. If you get upset, then it's your own fault. The best way to emasculate an ignoramus in the *dojo* is by being the most diligent and deferential person of all. That doesn't mean that you should try to become Japanese! Be yourself but abide by the Japanese rules and ideals of hard work and show respect.

That might even make you seem "more Japanese than Japanese" in some people's eyes, and then you will find the *dojo* bigot becomes your biggest fan. Strangely enough, it really does happen that way.

Left Foreign Kendo practitioners receive advice from a Japanese master at an international seminar.
Below Predominantly studied by women, Naginata, like all Budo disciplines, is practiced by people of all ages.

Dojo Politics

In spite of the much touted harmony and character-building attributes of Budo, *dojo* and federations can be nasty hotbeds of political dissent. Usually the *sensei* will try to keep any bickering in line but there is often more than one *sensei* and they may not see eye to eye. At a school club, an intensely frustrated *kohai* who resents a rambunctious *senpai* might cause some friction. Then there are power struggles much higher up in a federation. This won't have anything to do with you, but you will become inadvertently involved if your *sensei* is one of the stakeholders.

Some of the worst brouhahas involve succession issues in Kobudo schools. Political wrangling and infighting is a historical fact of life in all martial arts. In some cases, you might be seen as somebody's "ally" in a petty *dojo* dispute even though you are not.

If you do have opinions on an issue, my advice is to keep out of it altogether. Feign ignorance and don't be dragged into anything that smells of discord. You have enough on your plate getting on in Japan and don't need to be used as a pawn in something that probably runs much deeper than you could ever imagine.

Often these matters are brought to your attention in the Second Dojo. It's a time to tune out and just enjoy your beverage. Nothing good can possibly come from your involvement. Shaking your head innocently and saying *Wakarimassseeen* (I really don't [want to] understand) is the best way to escape getting hauled into *dojo* politics.

Training Expectations

Belonging to a *dojo* is a commitment. If you want to get good, you have to train. How much you train will depend on what else you are doing in Japan. If you work, your only options will be to head to the *dojo* in the evenings or at weekends.

Work has a horrible habit of taking over your life and you may have to cancel training more often than you'd like to. Work and "family service" are about the only accepted excuses for not turning up to trainings in Japan, but make sure to let your *sensei* or *senpai* know in advance as a matter of courtesy.

If you are in school, you really don't have an out unless you have classes.

When the club trains, you do too. Again, if you have to be somewhere else for whatever reason, make the seniors aware of when and why in advance. A cursory "Sorry, I was busy" after the fact will be thought of as insincere and put you even further on the outside. In the same vein, try not to be late for the start of training.

There will be periods when getting to the *dojo* is out of the question. The least you can do is maintain your level by revisiting the moves on your own for 10 minutes each night before you go to bed.

Also, go to the *dojo* with firm goals in mind for each training session. "Today, I'm going to get that footwork right." Or "I'm going to work on such and such *waza*." Quantity of training is important, but more so is quality and building on what you have learned.

Equipment

Depending on the Budo you've chosen, getting equipped can be a costly affair. Disciplines like Kendo, Kyudo, Naginata, Jukendo, Iaido and Kobudo will require purchasing weapons or protective armor which, although designed to protect your limbs, can cost an arm and a leg.

If you are just starting out, the *dojo* will usually be able to lend you equipment with the expectation that you buy your own if you decide to stay. At least purchase your own training uniform (*gi, hakama*, etc.) straight away. This will cost you $100–$200.

More people are buying Budo equipment online these days, which is convenient and inexpensive. But it's fun to find an actual store and practice your Japanese with the staff as they show you their wares. You might even get a decent discount.

Budo equipment should not be treated in the same way as common sports gear. Uniforms should be washed by hand and folded properly as if you were looking after your best suit. Protective gear should be dried in a drafty place away from direct sunlight and constantly checked for wear and tear.

This goes for your weapons as well. If they are not in tiptop condition, they could pose a danger to you and your opponent.

All weapons must be transported in a bag, otherwise you risk being arrested. Even wooden replicas must be handled like real weapons inside the *dojo* and out. Never, ever step over a weapon, or a person for that matter, and don't move something with your feet. That's considered to be quite uncouth in Japan.

The way somebody dresses in the *dojo* and looks after their equipment, is an indication of their understanding of Budo and respect for its traditions.

Above and right Getting equipped to start Budo is not always cheap. With the unarmed disciplines, you will only need a training top or bottom. Weapon Budo arts are a different matter. Don't fret. Most clubs will loan you the equipment at the beginning.

SETTING AND ACHIEVING GOALS

Personal progress is hard to gauge. Even though you are improving in the eyes of others, it is not so obvious to you. A perceived lack of development can be very frustrating and demotivating. How do you know where you are really at?

Keep a Training Diary

The best way to keep track of where you've been, where you're at and where you want to be is by keeping a training diary. Surprisingly few people do this. It does require a degree of discipline to scribble everything down and analyze each training when you are physically and mentally stuffed. The instant you say "I'll do it tomorrow" is the moment you lose to yourself.

Be sure to start the diary entry before training by writing your "Goal for today." After training, record what drills you practiced, who you trained with, things you did well, things you sucked at, impressions and random thoughts, plus those little gems that *sensei* imparted.

Strike while the iron is hot and the memory is still fresh in your mind. Read over your entry the next day and add any other reflections that retrospectively pop into your head. It will seem like a chore but you will be glad you kept it up when you see patterns in your improvement. Reading back on it in ten years' time is a blast, too. In this age of digital fragility, I highly recommend that you buy yourself a fancy paper diary with a nice cover and fill it in by hand. It's much more fitting for your odyssey. You will be more thoughtful when you write and it will last forever. It will become a genuine chronicle of great personal value.

Enter Competitions

Tournaments are a big part of modern Budo. Some people despise the mere idea of competition, seeing it as running counter to the ideals of Budo. The fact is, tournaments are invaluable

Competitors thrust it out in a Jukendo competition with local instructors watching in the background.

Naginata students listen carefully as they receive feedback from their instructor.

for making concrete goals and keeping tabs on your progress. It's amazing how many people excel in training but fall to pieces in a competition. They are quite often the ones who decry competition as not being "real Budo." Competition is the best way to measure your improvement and motivates you to implement strategies for further growth. At first, winning is a matter of pride and that is fine!

Nobody wants to lose and nobody should want to either. Such a defeatist attitude is not doing anybody any favors. Ultimately, though, the result is not as important as the process. This is a crucial point that you learn to appreciate after a few years of experience under your belt.

气剣体一致

BUDO CALLIGRAPHY:
Ki-ken-tai-itchi "Striking With a Unity of Energy (*ki*), Sword (*ken*) and Body (*tai*)"

Ken for sword (剣) is sometimes replaced with the ideogram for fist (拳), which is also read as *ken*.

Be sure to create clear goals for things you want to work on in the build-up to a tournament. This includes identifying technical improvements, working on your confidence and self-belief and finding out as much as you can about prospective opponents. Irrespective of success or failure, the postmortem is vital for pinpointing patterns and things to work on in training. All of this should go into your diary. Remember, win with humility and lose gracefully. Attitude is everything.

Where's my number goddammit? Either the worst or best moment in a Dan examination. If your number is up, then so is your grade. If not, then it's back to the drawing board.

KEY BUDO CONCEPTS: *Shitei-dogyo* 子弟同行
"Disciple and Teacher on the Same Path"

Shitei-dogyo is another old Buddhist saying that has become a part of Budo parlance. It means "The teacher and the student are studying on the same path." That might seem patently obvious but the finer nuances of this relationship are often missed. The teacher teaches, the student learns. The master imparts his or her wisdom on the techniques and principles of Budo and the disciple develops and becomes stronger.

The teacher, however, is conveying much more than meets the eye. The teacher's persona, temperament, passion, frustrations, imperfections, severity and kindness are all factors that affect the student in profound ways. Although the hierarchy in Budo seems unyielding and absolute, it actually conceals the fact that the teacher at the top is very much at the bottom. Teaching is not a one-way street. As the teacher teaches, the student learns but the teacher learns even more.

At least that's the ideal. It is precisely because the teacher is also striving to come to terms with the "Way" that the student can trust him or her to serve as a guide. It is through maintaining the humility to keep learning from everything and everyone that makes a great teacher and hence great students. Hopefully, even greater students. That is why in Japan there is the saying "Ears of rice bow deeply as they ripen." The deeper into the path s/he travels, the more the teacher realizes how much they don't really know. They are walking exactly the same path as their student, but in the grand scheme of things they are only a few steps ahead. As soon as this realization is forsaken, the teacher has veered from the Way. If the teacher veers, so too does the student. Neither can exist without the other.

Dan Grades
Despite what some might think, studying Budo is not about the quest for black belts or trophies. Like competition, however, the ranking system provides tangible goals to mark progress. This is why the system was introduced in the first place. It keeps you honest and on the right path. Although Dan grades might seem like an impossible dream, barring those who simply pay lots of money for them at a McDojo, they are very achievable in Japan. It really depends on the Budo, but in most cases you can expect to reach the level of *shodan*, the first black belt, within a year of serious study. You might be able to get to *nidan* (2nd Dan) after two years. A relatively skilled high school student can reach *sandan* (3rd Dan) by the time they graduate. Then it gets progressively more difficult and much more time is needed to prepare between each grade. To give an example from Kendo, a practitioner with the grade of 7th Dan will have to wait ten years before being eligible to take the 8th Dan examination, the high-

Key Budo Concepts:
Ippon 一本 "The Point"

On the scoreboard, *ippon* is "one point" but it is much more than this. *Ippon* is a work of art symbolizing life and death. To score the winning blow involves a definite process with a beginning, point of impact and follow through. In most sports, it is the moment of impact or the second the ball crosses the line that matters. What happens in the lead-up, and what goes on in the aftermath, is of little consequence as long as the "bit in the middle" is decisive.

In Budo, the point itself is not judged on impact. It is a process that includes what happens in the lead-up (was it a genuine creation or just a fluke?), and by the attitude after the fact (keeping calm and ready for counterattacks or more follow up regardless of the result—*zanshin*). In other words, the entire procedure is central to the success of the technique. Only when it has gone full circle will the referee call the *ippon* valid. Of course, hitting the target is crucial but is only a part of the deal. In other words, it is quite a subjective decision based on the personal experience, knowledge and aesthetic sensibilities of the referee. Theoretically, *ippon* means death—the killing blow that is born of courage, commitment and respect for one's enemy. There is no trickery, just a clash of wills in which the strongest prevails. The *ippon* should *never* be sullied with ridiculous victory poses or emotional tantrums. It's a sign of immaturity and disrespect to one's opponent and to the traditions of Budo.

Process for scoring Ippon

一本

Start/Finish
Apply/Withstand psychological and physical pressure to create an opening

Identify and seize the opening

Execute the *waza* with total commitment. A coalescence of mind and body and technique.

Precise Point of Impact

Follow through with continued physical and psychological vigilance

Hundreds of nervous Kendo practitioners wait for their number to be allotted before their examination commences.

est grade in Kendo, and the youngest possible age is 46. Even then, the pass rate is a minuscule 0.7 percent.

Although *shodan* in any Budo is a great achievement, it is by no means a license of mastery. Far from it! It means that you know how to do the fundamentals to a very basic level. It really only signifies the start of things.

The prospect of sitting an examination will keep you focused and on your toes. If you fail, there is a reason. You need to re-evaluate what you are doing wrong. It is disappointing but the silver lining is that you will learn from the experience. If you are successful, you will also realize how much further there is to go when your *senpai* brings you back down to earth!

In summary, it is easy to lose sight of what you are trying to achieve. That's why competitions and gradings are useful. Budo is not supposed to be *only* about winning matches and accumulating belts. This is something you will work out for yourself after a few years of succeeding and failing in these pressure cooker situations.

CHAPTER 6

SURVIVING JAPAN

How should one get on with getting on in Japan? This chapter introduces survival tips and observations drawing on my three decades of head-butting brick walls to attain a Zen-like "acceptance" of things. How can you enhance your study of Budo, make friends and behave in a way that will help break through prevalent stereotypes that all *gaijin* are proverbial bulls in china shops? It helps to actually stop being a bull in a china shop first and learn how to play the game by Japanese rules while keeping your identity intact. Some of the things I introduce here are likely to become dated pretty quickly. Japan is constantly changing but there are certain aspects of the culture that are timeless. Knowing beforehand about the various things you are likely to experience in Japan will greatly assist you in making the most of your time here. You will have good times and bad but the key is to keep an open mind, a sense of humor and to never forget your priorities. My Kendo teacher once told me "What you don't sweat when you're young will turn into tears when you are old." That means keep your chin up, roll with the punches and know that every adventure/encounter/ordeal is ultimately good.

Just another day commuting to and from work. You know you've been in Japan for too long when everything in this photo seems perfectly normal.

FINDING YOUR GROOVE

Living in Japan as a foreigner is a roller-coaster ride of emotions. The newbie finds each day full of stimulating surprises but gradually the sense of wonder turns into feelings of frustration, cynicism, ineptitude and ultimately what I refer to as "the rage." Life always has its ups and downs. These are just exacerbated when you are trying to make your way in a foreign land. But meaningful adventures were never supposed to be easy!

Getting to Japan

If you are coming from one of 66 countries that have an agreement with Japan, including the US, Canada, the UK, Australia, New Zealand and many European Union countries, you can stay for up to 90 days on a tourist visa that is granted on arrival. This means that you can't work but you can sure get to see the country. Visitors from other countries need to apply for a visa before they arrive. The budding *gai-sam* will be wanting to stay in Japan for longer, in which case you will need to ensure that you have the right permission. Check out the following government website for information on the various kinds of visas and how to go about getting one.

☛ **MOFA and Guide to Japanese Visas**

Regardless of the international airport you arrive at in Japan, the procedures for entry are the same for all foreign visitors. When you disembark, you will proceed to the immigration line for foreigners and hand over your passport and embarkation/disembarkation card filled in between movies on the plane. You will then be fingerprinted and photographed (anti-terrorism law) and receive your Residence Card if you have a visa to stay for more than three months. Clearing customs is simply a matter of handing over your yellow customs declaration card and being ready to say why you are in Japan and where you will be staying.

A Seriously Important Note About Medications

Read this carefully. No Drugs. I'm not just referring to hard drugs like cocaine and so on. That goes without saying. You won't get executed for bringing illicit drugs into Japan like some countries but it's the innocent mistakes that can ruin your adventure before you even start. Foreign prescriptions are not honored in Japan. This means that you need to check a medication's legality beforehand, and if it's okay you can only bring in a small supply—no more than one month's worth—with a letter from your doctor. Immediately go and see a Japanese doctor who can prescribe you the Japanese equivalent. There is a high chance that you won't be able to source the exact same medication in Japan. If it is absolutely integral to your well-being, you can apply for a *yakkan shomei* certificate to bring in more personal medication.

Be aware that over the counter medicines in your home country may very well be totally illegal in Japan. For example, anything with codeine in it is going to land you in hot water. It may be hard to believe that common medicines like Adderall are absolutely prohibited. Prozac is not available and cannot be brought in without permission. There are no exceptions, so look into it before coming. Contact the local embassy beforehand or face possible time in a Japanese slammer.

☛ **MHLW and bringing medicines into Japan**

Trains

Unless you have somebody picking you up, your first experience after getting off the plane will be riding a train. The Japanese train system is extensive and mind-bogglingly reliable, with an average delay time of about 18 seconds. The main delays are when some unfortunate soul has decided to jump in front of one. Trains run at regular intervals from around 5:00 am until 12:30 am. Japan Rail (JR)

The Japanese police have a zero tolerance policy regarding drugs. Just don't go there. Drugs, I mean!

People buying train tickets in Shinagawa Station in Tokyo. The map shows JR stations only. The underground subway system is so extensive it would fill in the remaining white space.

Japanese	English
Chintai bukken	Rental property
Apaato	Apartment (You can get one for as cheap as $200/month if you look hard.)
1K	One room apartment with kitchen
1DK	One room apartment with dining and kitchen area
1LDK	One room apartment with a living, dining and kitchen area
Manshon	Large apartment (Basically a condo. Bigger and much more expensive than an apartment. Not a real mansion.)
Ikkodate	Detached house (Harder to find in the cities these days but plenty going in the countryside.)
Fudousanya	Real estate agent
Kariru	To rent/lease
Ryo	Dormitory (Most universities have dorms.)
Geshuku	Board and lodging (Usually for students.)

is the biggest network in the country and they operate the Shinkansen bullet train—a plane without wings. There are also hundreds of private rail and subway lines connecting every part of the country. Most stations have information in English so navigation is pretty easy. Buy yourself a prepaid card (Suica, Icoca, Pasmo, etc.). They can be topped up any time and are usually interchangeable on the various lines, meaning you don't have to try and work out the fares between stops. Just touch and go.

Cheap Hotels and Airbnb

Some good news for Airbnb fans. Japan's upper house passed a bill in 2017 allowing private homes to be rented out for a max of 180 nights a year. Now renters don't risk breaking the law. Over 20 million tourists visited Japan in 2016 and 3.7 million stayed in Airbnb registered properties. This is the way of the future, especially considering government projections of 40 million visitors by 2020 for the Olympic Games. The government has even encouraged those kitschy, kinky "love hotels" to be converted into regular[ish] hotels to alleviate the expected shortage of accommodation. If you don't mind mirrored ceilings

and the like, these will surely be cheap alternatives for short-term stays. Capsule hotels at 3,000 yen/night are the cheapest if sleeping in self-contained coffins is your thing.

Apartment Hunting

With around 120 million people, Japan is the 10th most populous country in the world. The greater Tokyo area has a population of 26.5 million, which makes it one of the largest urban areas on the planet. But not to fear. There are plenty of places to live, even in Tokyo, which don't cost the earth. If you're a student, you might try a homestay (quite rare in Japan) or a school dormitory, which can be a lot of fun. If not, you may encounter a bit of discrimination and red tape before you find your castle. Just count to ten. The best thing is to go to a real estate agent who is used to dealing with foreigners. They will take care of most things but bring a Japanese speaker with you.

Be prepared for the following. In some cases, you might have to fork out five to six months' rent for an initial down payment. This will include the first month's rent, a security deposit (*shikikin*) and the inexplicable "key money" (*reikin*).

Unless you trash the place, the security deposit will be returned in full when

If you reside in the countryside, you might be able to rent a house relatively cheaply. If in a city, enjoy your new life in a rabbit hutch.

you move out. The "key money" is not refundable. It is like a signing bonus for the landlord! The equivalent of "I humbly thank you for allowing me to pay you rent and here is a token of my appreciation for all of the money I will pay to you from now." Some may forgo this obligation but many will not.

You will also probably need a guarantor. This is not because you are a foreigner—everybody needs one—but it makes things difficult if you don't know anyone. Even if you do, becoming a guarantor is a massive ask in Japan and causes a bit of awkwardness. I suggest you find a "rent guarantee company" (*yachin hosho kaisha*) to cover you. Ask the real estate agent. You will most likely end up in a closet-sized unit with a toilet, washbasin and tiny little bathtub for Lilliputians. But it's home for now.

Settling In

When you move into your new abode, never nail anything to the walls or do any DIY or its goodbye *shikikin*. Paper thin walls mean that you should refrain from being too loud, especially at night, lest you disturb the neighbors. Make sure you know the protocols for rubbish disposal. Every day is different and trash must be separated into recyclables, non-recyclables, bottles, etc., otherwise it will be left on the street and everybody will know it's yours (even if it isn't)!

You might get a visit from the police. They sometimes do the rounds to see who's new in the hood and are particularly interested in foreigners. Just smile and be nice. They might end up teaching you Budo at the local *dojo*.

Buy a cheap futon set for around $80, a microwave for $70, a water heater for $40, a book shelf for $20, a fridge for $150 and a small table, chair and nightstand for $80. That's all you need in order to function. You can purchase them new at a Japanese equivalent of Walmart (such as Kohnan) or go to a recycle shop near some university campus. By far and away the best places to buy cutlery, plates, cups and pretty much anything else are the ubiquitous 100 yen shops.

All foreign nationals who will live in Japan for a period exceeding three months must register at their local City/Ward Office within 14 days of moving into a new residence. This is very important, so don't forget.

Getting a Job?

If you're on a work visa, then you already have a job. If you're on a tourist visa, you're not allowed a job. If you're on a student or cultural visa, you're allowed to work for up to 20 hours a week but need permission from your Japanese college and are not permitted to work in certain industries, such as *mizu shobai* (entertainment business). If you are on a Working Holiday Visa, then you are allowed to do what you like except break the law. My first point of call if looking for employment would be gaijinpot.com. They have

It is becoming easier to use your signature these days but there will be times when you need a personalized seal. Make sure you don't lose it.

all of the information you need to get set up and you will find plenty of job listings.

When I arrived in Japan in the 1980s, English teaching was the easiest cash in the world. You could do it privately, at companies or for one of the corporate English schools, and were guaranteed to make a pretty penny. Anybody could find a gig paying in excess of $100/hour and all it involved was sitting down over a cup of coffee and making small talk about what you ate over the weekend. Everybody off the boat just walked into a job with people hell-bent on throwing money at them just to open their mouths.

The English teaching industry is still alive but quite exploitative. Most positions now require qualifications rather than simply "being not Japanese" and the remuneration is nowhere near what it was back in the day. If this is what you want/need to do, be prepared to work long hours for minimal pay and endure mind-numbingly tedious chitchat. The government-sponsored JET program, on the other hand, might be a nice foot in the door if you're a college graduate.

In any case, Gaijinpot will give you a good indication of the options out in the corporate world and the English teaching biosphere. If you are looking for an academic post in Japan (you have a Master's degree or higher), check out the JREC-In website. It's a government database listing positions at universities and research institutions.

☛ **Japan Exchange and Teaching Programme** ☛ **Gaijinpot.com**
☛ **JREC-In**

Insurance

If you have a Residence Card and intend to stay for more than three months, I strongly recommend that you sign up to a national Japanese health insurance scheme. Even if you have health insurance from back home, it won't be of much use at hospitals and clinics as they don't accept foreign policies for direct settlements. You will need to pay the full amount for your treatment first and make a claim after the fact. This can be a real nuisance if you don't have much cash. If you are working full-time at a company, you will be enrolled in the Social Health Insurance System. Students enroll in the National Health Insurance System. The rates are reasonable and it will cover the majority of your medical expenses. It is wise not to tempt fate.

☛ **Japan Healthcare Info**

Banks and Stamps

Economic superpower though Japan is, its banks are medieval institutions at the best of times. When you set up a bank account, you will need to be filthy rich in patience. Some of the rural banks are not used to dealing with foreigners and the paperwork will be confusing. Bigger banks in the main cities are slightly more bearable in terms of time and documentation but brace yourself for hassles. You will need your Residence Card for starters. Some banks will require a recent utility bill (electricity, gas, water) stating your current address and a *hanko* (aka *inkan*), a purpose-made personal seal with your name on it. As a foreigner, sometimes you will be able to get away with a signature but heaven help you if it's ever so slightly differently thereafter. It is easier in the long run

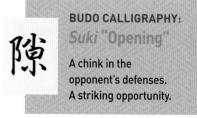

BUDO CALLIGRAPHY:
Suki "Opening"

A chink in the opponent's defenses. A striking opportunity.

to get yourself a *hanko*. There are two types of seals—unregistered and officially registered. You will only need the latter, a hand-carved seal registered with a certificate of authenticity, if you are planning on buying a house. Other than that, you can get away with a standard seal that can be purchased in stationary shops. Your name will probably have to be written in *katakana*, so you won't find it on a rack with hundreds of ready-made Japanese names. Order one, or go to a shop with a machine that can make you one on the spot. Never lose it. It is essentially your new signature. Store it with your passport.

Getting Connected

Gone are the days when you had to buy an NTT phone line for several hundred dollars to connect a telephone. Now, in the digital age, few people bother with landlines. Instead, all Japanese now own a *keitai denwa* (portable electric talker). Alas, for the foreigner the process for obtaining this most basic communication tool is infuriatingly difficult and expensive. Phone sales clerks are modern incarnations of the quintessential "used car salesman," gift of the gab sharks set to bamboozle you with fine print and hidden extra charges, even if you read and speak perfect Japanese! And they take a painfully long time as they systematically wear you down.

A recent change in Japanese law means that SIM cards must now be transferrable between companies, which was never the case before. This means that rigging your own smartphone for use in Japan may become simpler from now, hopefully. International students at my university are using their own phones in Japan.

☛ sunrise-net.ne.jp

Where would the world be without *sumaho* (smart phones)? These are particularly handy in Japan because most cities don't have street names. At least with these you can find your way around!

You can now get prepaid phones in Japan. Formerly illegal because "they might be used by [foreign] criminals," these may be an option if you are only planning to spend a few months here.

Why is it so difficult? Shops are legally required to verify the identity and home address of the customer, so you will need your Resident Card. Foreign passports with a hotel address are sometimes accepted. A standard subscription plan mobile, however, will entail a two-year contract and proof that you will be in Japan for that duration. Bring an empathetic Japanese friend with lots of spare time to bat for you.

The cost of your phone will typically be spread over the duration of the contract and is added to your monthly usage bill. Some retailers allow you to buy the phone outright (average cost is around $700), in which case you may get the service on a monthly contract, but this is not standard.

You can use your phone as a tethering device giving you ample GB of data each month. Additional data beyond your monthly quota will cost you, but there is a growing number of free wifi hotspots around the country. Another option for Internet usage is a portable wifi device that costs around $40/month. They will give you 5–20 GB of data to play with but the same stringent contract conditions apply. If you get cable in your apartment, then use as much data as you like, but again, be prepared for a minimum contract period. Once you get a phone, don't use it to ring folks when you are riding the train. This is very bad form in Japan.

Driving in Japan

Public transport in Japan is among the best in the world but if you live in the boondocks you might want to think about getting a car for convenience. You can use an international driving permit in Japan for a maximum of one year, but if you plan to be in Japan for more than three months, you are obligated to get a Japanese driver's license. This can be a piece of cake if you come from one of the more than 20 countries with bilateral agreements with Japan. You can simply go and get a Japanese license without having to take a written or practical exam. And you can ride a motorcycle up to 50 cc on a car license, but not an international license.

If you come from the US, get ready to fail the test several times, no matter how good your driving is. And be careful not to drive on the wrong side of the road! There is a handy 1,000-yen booklet published by the Japanese Automobile Federation that explains Japanese road rules in English. Definitely check it out. Also, you will need a GPS navigation system. The streets have no names!

Punishment for driving while intoxicated is swift and merciless. Zero tolerance. Passenger(s) and the bar that sold a driver alcohol are also subject to hefty penalties.

Bicycles are a very healthy option in Japan and are cheap. Be wary of hand-me-downs as you don't know where it came from. Japanese police are zealots when it comes to bikes. With an average of only two gun homicides a year, it seems that over 99.7 percent of police duties revolve around stopping cyclists and checking serial numbers. You will be stopped, asked for your Resident Card, where you got the bike from, what you are doing in Japan…. "I'm here to do Budo" is the best answer.

☛ **JAF and Rules of the Road**

LEARNING JAPANESE

A frightening prospect for many people coming to Japan is dealing with the language. It is possible to survive without speaking a lick of Japanese and many expats manage to do just that. I think it's a shame for anyone to fall into this trap because Japanese is a totally learnable language. This section offers some tips on how to get your head around Nihongo.

Is Japanese Hard to Learn?
No, Japanese is not hard to learn! It's all in the mind. Japanese people will tell you that theirs is surely one of the most difficult languages in the world to master, especially with all of the hidden nuances that must be, it is assumed, unintelligible to non-natives. Lazy or befuddled expats will agree. Poppycock I say, but learning Japanese does require hard work and diligence.

A common misconception is that you can eventually make sense of Japanese organically, that is, by just by just living in Japan. Don't believe it. Like Budo, you will not excel in the language simply through osmosis! You absolutely need some formal study to make sense of the basic grammar. You will need to memorize copious amounts of vocabulary, so get a beginner's textbook now.

Start by studying the basic vowel sounds: depending on your own English accent, a (as in ah), i (as in geek), u (as in Ooper-looper), e (as in egg) and o (as in OMG). The rest is about putting the pieces together. Also, be sure to learn the 48 *hiragana* and 48 *katakana* characters. Just keep writing them out until they stick. They can all be memorized in a couple of weeks, so the sooner the better. *Kanji* can come later.

Spoken Japanese
With a couple of hours of study a day, you will pick up enough Japanese to hold your own in basic conversation after about six months. There is no magic bullet or secret formula. It just requires chipping away at it and enjoying yourself as you make lots of embarrassing mistakes. Textbooks will teach you formal Japanese but what you hear in the course of daily life is informal, fast and quite different to what you study. This can be vexing. You will learn to say simple phrases and express your needs but will not immediately understand what is being said in reply. You will have no idea what two conversing Japanese are saying to each other and might start to get a little paranoid.

Don't be disheartened. Pieces of the puzzle will fall into place incrementally with time and patience. It starts with recognizing words here and there. A vivid imagination is useful to tie it all together and make educated guesses as to what is going on.

The most frustrating thing of all is the sinking feeling that you just can't get the hang of the lingo no matter how much

you try. It's nearly impossible to gauge your own progress. You may start to think that you're not progressing at all. Stick with it. I found the best indication of headway was when I started dreaming in Japanese. Everybody's different but it took me about six months to get to this stage.

Dialects and Politeness
One thing textbooks will never teach you are regional dialects, of which there are many. Depending on where you are based, the dialect may seem so thick that you doubt there is any connection at all with what you are studying. This won't be a problem in places like Tokyo, but go to Osaka and you notice the difference straight away. Learn standard Japanese first, then have fun with your local dialect later. Dialects add spice to life and Japanese love teaching you theirs. It is a matter of regional pride for many.

The other aspect of Japanese that causes confusion is the different modes of speaking. Even women's Japanese is slightly different. There are funny stories of big, burly American GIs who studied Japanese when stationed in Japan after the war. The problem was, their teachers were women. A real mismatch of machismo and feminine speech was met with gleeful hilarity by the locals. Textbooks will help you untangle gender-specific terms but there are not too many of them to worry about.

Levels of politeness, however, are a different matter. Honorific language is used to emphasize social rank, or the degree

Above *Desu*. "It is...." The sooner you start learning the language the better.
Left Almost, but not quite. Remember, we learn from failure, not from success.

of social intimacy. It depends on who you're talking to and where you sit in the scheme of things. Broadly categorized as *keigo* (literally, "honorific language"), there are three subcategories of *sonkeigo* (respectful language), *kenjogo* (humble language) and *teineigo* (polite language). The tone, prefixes and verb forms change depending on which category you are using, which in turn depend on who you are talking to.

To give an example, the standard form of the verb "to say" is *iu*, which is slangy-informal and used when speaking with friends, family or those lower in the pecking order. When speaking with somebody you don't know or don't want to offend, the polite form is *iimasu*. When talking to superiors (*sensei*, customers, bosses, gods, etc.), the respectful term is *moshimasu* or the even more gracious *moshiagemasu*.

I sense sighs of anguish. Don't worry! Polite language (*teineigo*), where all the sentences end in *desu* and *masu*, is all you need to really know. Even Japanese rarely get the *sonkeigo* and *kenjogo* right! The slangy stuff will be remembered quickly because it is ubiquitous but get a good formal grounding in the polite *desu–masu* language. You can't go wrong with that.

By the way, there is nothing like a four-letter word in Japanese. If you feel the need to curse, you have to snarl and roll your tongue with enough venom to kill a cobra!

The Accursed Kanji

Kanji can be fun or can be hell. It's up to you whether you enjoy deciphering trees and lamp-posts, but it will become an important part of your study eventually, so it's best to start sooner rather than later. Make it a hobby rather than a chore. Although you learn to read and write Japanese at the same time, your reading will always be better. This is simply because you will recognize the *kanji* you have learned but will be prone to forgetting how to write them. Especially in this age of texting and computers!

If you think studying *kanji* is troublesome, you're not alone. Japanese kids spend thousands of hours learning them as well.

Although the number keeps changing, there are now 2,136 official "General-Use" *kanji* learned by Japanese kids at school. About half of them are in common use. There is only one way to learn *kanji* and that is writing them over and over, thousands of times until they stick in your brain. Flash cards help also.

Learning *kanji* is like learning *kata*. There are specific stroke orders that should be adhered to if you want to write "neatly," but at the end of the day as long as it is legible.... There are also various readings for the *kanji*, so this adds to the confusion sometimes. I suggest you buy a *kanji* textbook or download an App and start learning the way Japanese kids do, incrementally, starting from the easiest ones. Get yourself a stack of blank grid notebooks, too. Use them to write each character in the squares and this will give you a sense of balance. You will increase your vocab as you learn *kanji*, so the learning process goes hand in hand. If I was asked to recommend one book, it would be *The Complete Guide to Japanese Kanji* by Kenneth Henshall and Christopher Seeley. Apart from the fact that both of these gentlemen-scholars were once professors of mine, the detailed explanations turn each *kanji* into a story making them fun and easy to remember.

Japanese Language Schools

Most of your Japanese study will be done on your own but it is good to get proper schooling if you can. Learning in a formal setting will keep you on the right track. If you are at a university in Japan, you will probably have to go to language classes anyway, so problem solved. What should you do if you are independent? Free or cheap Japanese lessons are usually offered at municipal offices by international exchange or volunteer groups around your community, and are typically held once or twice a week for a couple of hours. Alternatively, Japanese language schools are a booming business in Japan. Classes are usually 4–5 hours a day or around 20–25 hours a week. They can be pricey but certainly worth it to steer your linguistic ability in the right direction. In many schools you will probably find that most of the students are Chinese. The Chinese have a distinct advantage when learning Japanese because they know a godzillion *kanji* already. This makes their learning tempo fast and furious, while others may feel left behind in their wake, frustrated and disillusioned. Don't let it get to you. Ultimately, you have to improve at your own pace and the work you do outside the classroom makes all the difference.

☞ **Nisshinkyo and Japanese language schools**

Hints for Learning Japanese

Here are some exclusive *gai-sam* tips for getting to grips with the lingo. Despite the destructive potential for volatile brain cells when watching Japanese TV, it is nevertheless a fine way to hone your listening and reading skills. Most of the silly comments by so-called "talents" on a typical variety show are accompanied by big colorful manga-like subtitles. It can be fun trying to work out what's going on, followed by disbelief and disappointment when you do, but how often can you claim to be studying when watching the box? If anything, your powers of imagination and deduction will soar.

Go analogue and get yourself a little notebook. Write down new words you encounter each day. Do the same for things that you wish you could have said. Look them up when you get home and put each word into a sentence. Memorize the sentence rather than just the word. Also, try to write the sentences in *hiragana*. Learn the phrase or sentence in its past, present and future tenses. Set yourself a quota of three new words and sentences each day. See how long it takes you to fill the notebook up and review the content. It will be a good record of your progress.

Whenever possible, avoid the temptation to speak English. Japanese are happy to practice their English with you and things will go a lot smoother at the start because of it. But remember why you are in Japan! It's your responsibility and your duty to chuck yourself in the deep end and not succumb to laziness.

GF/BF! The best motivation to get good and have intimate fun with while learning rude words and slang (natural Japanese). But again, the point directly above applies here. All relationships involve a degree of give and take but the study of Japanese must always be your priority. The less English you speak, the more Japanese you will learn.

Copy how people speak, their intonation, pronunciation and mannerisms. Practice by talking out loud to yourself (when nobody's around).

Set a tangible goal like taking the Japanese Language Proficiency Test. The JLPT has five levels: N1, N2, N3, N4 and N5; the easiest one is N5 and the most difficult is N1. It can be awfully helpful to know your current skill level and to set future goals. This qualification is useful when looking for a job as well.

☛ **jlptne.jp**

By hook or by crook, make language study part of your daily routine.

Even 30 minutes a day can produce good progress, but the moment you get lazy....

Like Budo, there is no real end point. You won't feel as though you are improving but expect to reach a passable conversational level after six months, if you work at it each day.

Beware the "Expat Bubble"

You will meet people from all around the world in Japan. This is a wonderful part of living here. Being in a foreign land is a shared experience and expats find solace in each other's company. They understand what you are going though and are people you can confide in, boast about conquests and bitch about the trials and tribulations of Japan. Expat friends are the ones you can revel in the adventure with, bond in the brink and drink the evenings away speaking in English.

You need friends, but take care. Don't forget you are in Japan and Japanese friends are an important part of the experience. It goes without saying, right?

Truth alert. It is all too easy to live in the expat bubble in Japan, speaking only English and not even trying to fit in. The expat bubble can be a blast but it will wear your motivation down and eat away at your dream without you even realizing it. You will become lazy, self-righteous and an obnoxious know-all about Japan without having anything more than a rudimentary understanding of what is really going on. But that doesn't matter because you are in the bubble, only making reluctant forays outside of it when you really need to.

I know people who have been in Japan for three decades or more but can hardly string a sentence together in Japanese. Don't get

me wrong. They're not bad people. But the bubble has been known to numb the senses of many an expat and severely restrict the scope of their comfort zone. You may be content staying down the shallow end of the pool, doing just enough to get by. You may have some Japanese friends and acquaintances, even a Japanese spouse, but the lion's share of your communication will be conducted in English. This is okay if it's this path you choose, and good luck to you! But not if you came to Japan with a dream of exploring the world of Budo.

Ideally, it shouldn't make a difference where your friends come from, but if you're in Japan doesn't it stand to reason you'd at least have some Japanese friends whom you can converse with in their language? Joining a Budo club will help you immeasurably here, which is another good reason to start!

Ask yourself this from time to time: are you getting too comfortable in the expat bubble? Reality check. This is the opportunity of a lifetime to broaden your horizons, not diminish them. Go native as much as you can.

Japanese "Engrish"

English is the only foreign language taught in all Japanese schools. Now it's compulsory in elementary school. Businesses are increasingly reliant on the English skills of their staff and it is fast becoming a prerequisite to work at major companies. There are thousands of English words used in modern Japanese as "loan words," to the extent that whole sentences can consist

Japanese leprechauns. A strange thing about Japan is that locals will be caught rubbernecking foreigners but will flat out ignore Japanese weirdos!

of robotic-sounding English terms. The number keeps growing. So why, then, do Japanese people have a reputation for being poor English speakers? Why does Japan rank as one of the lowest scoring Asian nations in proficiency exams like TOEFL?

The first reason is ineffective English education, which focuses on passing exams rather than communication. The grammar-translation method of teaching is common and is rarely backed up with remedial communication practice. This is partly because many of the teachers in schools are not actually conversant in English. It's all about rote memorization of vocab and grammar. Thus, the Japanese are great at reading English but speaking is not typically their forte.

Japanese people are also frightened at the prospect of making mistakes. Anything other than perfect can mean humiliation, so there is little inclination for students to speak up in class through shyness and a fear of sounding silly. It takes some serious coaxing at the best of times.

Then, there are those who speak fantastic English because they've studied hard or lived overseas but are hesitant to showcase their special talent. After all, as the Japanese proverb goes, "The nail that stands out gets hammered down."

Japanese-English does have some interesting idiosyncrasies. In line with the *katakana* pronunciation, distinguishing between "l" and "r" is particularly problematic. An old banner hung across a prominent area in Tokyo in support of General Douglas MacArthur's presidential bid read, "We play for MacArthur's erection." You will find signs and fashion items everywhere emblazoned with the most bizarre, sometimes even profane English. This is a relished source of endless joy to humor-starved expats. English is very much a work in progress in Japan, but if you think you're safe making lewd comments in English about some exceptionally attractive girl/boy sitting opposite you in the train, watch out. The truth is that Japanese often understand a lot more English than they let on.

SIX KINDS OF GAIJIN IN JAPAN

1. GEEKUS NIPPONICA
Infuriating enthusiasm for everything Japanese, irrespective of whether it's good or bad. "If it's Japanese, then it's gotta be awesome" type of kid in a candy shop mentality that never penetrates beyond the surface. Japan can do no wrong. Uncanny but stilted knowledge about Japanese culture and history gleaned through manga and videogames. Inevitably popular with the locals.

2. JAPANDROID
Left his/her true identity at Narita Airport and dresses, acts and speaks like a Japanese. In fact, is often referred to as being more Japanese than Japanese and revels in the attention believing that this is the ultimate homage and acceptance of his/her successful assimilation. Shows disdain for lesser beings who just don't understand the profound depth of Japanese culture and will correct other *gaijin*'s Japanese without missing a beat. Aloof, and often embarrassed to be associated with *gaijin*. Also popular with the locals.

3. CHARISMA MAN
A dude who never had a girlfriend in his own country but suddenly finds himself a born again gigolo with more numbers registered in his phone than he knows what to do with. Consequently, he has a grossly overinflated opinion of his charismatic qualities and becomes an unashamed playboy overnight. He might teach English conversation and gets off on being called *sensei* by hankering students. Actually comes to believe he is *kakko-ii*. Held in contempt by Japanese men.

4. ANGRY GAIJIN
In a constant state of rage and usually starts each sentence with a four-letter profanity before launching into a diatribe about why Japan is so screwed up. A volatile specialist in the art of tea ("storm in a teacup-ryu"), nothing is too small to get worked up into a frenzy about. Not so popular with the locals and often intoxicated.

5. BUBBLE BROTHER
Generally harmless and content to cruise through life in Japan in the expat bubble as a happy *gaijin* with no inclination to learn the language or get their hands dirty messing with the culture. Often seen fraternizing in foreign-style pubs with Charisma Men boasting about recent conquests and a few angry *gaijin* venting about problems at work or how their Japanese wife doesn't show affection anymore. Not really noticed by Japanese and prefer it that way.

6. ZENLING
The Zenlings are focused, balanced, affable, able to play the game in Japan, speak the lingo and don't have a problem associating with other *gaijin*. Usually inconspicuous but can always be relied on to help people out when needed. Zenlings have a solid base of genuine social navigational skills based on hard work, cultural appreciation and experience but are humble and just not interested in blowing their own trumpet. *Gai-sam* should ideally fall into this category—the perfect gentleman/lady warrior-scholar. An enigma to the Japanese but appreciated.

SURVIVING JAPANESE STYLE

Living Japanese doesn't mean becoming Japanese. It is simply navigating the culture and living as a local does. There will be many things that don't make sense at first but every day is one of discovery as long as you keep an open mind.

Rice, Bread and Raw Stuff

The Japanese diet is lauded throughout the universe as being very healthy. This is confirmed by an average life expectancy of 83.3 years, which is pretty much the highest on the planet. Indeed, the traditional Japanese diet of fish, rice, seaweed and tofu kept those Japanese tummies tucked in tight. But, like many things in postwar Japan, the diet has changed considerably and not necessarily for the better. Japanese food now is high in fat, MSG, preservatives and salt and is processed beyond recognition.

One of the latest foreign words on everybody's lips in Japan is *metabo*. You guessed it, "metabolic syndrome," an indication that the Japanese lifestyle and diet is catalyzing an obesity epidemic, diabetes, heart disease, high blood pressure and cancer. Obesity is still a long way behind some countries in the West but is becoming a grave concern. Fast-paced infomercials sell consumers all manner of supplements and exercise machines to snare worried "health conscious" Japanese of all ages into working out in their living room (as they watch the infomercials). The health industry is booming in Japan, preying on consumers' guilty consciences and bulging bits. All the while, the aforesaid consumer may have eaten a couple of slices of two-inch thick toast smeared with margarine for breakfast, had a can of sweetened coffee and a cake for morning tea, a big bowl of rice with fried *karaage* chicken for lunch and then a bowl of salty soy sauce pork *ramen* with fried *gyoza* dumplings plus a bowl of filler rice on the way home from work/school. Oh, and probably a snack of instant noodles (Japanese invention) before bed after working out to the late night infomercials. I'm not joking.

It's not all bad if you want to eat healthily in Japan. Unhealthy food is popular because it's easy and filling. Fast lifestyle = fast food. If you make a conscious decision to cut back on the carbs and eat fresh vegetables, tofu, fish and healthy things, you can certainly do it. But that's the same everywhere, right?

Living on organic foods will still cost you a lot of money in Japan and your choices will be limited. As a country of Buddhists, one would think a vegetarian lifestyle would be easy but it can be challenging when you eat out. Meat is in everything. If you are intolerant to gluten, MSG or have other dietary taboos, then eating at Japanese restaurants is like walking through a culinary minefield and extreme vigilance is required. I had a Jewish friend who fell in love with *ramen* until I was compelled to inform him that the broth was often made of pork. I felt really bad telling him but he felt a lot worse. There is even pork extract in convenience store egg sandwiches! It is clearly stated on the label but that doesn't help if you can't read Japanese.

Japanese are also funny about their rice. They love the white polished variety, which means it's devoid of most nutrients before it gets chopsticked into the gullet. For centuries, white rice was a luxury item in Japan, enjoyed only by the nobility. The peasants made do with unpolished rice mixed with other grains to fill their stomachs. The aristocrats suffered from beriberi while the peasants were comparatively healthy, which was useful because they did all the work.

Even now, although metabo stalks the blobbing postwar generations, brown rice is not common at Japanese tables. Brown rice takes longer to cook and is a reminder of hardships endured during the war years when the country had to "make do" with that poor peasant mush. Ironically, that could have something to do with why the Japanese live so long at the moment. Good luck finding brown bread, too. Although it will be tempting to fill up on crap when running from wherever to training, remember the old clichés—"you are what

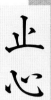

BUDO CALLIGRAPHY:
Shishin "Attached Mind

When the mind has become attached to something and come to a standstill, making it impossible to respond with fluidity.

you eat" and "your body is the temple of your mind." If you want to make the most of your Budo training, you have to eat properly. This means planning your meals in advance, going to the supermarket (rather than convenience stores) and buying vegetables and other healthy options to do a bit of cooking at home. It's too easy to fall into less than ideal eating habits in Japan if you're not careful.

As a member of a *dojo*, you will have to go out to restaurants on occasion and will be presented with all sorts of culinary delights: *tonkatsu cutlets*, *tempura*, *furaido poteto*, *sushi*, *sashimi* and other chewy raw things which you will not come close to recognizing—maybe even raw horse meat (*basashi*) and, dare I say it, whale (*kujira*). Oh, the moral dilemma. Fear not as nobody will force you to eat anything that you don't want to. In fact, Japanese don't really have any expectations that a foreigner will be able to appreciate the country's traditional and "unique" cuisine.

My advice is not to eat with your eyes. Close them if need be but take the plunge and experience the various pleasures on the plates. Not being fussy about what I eat is very useful as an expat in Japan. There is nothing I won't eat and Japanese people find this strangely entertaining. It might seem gross (especially to a vegetarian), but I even developed a penchant for raw chicken liver, raw pig uterus, broiled sparrow with crunchy beaks and legs attached, and the very phallic-like raw sea cucumber. I am also quite partial to fermented (rotten) soy beans called *natto*. They are sticky and stinky but make a fine substitute for marmite when put on toast! *Tako-yaki* (octopus balls) is another favorite but it's not what you're thinking. Hang on. If you are what you eat, then what does that makes me?

Anyway, my point is you just never know until you try but too many expats fall back on what they know, which is usually fast and greasy. Your Japanese friends will admire your adventurous spirit when you make the effort to try new delicacies. Some basic things to keep in mind:

- Say *itadakimasu* (eat a duck I must) before you start, and *gochiso sama deshita* (gotcha soul summer day shitter) when you have finished. ("Thank you for the food in which I am about to partake" and "Thank you for the delicious feast which must have taken some serious running around [on a horse] to prepare.")
- *Sushi* and *sashimi* are different things.
- Don't leave any rice in your bowl. One grain = one more rice plant that could have been cultivated.
- Slurp your noodles. It's okay. Spaghetti as well. And hot drinks.
- Don't be surprised when Japanese praise your magnificent chopstick technique. Foreigners aren't supposed to be able to use them.
- Raw is generally healthy, unless it's left in the sun.
- When invited to somebody's home for a meal, always take a gift of cakes or wine, etc. Never go empty handed, especially pertinent to Karateka.
- Don't stand your chopsticks up in rice. This makes it an offering to the dead and freaks people out.
- Speaking of death, eating too many convenience store rice balls (*onigiri*) will preserve your corpse like a mummy after you've shuffled off your mortal coil. Chemicals.
- Belching at the table is just not cool.
- Don't eat while you are walking. (I got punched in the mouth for doing that once.)
- Don't snort *wasabi* or mistake tubes of it for toothpaste.
- "Curry rice" is seriously Japan's best-ever invention.

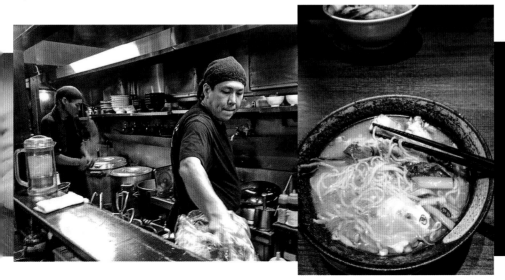

From far left Octopus balls, rotten soy beans on rice, sushi and a *ramen* noodle shop. In the popular noodle shops, the recipe for broth is always a well-guarded secret. Like old martial art schools, *ramen* shops are also kinds of *ryuha* in a sense. The correct protocol is to sip the broth first before adding extras like pepper to season it. Slurp away to your heart's content.

The Four Seasons in Japan

Japan is a country of four seasons. **Spring** is officially from February 5 to May 6 in Japan. It's a brisk but pleasant time of year ushered in by the blooming plum blossoms. These are followed by Japan's iconic suicidal *sakura* cherry blossoms, loved for their "grace in death," towards the end of March, starting in the southern regions and working their way up the country. The exact dates change each year and the state of the blossoms and timing is a popular topic of discussion among Japanese who wait in anticipation. The views in cities, parks and the mountains are splendid, with blankets of pink everywhere. The pink falls off the trees after a few days as the petals scatter to the wind and inevitable spring rains, only to leave a thick pink carpet on the ground. It is a wonderful time of year and people have a spring in their step as they celebrate the approach of warmer weather. It's another excuse to get sozzled under the cherry trees at the infamous *hanami* flower viewing parties. The only downside of spring in Japan is hay fever (*kafunsho*) caused by pollen from *Cryptomeria japonica*. The temperature is changeable, too, but you can usually make do with a light jacket and sweater and maybe a surgeon's mask to keep the pollen out.

Then comes the stifling **summer** from May 7 to August 8. A time of nappy rash, body odor and moldy training equipment. It begins with a slightly depressing, extremely muggy four-week rainy season. This is the time when Japanese farmers busy themselves in the paddies planting rice. Nothing dries in this period of incessant moisture and the *gai-sam* will have to get used to slimy *gi* and a fungal invasion of training gear. It goes from hot to hotter and even muggier in July. There is no respite from the summer heat in the *dojo*, or anywhere else for that matter. It is vital to keep hydrated and not to spend too much time under the air conditioner, as tempting and soothing as it is. Stores and banks will be freezing inside but walking in and out of shops can wreak havoc on your body due to fluctuating temperature extremes. If you live in a modern apartment, it will come equipped with an

air conditioner but it's better to make do with a fan most of the time. They are cheaper to run for a start, and it is not so much of a shock on the body as long as you don't have it blowing on your face when you sleep at night. Summer is the time in Japan when local communities hold their traditional festivals, so there is lots to do. Light cotton clothes are best, but remember it can get very chilly indoors! You will be constantly sweating and then freeze in air conditioning. Don't catch a summer cold (*natsu-kaze*) as they just won't go away. If you are not used to high humidity, summer can be a trying period. Thank goodness for "cool biz," a government initiative that makes it acceptable to wear short-sleeved shirts with no neckties in summer as a way of saving energy.

Fall is from August 9 to November 7. It is a fresh time of the year very similar to spring but the colors are different. Whereas spring is pink, fall is red, brown and yellow. This is brought on by the leaves changing hue and is another natural marker called *koyo,* which is greatly anticipated by the Japanese. Each night on the news, there will be reports of which areas are peaking in foliage and tourists flock to see the glorious maples and cedars that light up the hillsides with brilliant color. The wind becomes cooler and offers welcome respite from the heat of summer. Although not as humming as spring, fall is an exciting time for art exhibitions, concerts and sporting tournaments, where artists and athletes show off the fruits of their labors.

Winter shimmies in from November 8 to February 4. The further north you travel, the colder it becomes. Still, winter in Japan is comparatively mild in most places. It will still snow but rarely will it get deeper than the ankles. The mountains are a different matter and Japan boasts some world class ski areas. A typical winter's day will be quite dry and often sunny. You will need a good warm jacket, though. A cold day north of Tokyo will drop below freezing. Nights are even colder but life is good relaxing with your legs under a heated *kotatsu* table gorging on sweet mandarin oranges. You might need to get out that surgeon's mask again if you catch a cold so that you don't dribble and sneeze on other people. Millions of people, like a massive incision of surgeons, wear them as a preventative measure.

Convenience Stores

Nothing is more convenient than a Japanese convenience store and they are everywhere, conveniently called *konbini*. There are more than 55,000 *konbini* throughout Japan with Tokyo claiming over 7,000 of them. The average Japanese will visit a *konbini* 11 times a month to buy just about anything you care to name. That makes approximately 1,000 customers in each store in the country every day. Open 24/7, they are everybody's port of call for food, drinks, alcohol, cigarettes, contraception, toiletries, magazines, toys, amenities, stationary, concert tickets, faxes, photocopies and banking. You can even pay your utility bills at the good old *konbini*.

As if that wasn't convenient enough, there are nearly six million vending machines (*jido hanbaiki*) tucked away in every nook and cranny of the country. There is no such thing as an unlikely place to find a vending machine because they are literally everywhere and sell just about everything. The first vending machine was introduced in 1888 and sold tobacco. About 600,000 tobacco machines are around now but you need a swipe card to verify age before purchasing. You can also buy alcohol and every other beverage, hot or cold, food, snacks, ice creams, sex toys, mags, [used] underwear, hot salty octopus balls…. There even used to be one in front of Osaka Station that sold magic mushrooms but that disappeared in 2002 after the police realized that psychedelic fungi were Class A drugs in other countries!

An old friend of mine once found Virgin Cola in a vending machine. He'd read an interview with Richard Branson who jokingly promised anybody who could find a can of his unsuccessful beverage somewhere in the world would be given a free air ticket. He contacted Mr Branson's office with photographic evidence and claimed his prize in the form of a return ticket to London courtesy of Virgin Air.

It comes as no surprise to those who live here that Japan has the highest per capita rate of vending machines in the world. It is also no surprise that if there was ever going to be something as obscure as Virgin Cola somewhere on the planet, it would most likely be in the guts of a Japanese *jido hanbaiki*. What is surprising is how none get vandalized or ripped off for the cash and goodies contained within, testament to how law abiding the people are and just how sacred the venerated vending machine is. I have yet to come across one vending Budo equipment but a *gai-sam* would not survive without them for ice cold drinks in the midst of summer. (Did somebody say beer?)

A Dangerous Place to Live?

The question of safety depends on who you talk to and what scares you most—people or nature. In terms of mother nature's mauling of Japan, it is no secret that since its creation from the briny drips off Izanami and Izanagi's spear congealing in the ocean below, the archipelago has been subjected to all manner of cataclysm. A 2015 survey by a Swiss risk management company found that Tokyo is the second riskiest city to live in the world after Taipei due to its constant exposure to man-made and natural disasters. Osaka was not

far behind. Almost one-tenth of the world's active volcanoes are found here, with over 50 of them erupting in the last 100 years. There are 36 still classed as active and they vomit ash and lava every so often just to remind people that they're there.

Then, there are the dreaded earthquakes. The Japanese are quite blasé about the odd tremor because they happen all the time—around 1,500 each year. The most recent *really* bigguns were in 1995 in Kobe (The Great Hanshin Awaji Earthquake) and 2011 in the Great East Japan Earthquake remembered as 3/11. Following the magnitude 9.0 quake, 18,537 people were reported as dead or missing, which has cost the country between 16 and 25 trillion yen (so far), making it the world's costliest ever. You would never know now that Kobe was decimated in 1995 but Tohoku and affected regions of 3/11 are a different matter, especially with the Fukushima nuclear power plant meltdown still ongoing. Many little towns on the remote Tohoku coastline will never be brought back to life.

With earthquakes come the incessant danger of tsunami. Who can forget the images of 3/11 as the tidal wave ripped through the countryside swallowing everything in its path? Most of the victims of that tragic day were killed by the wave. It was not the first time. Whole villages have been washed away throughout Japan's history and centuries-old marker stones can be found in the foothills along the expansive coastline warning "never build below here." Why, oh why didn't they listen to their ancestor's advice?

The other common natural disaster that comes to Japan every year, peaking in the months of September and October, are typhoons. Called *taifu*, these are a fact of life here. You will get several days warning as they wind their way over the sea from the southern islands and head to the mainland. It is very much a hit and miss scenario, and you never know if they will land or not until the last moment. If you live in the cities, you'll wonder what all the fuss is about,

but exposed areas on railways and roads can be particularly dangerous. Schools cancel classes when typhoons strike so its students don't have to commute. The accompanying torrential rain also causes floods and landslides, washing away entire hamlets nestled in the mountains. Typhoons are becoming more powerful and numerous every year and there is nearly always human loss.

Nuclear Power Plants

For an expat from a staunchly anti-nuke country like New Zealand, I have always been suspicious of Japan's nuclear power for reasons that were demonstrated only too clearly in Fukushima. Japan is prone to earthquakes and tsunami. So why build nuclear plants along the coast, especially ones constructed along the lines of the old American model, which put the reactors underground to protect them from tornados? They might be good for America but it doesn't help when a whopping big wave engulfs the plant.

I'll never forget watching NHK in 1999. Three workers at the Tokaimura Nuclear Power Plant were preparing a batch of uranium-enriched fuel in a bucket for a fast breed reactor and all hell broke loose. Nobody knew the extent of the radiation leak. The NHK presenter broadcasting live didn't know what to say. "Ummm…. Please keep doors and windows shut until further notice." It was chilling.

That is just the tip of the iceberg in terms of the Japanese nuclear industry's incompetency. There have been many other incidents swept under that huge radioactive carpet, but the government insists nuclear power is the way forward. Japan is the only country in the world that has been both a victim of nuclear weapons and has suffered a catastrophic nuclear meltdown. One would think the Japanese people would be more vocal in their opposition but activism is summarily stifled. Popular broadcasters have been sacked for simply mentioning on air more or less what I am saying here.

Nobody really knows the extent of the fallout from Fukushima. If they did, those inconvenient truths will surely be buried under that glowing carpet again. One Kendo professor told me something interesting about Japan's attitude to the dangers of radiation. "We've already had two bombs dropped on our cities, and some victims of those blasts (*hibakusha*) are still alive and well today. So we're accustomed to it. Japanese are just resigned to the impermanence of things. If your time is up, it's up." Indeed, an attitude perhaps born of centuries of living with natural disasters.

Crime

From dangerous country to safe country—at least in terms of crime. There are few countries in the world where you can lose your wallet and expect it to be waiting for you at the police department. Leave your bag by the gate at the train station to go and buy a can of chocolate *matcha* tea at the convenience store, and it'll still be there when you get back. Even that embarrassing used handkerchief that fell out of your pocket and blew down the street—the one you pretended you didn't notice because you don't want it anymore—will be picked up by a discerning passerby and duly returned. Where else can you walk down a dark backstreet in the middle of the night, drunk, lost and volatile, but not have the slightest worry in the world that you'll be mugged? Japan is as safe as houses and many people in the countryside don't even lock their doors.

That said, the country is not completely free of crime. It does happen and you shouldn't tempt fate. Violent crimes are rare but Japan has its share of heinous lawbreaking committed by crazies, and the perpetrators can be very young indeed.

The conviction rate for murders and serious crimes is a staggering 99 percent! Are the police that good at solving crimes? Maybe, but they are also expert at coaxing confessions out of suspects, guilty or not. The rule of thumb in Japan is that you are "guilty until proven innocent." That's why you should never get involved in anything that even

smells of wrongdoing. There will be no quarter given. This is particularly alarming when you consider that Japan still has the death penalty.

As I alluded to before, the most "serious" crime in Japan is the pressing social issue of bicycle theft. At 6.6 thefts per 100,000 people, this makes Japan second only to the Netherlands among G20 countries. Of more concern is that this rate is rising. But don't worry. In between cajoling confessions, the police are at work protecting the streets by apprehending perps of this despicable blight on society. I suspect that more umbrellas are stolen than bikes, though.

Foreign crime stats are a favorite topic for politicians and the police, and the usual annual reports of "crime rate increases" draw sighs of condemnation. They never take into account that the number of non-Japanese is increasing, and that the majority of "crimes" are nothing more than visa infringements. Serious crime is lower among foreigners per capita than Japanese. You might get stopped for questioning by bored policemen every now and again but foreigners don't have too much to worry about in Japan other than keeping their noses clean—avoiding fights and not getting involved with illicit substances.

Speaking of fighting, low-level *yakuza* thugs (*chinpira*) are lunatics who should be avoided at all costs. They are identifiable by their gaudy clothes emblazoned with cartoon characters, ridiculous curly hairstyle called "panchi perm," tattoos visible under their shirts, the pinkie on their left hand missing, and a barefaced demeanor of rancor in both word and action. The pinkie thing is symbolic of

deference to the boss. You can't wield a *katana* properly without your left pinkie, so removal amounts to a pledge of allegiance in return for his protection. It is usually snipped off to atone for some transgression. "I'm sorry, boss, now you'll have to look after me."

"Yaks," as we expats call them, used to stand out like the red backsides on monkeys. They take a stealthier approach these days—not so ostentatious—but they are out there. As much as they would be laughed off the street in seedier areas of the US or elsewhere, your best course of action is to avoid eye contact and just ignore them altogether. Nothing good will come of putting a Yak in his place. Nothing.

The Economist announced in 2015 that, crime-wise, Tokyo was the "safest city in the world," with Osaka coming in at third place. All said and done, not bad for two of the world's biggest metropolises. But women should watch out for the occasional groper in crowded trains. Women even have their own carriages to avoid wandering hands. Shout *chikan!* if touched inappropriately and put the creep in a painful wrist lock. Another good reason to do Budo. Station police will be onto him like defensive linesmen at the next stop.

The "Mysterious" Japanese

Wareware Nipponjin.... ("We Japanese are unique because....") As much as this often heard conversation starter is a massive generalization, I myself must now generalize to paint an overall picture of the Japanese. They take great pride in the fact that their culture seems mysterious and untranslatable to anybody not imbued with Japanese DNA. They are intensely interested in what foreigners think of them but not too concerned if it's bad because, well … *gaijin* will never completely get it so it can't be helped. They are delighted with the exploits of their countrymen/women on the world stage. They believe they are a virtuous race of people with an inimitable sense of "hospitality," "politeness" and "humility." They are proud of their cutting-edge technology and their renowned traditional and modern arts and culture: anime, fashion, Budo, tea ceremony, Pokémon, Hello Kitty. The list goes on. The Japanese want you to know about the wonders of their culture but don't want to openly boast about it themselves as this lacks class. Boasters are seen as fools. They'd rather be told so that they can nod shyly with quintessential Japanese humility. (There are annoying exceptions to the rule, of course, especially when alcohol is involved.)

This is very much the attitude that permeates all walks of Japanese life. They are acutely aware of what others think of them and behave in a way not to draw the ire of observant eyes. It would not be acceptable to go home early when colleagues are slaving away at their desks, even if they are only pretending to work! One must be seen to do the right thing, even if it's a cause of considerable personal inconvenience. This includes avoiding conflict. There is rarely a straight yes or no given in response to a situation, more so if it's something that has never arisen before. There will be a lot of sucking air through teeth, umming and ahing, as black or white is substituted for a much more comfortable shade of gray. Thus, ambiguity is another virtue in Japan.

One's preferences are rarely voiced in case it seems too assertive. That's why it's so hard to work out what on earth is going on sometimes. Rule of thumb, it is often not what it seems.

Inside and Outside

It's not that Japanese don't have their own opinions! It's just that social decorum dictates that personal preferences are kept just that—personal. This attitude is represented by the notion of *tatemae* and *honne*, the contrast between one's true feelings and those which are displayed in public as one toes the party line. *Tatemae* is one's outside face, whereas *honne* is one's inside or private face. Everybody has their *honne* feelings about what is good or bad, but to reveal this is scorned as being emotional and lacking in civility.

The only people who will be told *honne* feelings are those in one's immediate circle of friends and family. This is the *uchi* group—those on the inside. All others belong to the *soto* group and are essentially outsiders. You have to be in the *uchi* before anybody really gives you the time of day but there are many levels of *uchi*. Japanese will see themselves belonging to the same *uchi* vis-à-vis foreigners, who will be *soto*. The level of dependence and disclosure is completely different between *uchi* and *soto*.

Even as a *gaijin*, which uses the same *kanji* for *soto*, you have an opportunity to become a provisional *uchi* member if you get married, for example, or belong to a school club or a *dojo*. You will become an *uchi* member of that group, and your peers (rather than *sensei*, *senpai* or *kohai*) will be your *uchi*-est *uchi* confidants with whom you can *honne* away (within reason) until the cows come home. That means that you will be expected to play the game and always show your *tatemae* public face to other outsiders lest you embarrass the group. *Gaijin* are cut a bit of slack here, but nobody likes a blowhard who keeps *honne*-ing to all and sundry. I call my *tatemae* face GPS—Gaijin Plastic Smile. It's more like a grimace caused by the pain of biting my tongue.

Reading Between the Lines

Culturally speaking, apart from being ambiguous at the best of times, the Japanese communication style is one in which silence says a lot. Silence is appreciated infinitely more than verbosity. Japanese will rarely open up about themselves and you will be left either frustrated or trying to read between the lines. Mind reading is another one of those mysterious powers that Japanese claim to have. It is called *haragei*—"stomach art." It basically means that as they are all on the same page in terms of knowing their *tatemae*, *honne*, *uchi*, *soto*, Ps and Qs, and things don't need to be said as they are [supposedly] known intuitively already—in their gut. That is why, so the argument goes, foreigners will never "get it" completely and insist on verbal confirmation for everything.

BUDO CALLIGRAPHY:
Yamato-damashii "The Japanese Spirit"

Commonly used to refer to the spiritual and cultural values of the Japanese people. It was first coined in the Heian period to differentiate Japanese from Chinese values and was named after Yamato, an old province and ancient name for Japan. The term came into prominent use from the Meiji period, where it was attached to the newly forming national identity of the Japanese people as they stepped onto the international stage. In the militaristic 1930s and 1940s, it came to represent "the brave, daring and indomitable spirit of Japanese people." It's still often used in the same context as Bushido.

Hear no evil, say no evil, see no evil. The famous "Three Wise Monkeys" of Nikko. The 17th-century carvings at the Toshogu Shrine were carved by Hidari Jingoro.

It's really not that mystical at all. It's more a matter of knowing how you should behave in certain situations, reading the context, expression, intonation, silence and the "scent" of the situation. For example, when you walk into the *dojo* with a hat on, a *kohai* will never say anything because it's not their place to do so. It would be deemed confrontational and inappropriate. A *senpai* may be more direct. They might say, "Hey, take your hat off in the *dojo*!" They may or may not tell you why. A mature *sensei* will most likely say something along the lines of, "Oh my, that's a nice hat." What s/he really means, if you can read the cues, is "Take that hat off when you walk into the *dojo*. It is very bad-mannered and you shouldn't have to be told. So this is a warning expressed to you in the nicest possible way to avoid conflict and not make you feel bad. You get my drift, right?" In fact, the politer the language becomes, the more trouble you know you are in.

You will learn with time. Nobody wants to lose face in Japan and people go to great lengths to help others avoid it, too. Making somebody else lose face means that a bit of your own face is also sacrificed. Of course, there is conflict in Japan as there is anywhere else but the desire to avoid open confrontation is why important decisions are seldom made on the spot. There is a process called *nemawashi*—joining the roots—in which all stakeholders are advised *offu-reko*

(off the record) beforehand. Consensus is gained first and it can then be voted on in a meeting to officially make it so. The meeting vote is little more than a formality, not a place to debate the pros and cons of an important policy, especially if it isn't covered in the manual. The *nemawashi* must also be done in the right way and order lest somebody up the pecking order loses face.

A Thousand Apologies

An indication of the myriad eggshells one must delicately walk on in Japan is the sheer number of words in the language used to say sorry—over 20 in fact. The most common is *sumimasen*, literally "[I feel so bad about this that] the matter will never end." Interestingly, words for sorry are also used to say "thanks." I've been here so long that I find myself saying "sorry" in English instead of saying thank you. People ask me what I am apologizing for. Even the common term for thank you—*arigato*—literally means "it is indeed difficult to reconcile [this favor]." Such is the

The deeper the bow, the sincerer the apology.

strong conviction that it's shameful to cause others bother, recipients of a favor express remorse for any trouble that the benefactor has been put to, even if s/he doesn't really feel that indebted and didn't ask for the favor in the first place.

A Perpetual Debt of Kindness

Perhaps saying sorry in lieu of thank you is a precursor to another complex aspect of human relationships in Japan—the concept of *on*. It means "favor" and everybody is connected in some way by an *on* bond. If somebody does you a favor, you must repay it with an ongoing intravenous drip of *on-gaeshi*—favor reimbursement. *On* can't be turned off. For example, an old school teacher will always be on your New Year card list because of what you learned at school. In fact, the Japanese post more than 35 billion New Year cards each year, some 30 cards for every man, woman and child in the country! Companies always send gifts to clients a couple of times of year. Even if there is no tangible *on* per se, cards will be sent out of *giri* (obligation) to keep the social wheels well oiled.

As a university professor, the members of my school's Kendo club never fail to send me a couple of boxes of beer. This is a token of their appreciation for my instruction, thereby confirming my place in the *uchi*. It shows that they are indebted to me. In turn, I send presents to all of my *sensei* through

my appreciation for their mentoring. The department stores make a killing with the *chugen* (summer gift-giving) and *ose-ibo* (winter gift-giving) seasons and push it for all they are worth.

Then there are the *giri*-chocolates that women are obligated to give to men in their workplace on Valentine's Day. Big money for the chocolate makers, especially when men have to reciprocate with white chocolate for "White Day" on March 14! When you go to a wedding, you will take a pretty envelope of cash for the happy couple. They will reciprocate with a "thank you for coming" gift at the end of the ceremony. If you are sick in hospital and somebody visits you, they will bring an envelope of get well money. You will have to reciprocate with a present worth half that when you get out to say thank you, I am alive and well. When you go on holiday, you may receive a parting gift of cash, which you would be wise to reciprocate with a souvenir worth half the amount. Get the picture?

You have to be *on* to it because it's an affirmation of interdependence and is an integral part of Japanese society. It gets very confusing as you get older, not just because of memory loss but because you will have so much *on* onboard that it's hard to keep up. At the very least, the *gai-sam* should remember your *sensei* at New Year and be sure to send a little note of thanks when somebody does something for you.

Doing the "Right" Thing

Right thing for who? The individual or the group? The Japanese word for human (*ningen* = 人間) is written with the *kanji* meaning the "interrelatedness of people." Children in Japan are taught the importance of playing by the interdependence appreciation rules. It starts with the family but spreads to bigger groups like the neighborhood, school, village, club, company and even the whole nation. With belonging comes *giri*—social obligation. But this becomes onerous when *giri* dictates that a person must fulfill his or her obligations in a way that is beyond their capacity or is in conflict with their "human feeling" (*ninjo*).

For example, let's take the Samurai Romeonosuke, who falls in love with Jurietteko from an enemy clan. Romeonosuke feels conflicted between his obligation to serve and die for his lord and the irrepressible human feelings he has for Jurietteko. What is a love-struck Samurai to do? The only solution is to commit double suicide—a common theme in Japanese literature for centuries. That way, everybody saves face. Quite simply, there is always *giri* pressure at all levels of society to "do the right thing" even if it means your own downfall or concealing your true feelings on a matter. How closely this ethic is adhered to in Japan (especially by politicians) is a matter of contention but certainly accounts for the high rate

KEY BUDO CONCEPTS: *Kyojitsu* 虚実 "Hole and Whole"

Kyojitsu is a word made up of two contrasting *kanji*. *Jitsu* (whole) refers to the condition of being fully primed mentally and physically. Cocked like a gun with a hair trigger or the USS *Enterprise* with full shields on and photon torpedoes armed. *Kyo* is the opposite of *jitsu*. It refers to "holes" in mental or physical posture. Simply put, *jitsu* means guarded and *kyo* unguarded. If both you and your opponent are in a state of *jitsu*, this will result in a stalemate. *Jitsu* will clash with *jitsu*. If *kyo* attacks *jitsu*, *kyo* will come off second best. If *jitsu* attacks *kyo*, then goodbye *kyo*. As you face off with an opponent, it is crucial to be able to identify *jitsu* and *kyo* and mask it in yourself. Avoid striking the opponent when s/he is in *jitsu* mode and zero in on their *kyo* state. Ideally, you should be able to stay in *jitsu* for the entire encounter but a strong opponent will be able to unsettle your mind and you will oscillate between the two.

Stronger and longer *jitsu* comes with years of training but every move you make will result in a hole somewhere. For example, when you are about to unleash an attack, this will become evident in subtle movements of your posture or hands and once you start you can't stop. A strong opponent may coax you into making a move so that they can pick off this tiny little hole as it manifests. In other words, showing a hole to entice the opponent into the *jitsu*. The four illnesses of the mind—fear, surprise, doubt and hesitation—are also good examples of holes in one's spiritual armor that will lead to one's demise if capitalized upon by the opponent's *jitsu*. The act of pressurizing the opponent into a state of *kyo* is called *seme*. This is another word you will hear often in Budo.

The receiving and giving of gifts in Japan comes with its own protocols of etiquette.

of suicide when scandals erupt, that is, when people are caught out.

Japan is a "system" with fascinating idiosyncrasies. It's said that the system is predicated on the ideal of maintaining harmony (*wa*) and the Japanese will do anything to circumvent havoc. Japanese like order and feel secure when the system is running smoothly, even if it requires superhuman effort to hold one's tongue. Drinking parties are one of the few pardonable opportunities to tell your superiors what you really think.

You will see homeless people living under blue tarpaulins and cardboard boxes in parks. They are rarely talked about, or to. These are people who have opted out of the system. Some suffer from mental illness and have no recourse to treatment. Others just got tired of the "corporate warrior" lifestyle and the unrelenting pressure to play by the suffocating rules.

It's easy to see where their frustration arises with the constant barrage of instructions invading your ears in Japan. Wherever you go, there are speakers blurting out a never-ending string of high-pitched "Thank you," "Be careful," "Watch out for suspicious packages or behavior," "We look forward to serving you again." Don't get me started on the noise pollution from loudspeakers on campaign vehicles at election time or right-wing propaganda buses on public holidays like the Emperor's Birthday. Then, there are the cuckoo chimes blaring across the countryside telling you it's "7 am [so get out of bed lazybones]." Even vending machines tell you what to do! Unfortunately, nannying is also a highly refined art form in Japan.

The author at a *yabusame* event. My job was to signal when arrows hit the target. Nobody told me I was the target. Maybe they did and I misinterpreted it. That happens a lot in Japan.

Dealing With Culture Shock

Culture shock is not always a bad thing. It's an opportunity to challenge yourself as you get to grips with a different culture and environment. Culture shock in Japan, however, is about as testing as it gets. Simple tasks can take days, if not weeks to complete because of some hidden barrier that everybody else knows about except you. You start to feel you're the only one out of step. This is compounded by language issues and unwritten rules of interpersonal relations that seem designed to make *gaijin* feel inadequate and unable to fathom the depths of Japanese culture.

There are distinct stages of culture shock that the *gai-sam* will experience. Everybody is different but the following account is what I went through in my first year here as a 17 year old. It's a one-year cycle of what to expect, more or less, when the reality of living in Japan starts slapping you in the face.

Before coming to Japan, I was nervous and excited at the same time. This is the "Preparation Stage" of culture shock. In other words, it starts before you even get here. It's when you organize visas, plane tickets, start reviewing some basic Japanese phrases and hopefully buy this book so that you know what you're in for.

After arriving in Japan, everything was new, fresh, stimulating and exciting. I discovered what a love hotel was (from the outside). I was amazed by all the pristine cars on the road. The food was an adventure, the people were unbelievably kind and all was good. I loved the attention. I felt like a celebrity and had never talked to so many girls before! This blissful existence lasted about three months. It was the "Honeymoon Stage." But like marriage things begin to change. The buzz I felt faded as I settled into a routine.

Next is the "Participation Stage," which entails covering your ineptitude to do any simple task without help. You would like to be independent but you keep screwing up. You can't write your own address when trying to open a bank account, work out the rubbish days or even hold the most basic of conversations. You lose your confidence, get sick of eating the local food and hot under the collar with the thousands of drones crammed onto the platform at your local train station. You start to doubt the reasons you are in Japan and hanker for the company of English-speaking expats.

After three months or so, the Participation Stage gradually worsens and you descend into the "Rage Stage." This is culture shock at its nastiest. You hate Japan. You hate the food. You hate the busybody Japanese always trying to interfere and tell you what you can't do. You hate how people, even girls, won't stop staring at you. You don't know who you can trust and you are totally fed up with your lack of progress in learning the language. You are jaded at forever being in the dark about what is going on around you and then convince yourself that you don't care anyway because it's all crap. You know you shouldn't feel like this but you can't stop. It doesn't help when it suddenly gets so goddam hot every day. Wild horses aren't going to get you into the *dojo* when you are this far gone and nobody is going to make you.

My first experience of the "Rage Stage" was not pleasant. I felt very isolated and lonely. I lost sight of who my friends were and couldn't communicate my frustration and concerns properly. It was close to depression, and can trigger such a condition in some people, so never be afraid to seek help. (Beware! The expat bubble beckons more than ever at this juncture.)

Fortunately, this phase doesn't last forever. After a few miserable months of hating my life, I started to get over it. In time I found my mojo again and started to make sense of it all. My language skills were still only basic but I was able to communicate with more confidence. It's difficult to keep motivated but you must somehow keep up the language study during the Rage Stage. This will help you focus on something positive and it will pay dividends by bringing you into the "Post-rage Stage." You will not be 100 percent but you will have established your own rhythm and be able to see things for what they are.

After two or three months of the Post-rage Stage, you fall back into the Rage Stage again. This time however, you know that what goes down must come up. It's just a matter of battening down the hatches and sitting out the storm. The second Rage Stage is nowhere near as bad as the first and it doesn't take long to snap out of it.

If you are in Japan for a year, it will probably be about time to go home. This heralds the "Return Stage," which is quite confusing. You want to go home to see your friends, family and pets but you also feel that you should stay a little

KEY BUDO CONCEPTS:
Shizentai 自然体 "Natural Stance"

Often translated as "natural standing position," *shizentai* is to stand up straight but not to attention. Attention is far too rigid. *Shizentai* is not only one's natural stance, it is also a mindset. You are always alert and ready to go with the flow. You are in a state of *mushin*, ideally, without a physical or psychological leaning in any particular direction. The feet are spread slightly apart, limbs are relaxed, and power is centered in the *seika-tanden* (T-spot) just below the navel. The ideal *shizentai* stance augments both stability and mobility.

longer. Fully conversant in Japanese by now, you can say most things you need to without much trouble. Because of this, you have many insights into Japan that you didn't before. Just as things get interesting, you have to go home. A bittersweet time.

The first six months in Japan seem like an eternity but the last six, especially after the "Rage Stage," will fly by so quickly it'll be over before you know it. You are more confident in yourself. You have a foreign language under your belt. You have endured a bit of stress along the way but it has made you stronger, more tolerant of others and more open-minded about the ways of the world. Hopefully, you'll have had a great Budo experience and a *shodan* in some discipline as a nice "souvenir."

It isn't over though. When you do get home, you enter the "Post-return Stage." You have just spent a year in Japan and you have changed whether you think so or not. It all seems like a dream and you'll wonder if you'd really been to Japan at all.

In my case, some of my close friends did not get it. They became tired of me blabbing about the incredible time I had and the things I learned. I started to feel removed from my own circle of friends but eventually moved on and made new ones. Of course, I was still a teenager with quite a bit of growing up to do.

In any case, looking back on my first year in Japan, I can categorically say it was thanks to joining the school Kendo club that I could break through barriers and make something of my time here. True, Kendo was hard and some days I hated it, but it was the friends that I made in the club that enabled me to see Japanese people as no different to me. I had my *uchi*.

I'm glad there was no expat bubble way back then because I'm sure I would have succumbed to the comfort of hanging out with "people like me" and let the greatest opportunity of my life slip me by. That's another great reason to do Budo in Japan.

I've lived in Japan for 30 years now and still get "raged out" every so often. This comes from being fully exposed to two completely different cultures so I don't see it as necessarily a bad thing. At least, it's nothing that a decent session down at the *dojo* won't fix. There is a lot to be said about the cathartic properties of Budo for releasing pent-up frustration and stress. Everything gets put back into perspective pretty quickly.

理念

BUDO CALLIGRAPHY: *Rinen* "Ideology, Concept or Philosophy"

In the case of Budo, *rinen* points to the ideal of "personal development."

CULTURAL VITAMINS FOR THE BUDO SOUL

Doing only Budo makes Bob a dull *gai-sam*. There is much to be enjoyed in Japan and if you look carefully you will be able to see a myriad of commonalities running through the lifeblood of Japanese culture. Exposure to other aspects of the culture will help you appreciate Budo more and vice versa.

Temples and Shrines

There are over 2,000 temples and shrines in Kyoto alone. What is the difference? Shrines are called *jinja* or *jingu* and serve the Shinto religious tradition. They have a big *torii* gate that you walk through to enter the precincts. Temples are called *o-tera*. Anything ending with *-ji* is a Buddhist temple and may have a big *sanmon* gate. These are identifiable by the fierce temple guardian statues called *niozo*. Japan's religious history is a fascinating subject and one in which Buddhism and Shinto, the indigenous religion, have formed a tight syncretistic relationship. Bodhisattvas were *kami* (Shinto deities) and *kami* were

Bodhisattvas. This relationship was largely sabotaged during the Meiji period with the movement to purge the indigenous Japanese spiritual tradition of foreign Buddhist influences. Still, you may still see a *torii* in a temple and Buddhist trappings in a shrine.

There are certain procedures to be followed when visiting a shrine. Once you pass through the *torii* you are in the domain of the *kami* enshrined there. Not many people do it anymore but it's good form to bow as you enter, just as you would when entering a *dojo*. Avoid walking down the center of the main path as this is an affront to the *kami*. Purify your hands by taking the ladle in the basin and pouring water over your

left hand, then your right. Rinse your mouth without drinking the water. Finish by washing the ladle handle. This is all done with one scoop of water and is to wash evil impurities from mind and body. *Kami* don't like impurity.

When you arrive at the altar, throw a coin into the offering box, ring the bell to announce your presence to the *kami*, bow twice, clap your hands together twice to show respect, bow one more time and then move out of the way for other worshippers. When you bow to the *kami*, you are not supposed to make a wish, just be sincere in heart. Then you go and buy an amulet. The *kami* of each shrine is known for a particular domain, such as study, safe birth, traffic safety and success in sports.

Visiting a temple doesn't require such a ritualistic approach but you should purify your hands and mouth in the same way as at a shrine. Then head to the altar, make a small donation in the box, offer some incense and put your hands together in prayer. You don't clap at a

KEY BUDO CONCEPTS: *Ichigo ichie* 一期一会 "One Time, One Meeting"

Ichigo ichie means one unprecedented, unrepeatable moment—a meeting with a person that is so special that it can never be replicated. It is living for the moment and appreciating each and every second. It's so easy to take things for granted but with a dose of *ichigo ichie* thrown into the mix life will be vibrant and relationships cherished. I am reminded of a vignette in *Hagakure* that says, "All encounters will be like meeting for the first time and the rapport will be easy to maintain. This is the same for married couples as well. If you remain as thoughtful as when you met for the first time, there will be no reason for you to quarrel." Indeed, this is the key to martial and marital bliss.

It is a term often quoted in the world of tea but it is especially pertinent to the martial arts as well. Harking back to the days of the Samurai who could perish with the swoosh of a blade, each and every movement had meaning. Students of Budo who give up half way through a technique because it failed are told to see the technique through to its conclusion as there is no second chance in the heat of combat. Making mistakes is a part of the process that makes you stronger and should be appreciated as such. There is no reset button in Budo, just like there is no eraser in calligraphy. Each technique is decisive in its own way, for different reasons. Related to this idea is always striving to score the first *ippon* in a match or training. The *ippon* figuratively means death and there is no going back. The first strike is supreme, but all strikes thereafter must be also thought of with the same solemnity as the "first strike"—unprecedented and unrepeatable.

From far left From the sublime to the ridiculous. Japan is a cultural theme park that constantly blows your mind. My friend Randy is to the left.

temple. When in doubt, stand back for a minute and watch what the locals do and copy them. If you have your own religious beliefs, following these protocols is a sign of respect to the tradition but there is no imperative to do it.

Tea Anyone?

A close Canadian friend of mine, Randy Channell (Soei-sensei), is a tea guru in Japan. His *sensei* asked him to serve tea at a big wedding in Yokohama with hundreds of guests. As soon as he walked in the door, his *sensei* immediately said "Okay.... You're up!" Confident to the point of cockiness, Randy strode into the room full of guests only to see it was set up to do a procedure he hadn't done in years! Panic set in as he tried to remember the proper order. Then, disaster.... He knocked over the container with the tea! Doesn't sound like much of a big deal but a Samurai never drops his sword. He looked up and all he could see was the discerning face of his *sensei*. He struggled through the procedure, apologized and immediately asked to serve the next group. This time it went off without a hitch. His *sensei* was even more relieved than Randy. "Way to go, Randy-san! Let's go get a coffee."

The tea ceremony is an occasion all foreigners in Japan get to experience at some time. The Japanese believe it to be the quintessential cultural experience. Called *sado, chado* or *chanoyu*, the "Way of Tea" is a world unto its own. Originally introduced into Japan by Buddhists, by the thirteenth century the tea ceremony was enjoyed primarily by Samurai but became widespread among other members of society by the sixteenth century. As with everything in Japan, there is a correct way of participating in the ceremony. It is very much

a *kata* for both the host and the guest. There are different kinds of ceremony depending on the school and occasion. A standard ceremony is called a *chakai*. It will involve consuming a small sweet, a bowl of tea and, depending on how many other guests there are, about 30 minutes (if you're lucky) of knee-numbing *seiza*.

Subject to where you sit in the tiny tearoom you will have slightly different roles to play in the production. Don't worry, the host will guide you through it, but you will have to utter some tongue-twisting Japanese phrases. After being seated, sweets will be brought in by assistants and placed in front of all the guests. It's polite to come prepared with your own square piece of *washi* paper to put the sweet on and a special giant toothpick to eat it with. It'll be really sweet to get those taste buds ready for the extraordinarily bitter green tea.

The tea will then be made one bowl at a time and placed in front of each guest. When you get yours, bow to the person after you in line and beg their pardon for partaking first. Hold the bowl up in gratitude to the host, place it in the left palm at chest height, turn the bowl clockwise twice, drink it in three sips without burning your lips and finish with a loud slurp. Wipe the rim where your lips touched it, turn the bowl again two turns anti-clockwise and put it down on the *tatami* to admire its exquisite beauty. Don't worry. Just follow what those in the know are doing.

The *chakai* is an artistic production of the host and every little spatula, tea whisk, bowl, calligraphy in the *tokonoma* (room's alcove), flower arrangement, and sweet will have significance for the season and event. Some accouterments are priceless. A simple bamboo tea scoop, for example, made by a famous tea master a hundred years ago can cost tens of thousands of dollars if it has a box with a signature of authenticity. But value is not what makes it important. You must admire each item for the part it plays in this "once in a lifetime" experience. It's terribly impolite to actually ask how much something costs and

KEY BUDO CONCEPTS: *Heijoshin* 平常心 "A Normal State of Mind"

Heijoshin means maintaining one's normal state of mind at all times, that is, coolness in the face of adversity. It is to "keep calm and carry on." This is the only way to make sound judgments when things aren't going your way and is particularly important when an opponent is trying to beat the living daylights out of you. As Funakoshi Gichin said, "It's only the tranquil mind that can allow for fair and clear judgments free of error." If you can do it in the *dojo*, then hopefully you can carry that strong unfettered mind in the course of everyday life as well. According to Yagyu Munenori's *Heiho Kadensho*, the Way is only achievable by maintaining one's "everyday mind" where you are free from surprise, doubt, fear, hesitation, greed or avarice. "An archer releases his arrow precisely when he is not conscious of shooting and shoots with an everyday mind. The man of the Way is like a mirror and he contains nothing in his body–mind and is clear. His mind is empty but lacks nothing. It is just an everyday mind. He who does everything with this everyday mind is a Master."

better not to know anyway! And don't drink too much of the tea. It'll give you the shakes and keep you up all night.

Shodo Calligraphy

Shodo is an art form which uses charcoal ink and a brush to write calligraphy as an expression of spiritual depth and beauty. Initially, the student calligrapher must master the basic forms, a stage known as *shin* (真 = essence). When the basic form becomes ingrained, an individual style develops called *gyo* (行 = running style). Following years of intensive practice, the student creates a distinctive cursive style referred to as "grass writing" (草 = *so*). This cursive style is abbreviated and the characters linked, resulting in a highly artistic curvilinear form of writing. The art of calligraphy is often compared to Budo. The calligrapher assumes a special posture (*kamae*), the breathing is controlled and each stroke of the brush is made with the mind in a state of *mushin*. That's why the "Way of Writing" is an excellent hobby to take up in Japan even though it's a lot harder than it looks.

Zen and the Art of Meditation

Although Budo is not Zen, the practice of Zen meditation is immensely beneficial to the Budoka. Why? It is the ultimate chillax! It brings serenity to a hot Budo head. Zen provides a pathway into the deepest reaches of the mind and helps contextualize the physicality of Budo and its underlying spirituality. Meditation is something that you can do on your own without having to experience the formalities of a Zen temple. Still, it is something that should be on all *gai-sam* bucket lists.

When the novice goes to the Zen hall for a round of *zazen*, s/he will be taught to focus on breathing—short deep breaths through the nose and long exhalations from the stomach (*hara*)

Above One of the fascinating aspects of living in Japan is that modernity and tradition go hand in hand.

Left Calligraphy is a lot harder than it looks. You will be able to find a private school in most neighborhoods in Japan.

Wabi and *Sabi* 侘寂 "Flawed Beauty"

Wabi-sabi is a Japanese aesthetic based on the acceptance that everything is here for a fleeting moment and that there is great beauty in sadness and imperfection. This notion derives from Buddhist ideals of impermanence, suffering and emptiness. In other words, nothing will last forever, nothing is ever complete and nothing can ever be perfect. This aesthetic appreciates the asymmetrical or irregular shape of things and simplicity. *Wabi* (侘) originally meant the lonely solitude that was experienced through living in the wilderness away from mundane concerns of communal living but now means "rustic minimalism." Its partner, *sabi* (寂), refers to the beauty felt in imperfections that arise as an object, human or otherwise ages. It's a celebration of decay. It was the Japanese nobles in the Muromachi period who adopted this aesthetic of "flawed beauty" as something joyful and to be admired rather than spurned. It was seen as a part of the road to enlightenment. Whereas Western Renaissance art looks for symmetry and realism, the *sabi* aesthetic seen in Zen art values economy in brush strokes and color (no color, in fact). Gardens are another good example. Think of the quintessential garden in a European aristocrat's manor with its perfection in form and pattern symmetry compared to the random order and the highlighting of defectiveness and space in a Zen garden. The tea bowl that is chipped is not to be discarded. Rather, it is seen as even more beautiful than before. Maybe this is why martial artists like to have their black belts so worn out that they actually look white.

through the mouth until there is no more air left and the body naturally breathes in again. The eyes are neither shut nor open. The full or half-lotus seated position is difficult if you are not flexible, but as long as you have three points touching the floor and your back is straight, then you don't have to concern yourself. *Seiza* is fine and sitting on a special cushion helps.

Your brain will do its absolute best to blind you with as much random *mushin*-inhibiting dross as it possibly can. You may be encouraged to count your breaths. This is remarkably effective for reining your mind in but don't expect some great epiphany. In fact, hoping for *mushin* is actually the antithesis of it. An American Zen priest in Kyoto once told me that you can't stop random thoughts but you can hone your concentration to zero in on the start of thoughts, "Just like the bubbles that appear on the surface of the ocean when Godzilla is arising." Practicing this will lead to "one-pointedness" of mind, which is a huge leap.

Another thing he told me is that there is no sudden transition into being an enlightened being for the rest of your life. There are just moments when you are temporarily elevated to a superlative realm of understanding.

At this point, the practitioner may be taught more advanced techniques such as contemplating the enigmatic nature of a *koan* riddle or just observing what is going through your mind. It depends on the school of Zen, but is generally divided into introspection with *koan* as per Eisai's Rinzai sect or "just sitting." Dogen, patriarch of the Soto sect, said that *zazen* is "Sitting fixedly, thinking of not thinking. How do you think of not thinking? Non-thinking." Huh?

Try to focus on that all-important "center" and stay there until you aren't thinking about it anymore. While you are doing this, the most amazing thing will happen. You will find that your sense of time becomes completely warped. When the priest rings the bell to signal the end of the session, what you thought was 15 minutes is actually an hour. It is incredible.

Given the high-paced lifestyle that typifies Japan, *zazen* is a welcome respite.

Ten Places in Japan Every Gai-sam Should Visit

1. **Kyoto during Golden Week** Golden Week is string of public holidays all joined together at the end of April and first week of May. Kyoto is buzzing with Budo activity during Golden Week. You can go and see the famous Kyoto Enbu Demonstration Taikai for Kobudo arts, Iaido and Kendo at the historical Butokuden *dojo* next to the Meiji Shrine. There are plenty of martial arts equipment shops around there, too. You can see *yabusame* and classical martial arts demonstrations at the Shimogamo Shrine. Visit Kuramadera Temple, the legendary source of west Japan's martial traditions.

2. **Nippon Budokan** Nestled in Kitanomaru Park in central Tokyo, the Nippon Budokan is the most famous *dojo* in Japan. It's used more for music concerts actually, but the building is magnificent. Have a coffee in Café Budo. Also, go and check out Yasukuni Shrine across the road. You might even get to see a whole bunch of right-wing xenophobes dressed in old military uniforms. Truly bizarre. The museum there is interesting also.

3. **Kashima Jingu Shrine** and **Katori Jingu Shrine** The Kashima Jingu Shrine is located in Ibaraki prefecture and the Katori Jingu Shrine in Chiba prefecture. They were places of pilgrimage for Samurai and are of immense historical importance in the history of martial arts. Be sure to buy a special Budo *omamori* (amulet).

4. **Hiroshima** and **Nagasaki** Just go. Beautiful cities with a tragic past.

5. **Zanshin Bar** in Tokyo and **Dojo Café** in Okinawa are Budo-themed bars. What could be better? Zanshin Bar is located in Ikebukuro in Tokyo and the Dojo Café is run by a *gai-sam* Karateka in Okinawa.

6. **Mt Fuji** Japan's most iconic mountain. Any *gai-sam* worth their salt should climb it once. The climbing season is August and September.

7. **Meiji Shrine** On November 3, the Meiji Shrine in Tokyo is the venue for the Culture Day classical martial arts demonstration. Very colorful and exciting.

8. **Kodokan** Near JR Suidobashi Station in Tokyo, the Kodokan is the HQ for Kano Jigoro's Judo. Given the influence Kano had on the development of modern martial arts, the Kodokan is definitely worth a visit. There is an interesting little museum inside.

9. **Yagyu-no-Sato In Nara** Yagyu-no-Sato is an eerie but stunning little piece of countryside steeped in history. It is where the Yagyu Shinkage-ryu style of swordsmanship emanated. See the *itto seki*, a giant rock that was split in two by Yagyu Sekishusai when he thought he was being attacked by *tengu*. (Magic mushrooms were legal back then.)

10. **Reigando** This cave in Kumamoto prefecture is where Miyamoto Musashi brushed his opus, *Gorin-no-sho*, in his dying days. An inspiring place.

Published by Tuttle Publishing, an imprint of Periplus Editions (HK) Ltd.

www.tuttlepublishing.com

ISBN: 978-4-8053-1375-6

Distributed by

North America, Latin America & Europe
Tuttle Publishing
364 Innovation Drive
North Clarendon, VT 05759-9436
U.S.A.
Tel: 1 (802) 773-8930
Fax: 1 (802) 773-6993
info@tuttlepublishing.com
www.tuttlepublishing.com

Japan
Tuttle Publishing
Yaekari Building, 3rd Floor
5-4-12 Osaki
Shinagawa-ku
Tokyo 141-0032
Tel: (81) 3 5437-0171
Fax: (81) 3 5437-0755
sales@tuttle.co.jp
www.tuttle.co.jp

Asia Pacific
Berkeley Books Pte. Ltd.
61 Tai Seng Avenue, #02-12
Singapore 534167
Tel: (65) 6280-1330
Fax: (65) 6280-6290
inquiries@periplus.com.sg
www.periplus.com

21 20 19 18   7 6 5 4 3 2 1
Printed in China   1803RR

This book is dedicated to Denis Gainty (1970–2017)

Afterword

Japan: The Ultimate Samurai Guide is the culmination of three decades of living and training in Japan. It was written as a resource for people interested in embarking on their own journey to study the Japanese martial arts. I have purposefully kept the text informal and as accessible as possible. There is much to absorb, but through my experiences to date I am confident that the information I have included will provide the foundations for a fruitful pursuit of Budo. Certain sections will be of more interest to readers than others, depending on their personal circumstances and understanding of Japanese culture.

I would like to thank Kansai University in Osaka, Japan, for granting me sabbatical leave during which I was able to write this guide. I also am indebted to the following people for their assistance: Dr Blake Bennett, Jon Braeley (Empty Mind Films), Jeff Broderick, Bruce Flanagan, Michael Ishimatsu-Prime, Trevor Jones, Dr Sean O'Connell, Bryan Peterson, Masashi Kan Shishikura, Baptiste Tavernier, Remi Yamaguchi and Yulin Zhuang. All provided me with editorial help, useful feedback on the content and a wonderful selection of photographs and images to include. Collectively, this group of esteemed martial art colleagues is known jokingly as the "Budo Union of Martial Scholars," or BUMS for short. It's what we do. I sincerely hope that you will join us.

"What you don't sweat when you are young will become tears when you are old."
—Tsurumaru Juichi, Kendo Hanshi 9th Dan

Photo Credits

Jon Braeley (Empty Mind Films), Jeff Broderick, Bunkasha International, Randy Channell, Bruce Flanagan, Kendo World Magazine, Masashi Shishikura and Yulin Zhuang. Dreamstime.com—*pp14* © Shalyginandrey; *23* © Akiyoko74; *24* © Innast; *25* © Joeygil; *29* © Combodesign; *30* © Nyiragongo70; *75* © J. Henning Buchholz; *90, 102* © Cowardlion; *93* © Stef22; *123* © Tupungato; *124* © Akiyoko74; *126* © Leigh Anne Meeks; *127* © YaoRusheng; *130* © Mr Sugiyono, © Caimacanul; *134* © Greir11; *136* © Tom Wang; *137* © Eagleflying. Pixtastock.com—*pp 9* © takezo; *11* © pekamaro; *12* © ky1227ky; *22* © aodora, © HitToon, © cybister, © prof204775; **23** © gokurakutonbo; *27* © KUCO; *29* © kensan; *31* © road; *front cover, 38* © kuranosuke; *49* © prof212305; *53* © polo; *59*; *63* © splav; *front cover, 68/69* © prof1708; *72, 74* © mochidigi; *back endpapers, 92* © sanukiudon49; *98* © SENBA; *100* © mo3, © sheila1; *101* © kohei24, © seaside, © nakase; *105* © photozy; *111* © sprvtec; *122* © dagobah; *126* © goripppa; *130* © ikuo; *134* © prof201661; *136* © kumachan; *137* © xiangtao; *140* © BabyChameleon; *142* © Noriaki-S, © happykazumi. Shutterstock.com—*front endpapers, pp 26* © blue-hand. Wikimedia Commons—*pp6/7*.

Illustrations by Jeff Broderick. Jeff started martial arts in Canada in 1991 and moved to Japan in 2000. He has been living there on and off ever since. He currently lives in Tokyo where he divides his time between his work as a university English teacher and his hobbies (art, photography, writing, metalworking and Budo).

ABOUT TUTTLE: "Books to Span the East and West"